McDonnell Douglas F-15 Eagle

Supreme Heavy-Weight Fighter

Dennis R Jenkins

McDonnell Douglas F-15 Eagle
© 1998 Dennis R Jenkins

ISBN 1 85780 148 2

Published 2002 by Midland Publishing
4 Watling Drive, Hinckley, LE10 3EY, England.
Tel: 01455 254 490 Fax: 01455 254 495

Worldwide distribution:
Midland Counties Publications
4 Watling Drive, Hinckley, LE10 3EY, England
Tel: 01455 233747 Fax: 01455 233737
E-mail: midlandbooks@compuserve.com

This work is an updated and expanded edition of
the *Aerofax Datagraph 6* by the same author,
originally published in 1990.

Design concept and layout © 1998
Midland Publishing Limited and Dennis R. Jenkins

Printed in England by
Ian Allan Printing Ltd, Riverdene Business Park,
Molesey Road, Hersham, Surrey, KT12 4RG

Aerofax and Midland Publishing are imprints of
Ian Allan Publishing Ltd.

The author and publisher would like to thank:
Mick Roth; Todd Enlund; Stefaan Vanhastel; Terry
Panopalis; Chris Salter; Masahiro 'Scotch' Koizumi;
Tsahi Ben-Ami; Patrick Nieuwkamp; Chris M Reed;
Malcolm Hayes; David Sargent; Kevin Taylor;
Sigmend S Grudzinski, USAF/Rome Lab; Wesley B
Henry and Tom Brewer, Air Force Museum; Dave
Phillips and Paul Tobin, McDonnell Douglas
(Boeing); C E 'Bud' Anderson; Wendall 'Wendy'
Shawler; Terry Vanden-Heuvel, AMARC; LtCol Roger
Smith; Cheryl Agin-Heathcock and Tony Landis,
NASA/DFRC; Frederick Johnsen, AFFTC History
Office; Jay Miller; and Mary E Jenkins.

Contents

Title page: **F-15C from the 32nd TFS displays an early air-to-air configuration.** US Air Force

Below: **The 71st TFS from Langley AFB, Virginia, lines up at Nellis AFB, Nevada. The squadron commander's F-15C (83-0030) is in the foreground.** Mick Roth Collection

Opposite page: **Fifteen years after production of the F-15 began, the F-15E 'Mud Hen' arrived on the scene to show Saddam Hussein that air power could still decide the outcome of even the 'mother of all wars'. Unlike previous F-15s, the Strike Eagle is optimized for air-to-ground combat, but it has given up little of its air-to-air capabilities along the way.** McDonnell Douglas

Introduction

In 1990 the McDonnell Douglas F-15 Eagle seemed to have run its course. Several things were conspiring against the Eagle: the United States Air Force's interest had turned to its newest fighter project, the F-22; the breakup of the Soviet Union had seemingly eliminated the need for a large standing military; and problems integrating the LANTIRN and ALQ-135B systems on the F-15E were creating bad press. Twenty year old aircraft with troublesome electronics that cost $46 million a copy were not 'politically correct', and the US Congress refused to fund any further purchases.

Things changed in 1991. A largely unknown minor dictator named Saddam Hussein invaded a small Middle East country called Kuwait, and the United States led a coalition that would amount to the largest armed force since World War II to drive Saddam back to his desert home. And the F-15 would play a large part.

Air superiority variants in both United States and Royal Saudi Air Force service combined to rack up a 36:0 kill-to-loss ratio. These included five victories against the much heralded MiG-29, although the circumstances certainly did not favor the Russian aircraft. And the Mud Hen, as the F-15E became known to its ground crews, proved itself as one of the premier strike-interdiction aircraft, even though LANTIRN pods were in short supply and the ALQ-135B really did not work very well.

The US Congress relented on its earlier refusal to fund further F-15E purchases for the USAF, and Israel and Saudi Arabia ordered a combined $11 billion worth of Eagles and support. Japan also continues to manufacture F-15s, and further purchases are expected from South Korea and possibly others.

The F-15 has always been something of an enigma. It is too large and heavy to truly consider a fighter. But it could outperform any of its contemporaries, and holds its own against aircraft 20 years newer. It bristles with the latest radar and electronics, yet has the simplest wing of any fighter of its generation. Fitted with troublesome engines, the Eagle earned the distinction of being the safest fighter in the history of the Air Force. Considered by many to be outclassed by smaller and lighter fighters, almost 100 kills to no air-to-air losses graphically disputes this.

Visually the F-15 has never been much to celebrate. The Compass Ghost paint scheme, although reportedly extremely effective, is dull almost to the point of boredom. USAF Eagles have seldom been seen in colorful markings.

This boredom rapidly fades when the F-15 takes to the skies. Like the Phantom before it, the sheer size and noise excites onlookers. And the performance, especially in the vertical, is outstanding. Streak Eagle managed to climb to 30,000 meters in under 3.5 minutes!

Where the Eagle goes from here is uncertain. The Air Force has again embraced the aircraft, but stands committed to replacing it with the F-22 soon after the turn of the century. Several projects hold the promise of breathing new life into the Eagle. The F-15 ACTIVE being flown at NASA Dryden has multi-dimensional thrust vectoring nozzles, greatly enhancing maneuverability. A new radar is being developed to retrofit early aircraft, and the integration of the AIM-120 AMRAAM significantly enhances its future kill probability. Beginning in 1997, a new short-range missile is finally being developed and will undoubtedly find use on the F-15.

The foreseeable future shows new F-15s rolling off production lines in both St. Louis and Japan, albeit at a very low rate. In most probability an entire new generation of fighter pilots will fly the Eagle well into the next century.

Dennis R Jenkins
Cape Canaveral, Florida   June 1998

3

Acronyms and Abbreviations

AAA	Anti-aircraft Artillery
AB	Air Base
ACM	Air Combat Maneuvering
ACMI	Air Combat Maneuvering Instrumentation
ACTIVE	Advanced Control Technology for Integrated Vehicles
ADC	Aerospace Defense Command
ADECS	Advanced Digital Engine Control System
ADTAC	Air Defense Tactical Air Command
AECS	Advanced Environmental Control System
AFB	Air Force Base
AFCS	Automatic Flight Control System
AFDT&E	Air Force Development, Test & Evaluation
AFTI	Advanced Fighter Technology Integration
AI	Air Intercept
AMAD	Airframe Mounted Accessory Drive
AMSA	Advanced Manned Strategic Aircraft (became the B-1)
ANG	Air National Guard
AOA	Angle of Attack
ASD	Aeronautical Systems Division
ATA	Advanced Tactical Aircraft (A-12)
ATF	Advanced Tactical Fighter (YF-22/YF-23, now just the F-22)
AWACS	Airborne Warning and Control System(Boeing E-3 Sentry)
BVR	Beyond Visual Range
Capt	Captain
CDR	Critical Design Review
CDT&E	Contractor Development, Test & Evaluation
CFT	Conformal Fuel Tanks
CFP	Concept Formulation Package
CMD	Countermeasures Dispenser
Col	Colonel
CONUS	Continental United States
CPIF	Cost-Plus-Incentive-Fee (contract type)
CRT	Cathode Ray Tube
CTF	Combined Test Force
DCP	Development Concept Paper
DEEC	Digital Electronic Engine Controls
ECM	Electronic Countermeasures
ECCM	Electronic Counter-Countermeasures
ECP	Engineering Change Proposal
ECS	Environmental Control System, Expendable Countermeasures System
EDT	Eastern Daylight Time
EM	Energy Maneuverability

EWWS	Electronic Warfare Warning System (AN/ALQ-128)
FAST Packs	Fuel and Sensor Tactical Packs (now CFTs)
FBW	Fly-by-Wire
FDL	Flight Dynamics Laboratory
FIS	Fighter Interceptor Squadron
FPIS	Fixed-Price-Incentive-with-Successive-Target (contract type)
FS	Fighter Squadron
FW	Fighter Wing
FWS	Fighter Weapons Squadron
FWW	Fighter Weapons Wing
F-X	Fighter-Experimental (F-15)
F-XX	Alternate F-X concept by Sprey
FY	Fiscal Year (United States)
GE	General Electric Company
Gen	General
GFE	Government Furnished Equipment
GSE	Ground Support Equipment
HIDEC	Highly Integrated Digital Electronic Control
HUD	Heads-Up Display
IAI	Israeli Aircraft Industries
ICMS	Internal Counter Measures Set (AN/ALQ-135, -135B)
ICS	Internal Countermeasures Set
IDF/AF	Israeli Defense Force/Air Force
IDG	Integrated Drive Generators
IOC	Initial Operational Capability
JASDF	Japanese Air Self Defense Force
JEPO	Joint Engine Project Office
JFS	Jet Fuel Starter
JTF	Joint Test Force
KFP	Korean Fighter Program
KIAS	Knots Indicated Air Speed
kW	Kilo-Watt
L/D	Lift to Drag ratio
LANTIRN	Low Altitude Navigation and Targeting for Night
Lt	Lieutenant
LtCol	Lieutenant Colonel
LTV	Ling Tempo Vought Corporation
MajGen	Major General
McAir	McDonnell Aircraft Company
MDA	McDonnell Douglas Astronautics
MHz	Megahertz
MMH/FH	Maintenance Man Hours per Flight Hour
MSIP	Multi-staged Improvement Program
MTBF	Mean-Time Between Failures
MTD	Maneuvering Technology Demonstrator (usually S/MTD)
NASA	National Aeronautics and Space Administration

NFOV	Narrow Field of View
OSD	Office of the Secretary of Defense
P&W	Pratt & Whitney
PACAF	Pacific Air Forces
PCA	Propulsion Controlled Aircraft
PDR	Preliminary Design Review
PRF	Pulse Repetition Frequency
PSC	Performance Seeking Control
QOR	Qualitative Operations Requirement
R&D	Research and Development
RFP	Request for Proposals
RPRV	Remotely Piloted Research Vehicle
RSAF	Royal Saudi Air Force
RTD	Reconnaissance Technology Demonstrator
RWR	Radar Warning Receiver
SAR	Synthetic Aperture Radar
SPO	System Project Office
SRFCS	Self-Repairing Flight Control System
SRV	Spin Research Vehicle
STOL	Short Take-Off and Landing
S/MTD	STOL/Maneuvering Technology Demonstrator (NF-15B)
TAC	Tactical Air Command
TACAN	Tactical Air Navigation system
TAWC	Tactical Air Warfare Center
TCTO	Time Compliance Technical Order
TDP	Tactical Development Plan
TEWS	Tactical Electronic Warfare System
TISEO	Target Identification System, Electro-Optical
TFS	Tactical Fighter Squadron
TFTS	Tactical Fighter Training Squadron
TFTW	Tactical Fighter Training Wing
TFW	Tactical Fighter Wing
TFX	Tactical Fighter, Experimental (F-111)
TS	Test Squadron
TTS	Tactical Training Squadron
TTW	Tactical Training Wing
TW	Test Wing
UHF	Ultra-High Frequency
USAF	United States Air Force
USAFE	United States Air Forces, Europe
V/STOL	Vertical/Short Takeoff and Landing
VFX	Navy Fighter, Experimental (F-14)
VHF	Very High Frequency
WFOV	Wide Field of View
WG	Wing (formerly TFW/FW)
WRALC	Warner-Robbins Air Logistics Center

Chapter One

Program History

Above: **The North American F-86 Sabre was the last fighter designed primarily for air-to-air combat until the advent of the F-15. The Sabre turned in a superb performance during the Korean War against a smaller and lighter adversary. Later models of the Sabre were developed into all-weather fighters and ground-attack aircraft, a parallel that would be followed by the F-15.** Peter Steehouwer

During the Korean war, the United States Air Force (USAF) racked up a 7:1 kill-to-loss ratio using North American F-86 Sabres against Soviet-built MiG-15s. The overall USAF versus North Korea kill-to-loss ratio was an even more impressive 10:1. The F-86 had first flown in May 1947, and looked every bit a fighter in the tradition of the P-51 Mustang. In fact, the Sabre was the only US jet aircraft to see significant service that had been designed primarily for aerial combat (albeit, as a fighter-escort), all others having been designed either as fighter-bombers or high-speed interceptors. The F-86 had all the makings of a classic fighter: a high cockpit with a bubble canopy provided excellent visibility for the single pilot, and a large

wing resulting in relatively low wing loading (56 pounds per square foot – only 6 pounds more than the P-51). These virtues contributed greatly to the outstanding kill ratio achieved in Korea.

'Project Forecast', a 1963 Air Force attempt to identify future weapons requirements foresaw such notable developments as the C-5A and B-1 programs. Directed by Gen Bernard A Schriever, commander of the Air Force Systems Command (AFSC), *Forecast* proved somewhat less clairvoyant regarding future fighter programs. It predicted that USAF fighter needs in the 1970s and 1980s would be best met by missile-armed F-111 and F-4 variants '... optimized for the air-superiority role ...', and that strategic bombing from aircraft able to fly faster and higher than the enemy would ensure air-superiority. Almost as an afterthought, Forecast added that '... the counterair force must be able to destroy aircraft in the air ...' at long ranges using advanced weapon systems. And so, American designers got sidetracked from developing true fighters by the magic of radar and electronics. These, coupled with the advent of seemingly workable beyond-visual-range (BVR) missiles, made the traditional 'dogfight' appear to be obsolete. All future bat-

tles would be fought without ever seeing the enemy, or so they thought.

The first opportunity to use this new technology, and an entire generation of aircraft built around it, came in Vietnam. It did not work. Not only were the new electronics and missiles unreliable, the entire battle scenario was vastly different from the exercises of the late 1950s and early 1960s. The major problem was that the enemy did not cooperate. During the 'war-games', the bad-guys had always approached from one side, the good-guys from the other. All the blips on the radar 'over there' were the enemy, and fair game to fire at. The real world didn't work that way since friends and enemies were interspersed in the same air space. To tell the players apart, Identification, Friend or Foe (IFF) systems were developed, but they too were somewhat unreliable, forcing the pilots to make visual identification prior to engaging. These problems with tactics and equipment, coupled with unbelievable political considerations, conspired against the American fighter pilot and created the rather dismal 2.5:1 USAF kill ratio in Vietnam. It was increasingly obvious that fighter-bombers (F-4, F-100, and F-105) and interceptors (F-102, F-104, and F-106)

Left: **During the early F-X concept definition phases, there was considerable support for small, lightweight, fighters. Most contractors, however, remembered the USAF's unhappy experience with the Lockheed F-104 Starfighter and elected to develop heavier all-weather fighters. These analyses largely missed the point, however, by not looking at whether it had been the F-104, or the Air Force tactics and policies, that had caused the USAF's unhappiness.** Denny Lombard, Lockheed Martin Skunk Works

were not destined to be good fighters, and at the time nobody was sure what the F-111 TFX would ever be good for, though it ended up being an excellent strike/interdiction aircraft.

On 7th January 1965, Secretary of Defense (SecDef) Robert McNamara allocated $10 million in FY66 funds to modernize the existing tactical aircraft force. At the same time he directed the Air Force to consider developing a new fighter '... optimized for close air support and useful in ground attack ...', and to 'assume' tactical air-superiority in all planning. Secretary of the Air Force (SecAF) Eugene M Zuckert and Air Staff officials were disturbed by McNamara's instructions to 'assume' tactical air-superiority in their planning

A study entitled *Force Options for Tactical Air* had been initiated in August 1964 under LtCol John W Bohn, Jr. to critically assess the Air Force's reliance on high-cost, high-performance tactical fighters. Completed on 27th February 1965, the study found that aircraft such as the F-111 were far too costly to be risked in a limited (ie; non-nuclear) war and recommended the acquisition of a mix of high- and low-cost aircraft as the most economical method of strengthening the tactical force. For the low-cost role, the study narrowed the candidates to the lightweight, comparatively inexpensive, Northrop F-5 and the LTV/Navy A-7. Both seemed equally acceptable; the A-7 could carry a greater payload and offered commonality with the Navy, whereas the F-5 had a superior air-to-air combat capability. The Air Force Chief of Staff, Gen John P McConnell, was briefed on the study on 9th March, and Zuckert and his staff two days later. McConnell subsequently advised Zuckert that the Bohn study clearly showed the folly of 'assuming' air-superiority and, in support of this view, he cited recent Defense Intelligence Agency estimates that new Soviet interceptors posed a significant threat beyond the capability of existing US forces to counter.

With this in mind, the Air Force began studying the basis for a new medium-cost fighter during April 1965. LtGen James Ferguson, AF Deputy Chief of Staff for R&D, established an Air Staff working group under BrigGen Andrew J Evens, Jr., Director of Development, and Dr Charles H Christenson, science advisor to the R&D deputy. This group conducted prerequisite studies for a Fighter-Experimental (F-X) that would cost between $1-2 million each with a production run of between 800 and 1,000 aircraft. The contemplated fighter would possess '... superior air-to-air, all-weather ...' capabilities, and was envisioned as a single-seat, twin-engined fighter stressing maneuverability over speed, with an initial operational capability (IOC) date of 1970. As a result of this study, on 6th October 1965, the Tactical Air Command (TAC) released Qualitative Operations Requirement (QOR) 65-14-F outlining the need for a new air-superiority fighter emphasizing an '... aircraft capable of out-performing the enemy in the air ...'. Other desired features included a high thrust-to-weight ratio, an advanced air-to-air radar, a top speed of Mach 2.5, and an armament consisting of infrared short-range and radar-guided BVR missiles.

During the summer and fall of 1965, the Air Force continued to wrestle with the F-5 versus A-7 issue. The Office of the Secretary of Defense (OSD), particularly the Systems Analysis Division, was still enamored of the 'commonality' principle wherein the Air Force and the Navy would possess a combined tactical force comprised of F-111, F-4, and A-7 aircraft. In July, McNamara directed OSD and the Air Force to begin a joint study to select either the F-5 or the A-7 for the close air support role. At the same time, but on a lower priority, he endorsed the Air Force's work on developing the new F-X fighter. On 5th November, the new Secretary of Defense, Dr Harold Brown, and Gen McConnell proposed acquiring eleven squadrons (264 aircraft) of A-7s. Although criti-

cized in some Air Force circles as a capitulation to the OSD, the decision to buy the A-7 was in fact a sensible compromise that ultimately cleared the way for approval of the F-X, which could now be justified as a '... more sophisticated, higher-performance, aircraft ... as an air-superiority replacement for the F-4 ...'.

However, under considerable political pressure, the F-X statement of work was revised to call for an aircraft with the '... best combination of air-to-air and air-to-ground characteristics ...' versus the previous QOR-65-14-F air-superiority description. Although this changed the basic character of the aircraft, it did gain enough support in the OSD to allow the Air Force to launch a major effort to acquire the new fighter.

In response to the revised statement of work, the TAC commander, Gen Gabriel P Disosway and his counterparts in the United States Air Forces, Europe (USAFE) and the Pacific Air Force (PACAF) issued the first aptly named '12-star letter' (three four-star generals) that stated simply that air-superiority would be severely jeopardized if the F-X were designed to accommodate both air-to-air and air-to-ground missions. They strongly urged the Chief of Staff to endorse air-superiority as the primary mission of the F-X. Although the 12-star letters received high-level consideration, Headquarters USAF decided to follow the path of least resistance, that is, to continue to study and justify a fighter capable of handling both the air-superiority and ground attack missions.

Concept Formulation Phase

On 8th December 1965 a Request for Proposals (RFP) was released to 13 manufacturers for initial parametric design studies. The RFP specified an aircraft that combined good air-to-air and air-to-ground capabilities, despite the still widely held belief that what was really needed was an air-superiority fighter. Proposals were received from eight companies, and on 18th March 1966 contracts were awarded to Boeing, Lockheed, and North American for a four month Concept Formulation Study. One other company, Grumman, participated in the study on an unfunded basis.

After considering the effects of five variables – avionics, maneuverability, payload, combat radius, and speed – on the F-X in terms of weight and cost, the contractors came up with some 500 proposed designs. To accommodate the dual air-to-air and air-to-ground requirements, the contractors agreed that the

F-X needed avionics comparable to the F-111's Mark II system. Moreover, they understood that multi-purpose meant the use of a variable-sweep wing and that a high-bypass ratio turbo-fan engine seemed preferable to a low-bypass engine. All of the designs called for armament including a M61 20mm cannon with 1,000 rounds, four fuselage mounted BVR missiles, and a 4,000 pound external stores allowance. Finally, all the contractor designs favored podded engines over fuselage mounting to avoid the inlet distortion problems encountered on the F-111. The typical design weighed more than 60,000 pounds and required the use of exotic materials to obtain a top speed of Mach 2.7. The aircraft would have a wing loading of 110 pounds per square foot, and a 0.75:1 thrust-to-weight ratio. Total R&D costs were estimated at $760 million in FY67–72.

Energy Maneuverability
The Air Force was not totally satisfied with the results of the study, and did not further pursue the proposals. Since the final RFP had specified an aircraft capable of both air-to-air and air-to-ground operations, what emerged was one optimized for neither. The new commander of AFSC, Gen Ferguson, and his development planners, MajGen Glenn A Kent and BrigGen F M Rogers, sensed that the F-X requirements were '... badly spelled out ...'. They subsequently were able to persuade Gen Disosway to modify his requirements, thanks in a large part to the work of Maj John R Boyd.

In October 1966, Boyd joined the Tactical Division of the Air Staff Directorate of Requirements and, when asked to comment on the just completed F-X proposals, he summarily rejected the designs as inappropriate to the task. A veteran combat pilot of the late-1950s, and author of the air combat training manual used by the Fighter Weapons School at Nellis AFB, Boyd was well qualified to assess fighter aircraft. In 1962, while completing an engineering course at Georgia Tech, he had studied the energy changes incurred by an aircraft during flight. Boyd hypothesized that a fighter's performance at any combination of altitude and airspeed could be expressed as the sum of its potential and kinetic energies, and its capability to change these energy states by maneuvering. With this idea as a departure point, Boyd thought he could describe how well a fighter could perform at any point in its flight envelope. If the hypothesis were true, this could be used to compare the performance of competing aircraft and determine which one was superior to the other at any point in the flight envelope.

By establishing a standard for comparison, Boyd could accomplish two significant things: he could compare the flying characteristics of existing fighters and derive better combat tactics; or he could evolve an improved design for a truly superior fighter.

While elegant in its simplicity, and computationally straight-forward, Boyd's energy-maneuverability theory required millions of calculations, something that could only be accomplished by the large main-frame computers of the 1960s. But computer time was expensive and Boyd had no official authorization or budget to pursue his theory.

Boyd continued his energy-maneuverability studies at his next assignment at Eglin AFB, even though his billet was as a maintenance officer. At Eglin he met Thomas Christie, a mathematician who also saw promise in the energy-maneuverability theory and who had access to a high-speed computer. With Christie's help, Boyd gained access to the computer and an elaborate cover story was concocted to disguise the actual use of the computer time. Initial comparisons centered on the MiG-15 and F-86 used during the Korean War. Later work included comparing MiGs with the F-4 Phantom II used in Vietnam.

For their irregularity (ie; working outside authorized channels) both were severely criticized. However, with the help of Air Proving Ground Center Vice Commander BrigGen Allman T Culbertson, Boyd and Christie fought off repeated attempts to terminate their studies and published an official two-volume report on energy maneuverability in May 1964.

Much to the dismay of many, including the aerodynamic engineers at Wright-Patterson AFB, Boyd's energy-maneuverability theory proved to be quite accurate. It provided a convenient method for translating tactics into engineering specifications and vice-versa. The energy-maneuverability theory would revolutionize the way designers looked at fighters.

Although the energy-maneuverability theory did not represent anything new in terms of physics or aerodynamics, it provided planners and developers a formalized method to compare competing aircraft directly, and to demonstrate the effects of design changes on aircraft performance. Applying this method, a model was designed that would demonstrate the effects of specific requirements on the F-X design. By the spring of 1967, through the efforts of Boyd and others, the projected weight of the F-X had been reduced from 60,000+ pounds to slightly under 40,000 pounds. The proposed engine bypass ratio had been lowered to 1.5, the thrust-to-weight ratio increased to 0.97:1, and the top speed scaled down to a range of Mach 2.3-2.5. Research indicated a wing loading of between 60 and 80 pounds per square foot would be optimum, but it was still planned to use a variable-geometry wing. At this point, total F-X costs were estimated at $7.183 billion, including $615 million for R&D, $4.1 billion for procurement and $2.468 billion for operations and maintenance over a five-year period. Based on a 1,000 aircraft procurement, the average F-X flyaway cost was computed at $2.84 million per copy in FY67 dollars.

Domodadovo
The F-X formulation phase continued through the spring and summer of 1967. By March a three-part Concept Formulation Package (CFP) and a Technical Development Plan (TDP) were drafted to specify the F-X's rationale, cost, and development schedule. In June a complete CFP was issued and underwent a final 'massaging' during the late summer.

Then, in July 1967, the Russians held the famous Domodadovo air show where they introduced six new aircraft types, including the MiG-25 'Foxbat' (at the time thought to be the MiG-23), as well as several new versions of older aircraft. Soon afterwards, the Air Force submitted the F-X proposal to OSD as the new

Below: **Many various planforms were investigated by McAir during the F-X competition. The aircraft on the left of the fourth row down is obviously a Phantom II, while others bear a striking resemblance to the F-14 and F-22.** McDonnell Douglas

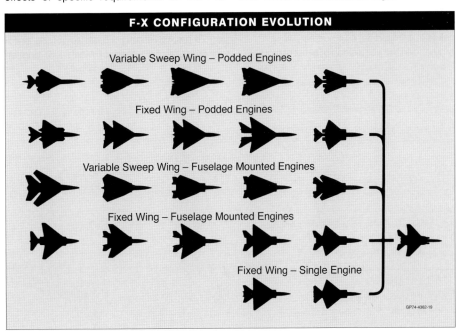

F-X CONFIGURATION EVOLUTION

Variable Sweep Wing – Podded Engines

Fixed Wing – Podded Engines

Variable Sweep Wing – Fuselage Mounted Engines

Fixed Wing – Fuselage Mounted Engines

Fixed Wing – Single Engine

GP74-4362-19

tactical fighter to replace the F-4. The Air Force argued for the importance of air-superiority, without which other aerial missions (close air support and interdiction)[1] would either be too costly or impossible to conduct. It was noted that although the multi-purpose F-4 was a capable air-to-air fighter, its continued effectiveness was doubtful in view of the new, advanced Soviet fighters.

Below, left: **This was the McAir design during most of 1967. The design exhibited higher than desired drag at low load factors. It would have satisfied the maximum speed and acceleration requirements, but not the maneuverability requirement, particularly the steady-state turn.** McDonnell Douglas

Below, right: **By early-1968, McAir had defined this 60,000+ pound variable-geometry wing design. Coincidentally, this design greatly resembled the proposal submitted by Fairchild. Widely separated engine pods contributed to low drag, but overall performance was less than desired.** McDonnell Douglas

Bottom, left: **Beginning to close in on the eventual design, this mid-1968 version featured a delta wing and intakes with pronounced lower lips. Noteworthy are the two-dimensional exhaust nozzles, something later demonstrated on the F-15S/MTD.** McDonnell Douglas

Bottom, right: **A modified delta planform was featured on this January 1969 concept. The air intakes bear a strong resemblance to the MiG-25, and two-dimensional nozzles are still shown.** McDonnell Douglas

This provided an impetus for the Air Force to solicit bids on 11th August 1967 from seven contractors for a second round of studies to refine the F-X concept. There were four main topics of discussion: validating performance in the wind tunnel; matching propulsion requirements to achieve the desired performance, including maneuverability; refining avionics and armament (missile, or guns, or both); and determining crew size (1 or 2). Contracts were awarded to General Dynamics and McDonnell Douglas on 1st December 1967 with four other companies, Fairchild-Republic, Grumman, Lockheed, and North American, participating with company funds. The study concluded in June 1968, and the results were reviewed by an Air Force team that analyzed the results and used them to rewrite the F-X Concept Formulation Package. More than 100 people participated in the review which was headed by Col Robert P Daly. The basic airframe issues were resolved quickly, but the composition of the avionics suite caused considerable disagreement. Specifically, the multi-purpose advocates attempted to retain such items as terrain-following radar and blind-bombing capabilities. They argued that future advances in technology would permit weight reductions acceptable to the F-X, but overlooked the costs and risks involved. This review was only partially successful, since many high-cost and high-risk items remained in the baseline.

Several significant events occurred in 1968 that helped shape the course of the F-X program. The Navy had become disenchanted with its version (F-111B) of the joint TFX program, and had initiated the study and develop-

ment of the VFX/F-14. Also, the Presidential elections in November guaranteed a change in the civilian leadership, both in the White House and the Pentagon. Since the Department of Defense still favored the concept of 'common' hardware, the Air Force decided to make the requirements for the F-X sufficiently different from the Navy's VFX to justify continued development. And, in an effort to get far enough along in development to protect the program from cancellation by the new administration, the Air Force decided to skip the prototype phase for the airframe, and proceed directly to full-scale development, a ploy also used by the F-14 program. The first true requirement for the F-X came in February 1968 when TAC's Gen Disosway issued ROC-9-68 (Required Operational Capability), which was a restatement of the original air-superiority QOR-65-14-F. In May 1968, the Air Force Chief of Staff, Gen McConnell, assigned the F-X as the Air Force's top priority development program.

In August 1968, the Air Staff issued a supplement to the CFP that not only updated the original, but also recommended some fundamental changes. For example, there no longer remained any ambiguities over the Air Force's air-superiority doctrine:

---

[1] Counterair (air-superiority) operations are intended to achieve and maintain air superiority and, if possible, eliminate enemy air interference. Interdiction involves the reduction or elimination of support for enemy ground forces by destroying his installations and disrupting his communications. Close Air Support seeks to provide fire support to friendly ground forces engaged in combat with the enemy.

'...it is sometimes held that air combat of the future will assume an entirely different complexion than that of the past. The Air Force does not share that contention. To the contrary, tactical applications of air-superiority forces will remain essentially the same for the foreseeable future.'

It further noted that the war in Vietnam had taught that smaller-sized aircraft could better escape radar and visual detection. The wing planform remained an open issue, although the 'representative F-X' described a swing-wing rather than a fixed-wing design.

The major subsystems – engine, radar, and weapons – would be selected on a competitive prototype basis to reduce potential risks. Cost estimates in the supplement included $1.162 billion for R&D and a 635 unit production buy at a flyaway cost of $4.68 million per aircraft in FY69 dollars.

The final task in the concept formulation phase was the preparation of an F-X Development Concept Paper (DCP). This described the F-X as a '...single-seat, twin-engine aircraft featuring excellent pilot visibility, with internal fuel sized for a 260 nm design mission, and ... a balanced combination of standoff [missile] and close-in [gun] target kill potential.'

The decision to include just one crew member was arrived at as much to differentiate the aircraft from the Navy's VFX as to save the estimated 5,000 pounds in additional structure and systems. The twin engine design was selected because it featured faster throttle response and earlier availability (interestingly, safety does not seem to have been a factor).

The DCP estimated expenditures at $1.078 billion for R&D and a flyaway cost of $5.3 million per aircraft based on a 520 unit production run.

In a letter dated 12th September 1968, Aeronautical Systems Division (ASD) Director of Engineering Standards, R F Semler, requested a designation for the new fighter. The Navy had earlier rejected the next available fighter designation (F-13) in favor of F-14 for the VFX. With superstition apparently also influencing the Air Force, Semler also declined the F-13 designation and requested F-15 instead.

F-X had a designation.

Dissension within the Air Force

Not all in the Air Force agreed that the F-15 was the aircraft to buy. One proposed alternative, dubbed the F-XX, was designed by Pierre M Sprey of the OSD office of Systems Analysis during July 1968. He believed that the F-15 was too expensive, incorporated too much high-risk technology, was unnecessarily complex, and would not achieve its advertised air superiority performance, a view shared by Boyd. Sprey's alternative was a 25,000 pound, single-seat, single-engine fighter designed specifically to fight in the sub/transonic region. It employed a fixed-wing planform and carried an internal gun and two Sidewinder missiles. Sprey's F-XX proposal shunned complex avionics, featuring

Above: **The North American entry was the runner-up in the F-X competition, and was actually the front-runner in certain categories. The design featured a gracefully blended wing similar to that later used on the YF-16. An AIM-7 Sparrow missile was mounted on each of the air intake corners, while two more were carried semi-submerged in the bottom of the fuselage.** Tony Landis Collection

Below: **North American repainted their mock-up several times. The large ventral intakes are reminiscent of the intake originally proposed for the YF-107, while the large bubble canopy featured excellent all-around visibility. Noteworthy is the use of a framed windscreen; North American was the only F-X competitor to do so.** Tony Landis Collection

instead a simple visual radar, easy and inexpensive maintenance, and a unit cost of only $2 million. The proposal also included a VFXX version for the Navy.

The Air Force and Navy were not impressed. They cited the short, unhappy experience of similarly equipped F-104s in Vietnam, and the limitations of the F-5, as examples of the inadequacy of lightweight fighters. But Sprey and Boyd were not alone in advocating lightweight fighters. Indeed, many experienced Air Force and Navy fighter pilots recommended that the best solution to the air-superiority problem was to '... buy MiG-21s!'. Simulations and flight tests during 1968 (including *Projects Feather Duster* and *Have Doughnut*) demonstrated the superior maneuverability of a lightweight fighter against F-4Es. Although the idea had considerable merit, and was later adopted for the YF-16 and YF-17 concepts, it was ill-timed. The F-14 and F-15 development programs were too far along to be sidetracked, and all the proposal succeeded in doing was uniting the Air Force behind the F-15.

Contract Definition

An RFP was released on 30th September 1968 to eight companies: Boeing, Fairchild-Republic, General Dynamics, Grumman, Lockheed, McDonnell Douglas, North American, and Northrop. Only four of the companies submitted proposals, and on 30th December three of them, Fairchild-Republic, McDonnell Douglas, and North American, were awarded $15.4 million contracts for the Contract Definition Phase. General Dynamics had been eliminated early during the evaluation process, but the Air Force was unable to further trim the competition to the previously planned two contestants. The technical proposals were due on 30th June 1969, with projected costs and schedules to follow two months later. The RFP gave the particulars for what the Air Force was looking for:

- a wing with low loading and optimized for buffet free performance at Mach 0.9;
- a high thrust-to-weight ratio (approaching 1:1 at combat weight);
- a long ferry range, i.e.; to Europe without aerial refueling;
- a one man cockpit and weapon system;
- a fatigue life of 4,000 flight hours under normal fighter operations;
- a low maintenance man-hours per flight hour (MMH/FH) ratio of 11.3:1;
- 360° visibility from the cockpit;
- self-contained engine starting with no ground support equipment required;
- a maximum gross take-off weight of 40,000 pounds for the air-superiority mission;
- a maximum speed of Mach 2.5;
- a long range pulse-Doppler radar with look-down/shoot-down capability; and
- low development risk.

The proposals were reviewed by the F-15 System Program Office (SPO) which had been organized within the ASD at Wright-Patterson in August 1966 with a charter to oversee both the F-X (F-15) and A-X (A-9/A-10) programs. When the priority for the F-X was raised in May 1968, the A-X project was transferred to a different office, leaving the F-X SPO free to concentrate on the F-15. In July 1969 Col (BrigGen-select) Benjamin N Bellis became the director of the F-15 SPO. Bellis had made his reputation in the development field with the Matador and Atlas missiles, and later managed the YF-12/SR-71 development project. In addition, he had written several Air Force management regulations and earned advanced degrees in aeronautical engineering and business administration. On 19th October the F-15 office became a 'super SPO' when Bellis was named Deputy for F-15. In reporting directly to the AFSC commander, he bypassed the entire ASD, which remained responsible for providing administrative support only. The SPO would eventually absorb the Joint Engine Project Office (JEPO) that was responsible for developing the F-14B/F-15 powerplant, further concentrating the decision making power.

One of Bellis' functions was to chair the Source Selection Evaluation Board (SSEB) that evaluated the three proposals. Eighty-seven separate factors under four major categories (technology, logistics, operations, and management) were considered, and the SSEB's ratings were forwarded, without recommendation, to the Source Selection Advisory Council (SSAC). The commander of the AFSC, MajGen Lee V Cossick, chaired the SSAC and this group used a set of weighting factors and evaluation criteria that had been established on 2nd June 1969 to evaluate the SSEB's ratings. All of this data, along with the SSAC's recommendation, was forwarded to the new Secretary of the Air Force, Robert C Seamans, Jr.

At the beginning of December 1969, Representative Otis Pike (D, NY) charged that the Air Force had violated the Air Corps Act of 1926 by withholding the weighting factors from the contractors. SecAF Seamans explained that the act allowed disclosure of the factors, but that such action was '... in no sense mandatory...', and that the act itself was obsolete. The Air Force's position was later vindicated by the General Accounting Office (GAO) which found itself in full agreement with the Air Force on the interpretation of the 1926 Act. There were no appeals of the eventual decision, and in fact, Fairchild-Hiller's (Republic's parent company) President, Edward C Uhl, endorsed the Air Force's handling of the F-15 competition as having '... been conducted in a most professional manner and ... fairly run.'

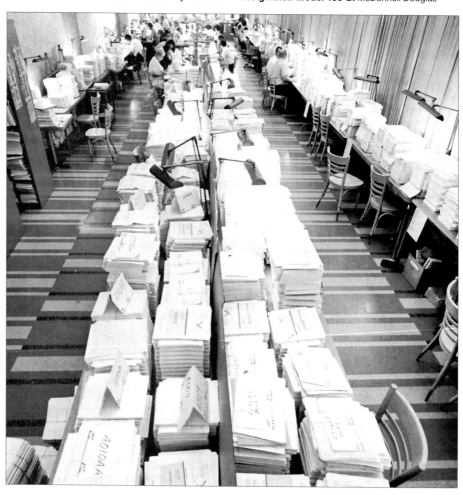

Below: **Donald Malvern led the McAir proposal team through the preparation of this 37,500 page submission. A total of 3.5 million man-hours were expended by the McAir team to design their Model 199-B.** McDonnell Douglas

Chapter Two

A Good Christmas Present

The F-15 contract was awarded to the McDonnell Aircraft Company (McAir) division of McDonnell Douglas Corporation on 23rd December 1969. The design McDonnell submitted (model number 199-B) was the result of 2.5 million man-hours of effort that had culminated in a 37,500 page proposal. The McAir proposal, and subsequent development effort, was led by F-15 General Manager Donald Malvern. The head of the McAir design staff was George Graff, with significant assistance by Bob Little, engineer and former chief test pilot. The contract which McAir received was a significant modification of the total package procurement policy that had received so much criticism in the Lockheed C-5A Galaxy program.

The terms, conditions, and restrictions of contract number F33657-70-0300 were spelled out in a 146 page document that was signed on 2nd January 1970. It combined a cost-plus-incentive-fee (CPIF) with a fixed-price-incen-

Below: **This was the winning McAir design. Noteworthy are the ventral fins and the two XAIM-82 short-range missiles mounted on the forward air intake station.** McDonnell Douglas

tive-with-successive-target (FPIS) arrangement which had three major items. The first item, which was the only CPIF portion, covered engineering and design of the aircraft; aerospace ground equipment and tooling; Category I flight testing; contractor support for Category II flight testing; plus structural, fatigue, and other pertinent testing. This item had a target cost of $588 million and a maximum 8% ($47 million) incentive fee. The first FPIS item included the production of 20 Category I and II test aircraft, plus spares and ground support equipment (GSE) and three static-test airframes, with a target cost of $469 million and a $42 million (9%) incentive fee. The second FPIS item covered the first wing of 107 production units, along with appropriate spares and GSE, and was budgeted at $646 million with a $58 million (9%) incentive fee. The not-to-exceed ceiling price on the first wing of production aircraft was $937 million, or 145% of the target cost. There originally were not-to-exceed ceiling options on the second and third wings of production aircraft, but between inflation and constantly changing USAF production requirements, these options ended up being renegotiated yearly.

Special provisions of the contract included

the demonstrated milestone clause, which required a technical demonstration to confirm the feasibility of the design before large sums of production money were committed. A 'total system performance responsibility' clause, which placed responsibility on McAir for satisfactory integration of the engines and all other government furnished equipment (GFE) was also included in the contract. The Air Force also specified that McAir was responsible for correcting deficiencies, without any price adjustments. These clauses were included in a successful attempt to preclude the massive failings of the F-111 and C-5A contracts. The Air Force could decide unilaterally whether McAir had met the commitments, and could delay funding or cancel the program if it desired. The contract also provided for more visible accounting methods, and required McAir to give 17 months notice if it determined that additional development funds would be required (17 months corresponded to the US government's budget cycle).

Initial planning centered on the eventual production of 749 aircraft: 432 to equip three 72-plane TAC wings, two 72-plane USAFE wings and one 72-plane PACAF wing; 108 for

transition training and proficiency; 54 for command support; 12 Category I test aircraft for continued testing; and 143 aircraft for attrition. It was planned that the eight Category II test aircraft would be brought up to the final operational configuration.

One of the major factors involved in allowing one aircraft to develop more lift in a turn than another is the wing loading. The other major factor is having enough thrust to overcome the additional drag generated during maneuvering. The air that spills from under the wing to the lower pressure on top of the wing disrupts the airflow and increasingly degrades the lifting capability as the angle of attack increases. This degradation is known as induced drag because it is induced by lift itself. In the years that had followed the development of the F-86, designers had purposely reduced the wing area to lower drag and enable higher top speeds. While this looked good on paper, experience had shown that few, if any, dogfights took place above Mach 1.2, and none had ever occurred at Mach 2.0.

The trade-off studies on the F-15 wing were designed around a lift-to-drag (L/D) ratio optimized for dogfighting at transonic and high subsonic speeds. Unfortunately, there was very little data available in this area since the last time any amount of research had been done on this subject had been in support of the F-86 project. McAir ended up keeping three wind tunnels busy for the better part of a year. and the ultimate wing was selected from some 800 analyzed configurations, with 107 of these tested in the wind tunnels. This wing was the antithesis of what the F-4 wing had been, containing no high-lift devices (slats, etc.), and control surfaces consisting of only simple ailerons and two-position flaps. The F-15 would spend 10,150 hours in the wind tunnel during its early development, in contrast to the F-4, which had spent just under 4,000.

New Engines
In December 1967, the Air Force and Navy agreed to conduct a joint engine development program for the F-14B and F-X. Their goal was to develop a high-performance afterburning turbofan Advanced Technology Engine (ATE, also called the Advanced Turbine Engine Gas Generator [ATEGG] program), drawing upon experience gained from the development of the lift-cruise engine of a still-born US-West German V/STOL fighter, the AMSA bomber program, and several demonstrator engine programs of the 1960s. The proposed new engine was required to produce 40% more thrust and weigh 25% less than the 12-year old

TF30 used in the F-111. New lightweight materials and improved designs promised more efficient compressor stage loading and higher turbine temperatures. The new engine was to generate more than 20,000 pounds of thrust and have a 9:1 thrust-to-weight ratio.

On 8th April 1968, RFPs were sent to the Allison Division of General Motors, General Electric (GE), and Pratt & Whitney (P&W). At the end of August, OSD authorized the award of two 18-month contracts totaling $117.45 million to GE and P&W. The competition was won by Pratt & Whitney on 27th March 1970, and a $448,200,000 contract was issued covering development, testing, and procurement of 90 engines. The Air Force and Navy had several significant disagreements concerning the management and procurement structures associated with the ATE program. The solution was the formation of a Joint Engine Project Office (JEPO), which was later absorbed into the F-15 SPO, with BrigGen Bellis reporting to the Chief of the Naval Materiel Command on matters concerning the Navy version of the engine.

The advanced afterburning turbofan was developed largely from the P&W JTF16 demonstrator engine of the mid-1960s and the Air Force version was to have less thrust but a longer interval between overhauls because of more stringent Navy emergency thrust requirements during carrier landings. The Air Force F100-PW-100 engine was to use the same gas generator section (core engine) as the Navy F401-PW-400, but the size of the fan (and hence total mass flow and bypass ratio), afterburner, nozzle and other significant components were not common.

P&W had to adhere to two major technical milestones: the preliminary flight rating test, which was completed in February 1972; and the final qualification test, which was completed under some controversy in May 1973. The first milestone cleared the engine for use during flight tests, while the second demonstrated its suitability for operational use. The F100 final qualification test is the only milestone the F-15 program failed to meet on time, the original schedule calling for test completion in February 1973. During this test, the F100 was supposed to run for 150 hours at various simulated altitudes and Mach numbers, but in February 1973, seven months after the F-15 had started flying, the test engine threw a fan blade which destroyed the fan section.

Nevertheless, in March the Air Force approved the production of initial F100s conditional on meeting the 150 hour milestone by May 1973. In an attempt to ensure P&W would meet the May date, Bellis deferred the high-Mach and high-altitude portions of the endurance test. Since it was not envisioned that the F-15 would ever actually operate at high Mach numbers, or at high altitude, this was an extremely practical decision, and Pratt & Whitney did complete the revised test in May. However, the commotion the decision caused within Congress, and among critics of the F-15, very nearly caused the entire F-15 program to be cancelled. The engine eventually passed the complete, unmodified, endurance test on 12th October 1973. The cause of the original failure was traced to a minor manufacturing defect in the prototype engine, plus some undetected rust contamination in the test chamber that had flaked off the walls and was ingested into the engine. However, the engine would continue to be a source of problems for the F-15, and eventually the F-16.

In November 1970, because of F-14 funding cuts, the Navy pared its engine request from 179 to 69 units. Since the larger number of engines set the original cost, this cut required a new formula with a higher price per engine for the Air Force. In the spring of 1971, the Navy further cut its order to 58 engines. An even more major problem shared by both the F-15 and the F-14 programs arose in June 1971 when Pratt & Whitney disclosed an unexpected rise in FY73 program costs for the engine. The total cost of the powerplant development was

Right: **After the Critical Design Review, McDonnell Douglas released this illustration that shows a fairly accurate picture of what the F-15 would look like at roll- out. Noteworthy is the black-painted radome.** McDonnell Douglas

then expected to be $63 million higher than first estimates, due in part to technical problems with the Navy version, additional testing requirements, inflation, and a decline in P&W's business base. Under the terms of the contract, P&W was to absorb 10% of the overrun, with each service responsible for 45%.

On 22nd June 1971, the Navy cancelled its option for the remaining 58 F401 engines for the F-14B, and lengthened F-14A production from 67 to 301 units (and eventually to 557). The Navy's action opened the engine contract for renegotiation, and significantly increased the unit cost for the F-15. The contract was rewritten in August 1971 to reflect the deferred Navy procurement of the F401, with the two services agreeing to split $110 million in overruns, while P&W absorbed $12.2 million. The new agreement covered the purchase of 59 R&D engines for $104,113,996 and 998 production units at a total ceiling price of $1,333,030,970, or $1,335,702 per engine. The procurement of additional engines for the F-16 program would eventually reduce the unit price to levels that had been anticipated with the F-14 buy. Only in late-1987 did the Navy finally get a new engine when the GE F110-GE-400 replaced the P&W TF30-P-412A/414As in the F-14B and F-14D.

During June 1971, P&W wrote a letter to the JEPO asking that the F100/F401 program be granted use of a B-45 engine test bed that had been used on numerous previous engine projects by both P&W and GE. The JEPO responded that the B-45 program would prove to be too expensive, and rejected the request. It is interesting to note that the proposed test program would have concentrated on the area of the flight envelope that has proven to be the F100's Achilles' heel.

The engine difficulties and the attendant cost overrun announced in June 1971 were caused mainly because a 'primary aerodynamic compressor' system installed in the first F100 engines had to be dropped and replaced with an 'advanced aerodynamic compressor' design. Both had been carried from the start of the program as potential designs, but the advanced version added about 100 pounds to the weight of the engine, and had been set aside due to stringent Navy weight requirements for the F401. Inferior operating performance with the primary aerodynamic compressor was discovered in the fall of 1970, and by the summer of 1971 the decision had swung in favor of the advanced version. The switch, which caused about a four month delay in the program, was no doubt a factor in the Navy's decision to cancel its production contract for the F401. Because of tight scheduling, the engines in the first five F-15 test aircraft (71-0280/0284) were Series-I (YF100) powerplants, which used the primary aerodynamic compressor. The first Series-II (F100) engine ran in a testbed during the spring of 1972 and all later F-15s were fitted with engines incorporating the advanced design.

New Weapons

It was decided early during conceptual development that the new fighter would employ a cannon and short-range missiles as its primary armament. Several studies indicated that a new cannon, using caseless ammunition, could be developed that would significantly improve the F-15's kill probability, despite the technical problems previously encountered by the Army with caseless ammunition. In mid-1968 contracts were awarded to General Electric and Philco-Ford for the development of a 25mm cannon using caseless ammunition. The perceived benefits of caseless ammunition were a faster, less complicated, firing cycle since there were no empty cases to remove, and the ability to carry more rounds for a given amount of weight since there were no heavy brass cases.

During an evaluation at Eglin AFB from July to October 1971, each contractor fired approximately 10,000 rounds from a prototype cannon. Philco-Ford was announced the winner, and began detailed development of the new GAU-7A cannon on 21st December 1971 with a $36,181,418 three year contract for 10 cannon and 160,000 rounds of ammunition. The caseless ammunition for the Philco-Ford design was developed and produced by Brunswick Corporation of Sugar Grove, Virginia. Technical problems with the ammunition and the attendant cost overruns caused the Air Force to abandon the project in November 1972, and subsequently the GE M61A1 Vulcan 20mm cannon was selected as the F-15's internal armament, although provisions for the 25mm cannon exist in all airframes except the F-15E (and its variants).

Missiles have not enjoyed a good reputation among fighter pilots, and the reason is that they have not performed very well. During use in Southeast Asia, only 18% of the AIM-9s fired hit their targets, while the success rate for the AIM-7 was even worse, at 9%. In March 1970, General Dynamics, Hughes, and Philco-Ford received contracts for the development of the XAIM-82A short-range dogfight missile to arm the F-15 and other aircraft. By September, rising costs, political pressures, and budgetary restrictions had forced the Air Force to cancel the contracts and fall back to the Sidewinder and Sparrow III. As late as 1980, a study released by the Defense Department concluded that the single-shot kill probability of the AIM-9 was 50% and that of the AIM-7 was 35% when in Navy service, and only 28% for both types[2] in Air Force service. The lower Air Force figure probably reflects the smaller and more agile targets the Air Force expects to meet in combat. Even in the mid-1990s, the US is just beginning the development of a successor for the AIM-9, although the AIM-120 AMRAAM is finally replacing the Sparrow.

Starting in March 1970, NASA conducted an early independent laboratory evaluation of the McAir design and found the F-15's subsonic drag level was higher than predicted by McAir. To correct this problem, designers removed the ventral fins and enlarged the vertical fins, along with significantly altering their shape. These changes produced the desired drag level and also enhanced stability slightly. The F-15 passed its preliminary design review (PDR) in September 1970, and the airframe critical design review (CDR) was successfully accomplished in April 1971. Changes from the original F-X design presented during the CDR included: increased height and area for the vertical fins and deletion of the ventral fins (as a result of the NASA study); horizontal tail surfaces and wings moved aft five inches to improve aircraft balance; redesign of the engine air intakes with cowl fences on the upper outer edge and a new cowl lip; and a more symmetrical nose radome to enhance radar performance. It was stated that the airframe would comprise 35.3% aluminum, 26.7% titanium, and 37.8% composites and other materials. The CDR package proposed an initial production rate of one aircraft bimonthly, increasing to one aircraft per month as the production staff acquired the necessary skills and experience to step-up to that rate with no increase in hours worked. It was planned to step-up to a maximum production rate of 12 aircraft per month. Structural testing of major subassemblies began in November 1971, with the first aircraft scheduled for roll-out in June 1972.

Congressional Reviews

Congress began to take several long looks at both the F-14 and F-15 programs during 1971 with the goal of eliminating one of them to save money. The aircraft were compared against each other and also against the MiG-25. Gen McConnell and Adm Thomas Moore, Chief of Naval Operations, agreed to present a unified view to Congress that the two aircraft were designed for different missions (air-superiority versus fleet defense). Nevertheless, several alternatives to the F-14/F-15 were proposed, including acceptance of one type by both services, or limited procurement of each, augmented by purchases of cheaper, less capable, lightweight fighters. Criticism of the F-15 also prodded the Air Force to look at other aircraft. Among the more interesting alternatives was a study by Lockheed Skunk Works' Kelly Johnson that combined the speed of the YF-12 with the maneuverability of the F-15. Eventually it was decided that the cost of developing such an aircraft would be prohibitive.

Fortunately for the F-15, development was more or less on track, and the only significant cost overrun (the engine) could be blamed on the Navy. However, the Air Force did agree to undertake the development of two prototype designs for lightweight fighters, and out of this program emerged the General Dynamics

[2] In contrast to its indifferent success in Vietnam, the Sparrow's performance in Desert Storm was difficult to fault, with 29 Iraqi aircraft claimed during the seven-week war, 67% of the total.

Above, left: **The first of the 3/8th-scale F-15 RPRVs is rolled out at Dryden. Like the real aircraft, these models originally had 'square' wingtips and smooth horizontal stabilizers.** NASA/DFRC

Above, right: **The third model continued to be used at Dryden as the Spin Research Vehicle well into the 1980s. Noteworthy is the elongated nose that was fitted to the vehicle late in its career.** NASA/DFRC

Right: **Dryden's ever-ready NB-52 carries one of the 3/8th-scale F-15 RPRVs to altitude in preparation for a test flight.** NASA/DFRC

YF-16 and Northrop YF-17. These fighters were very reminiscent of the aircraft proposed by Pierre Sprey during 1968 and would prove to be nearly equal to the F-15 in terms of performance, and substantially less expensive, although neither could match the operational firepower of the F-15. The YF-16 was subsequently selected for further development, and has enjoyed a healthy international production run despite a forced diversion away from its lightweight fighter origins (i.e.; more weapons, radar, avionics, etc.).

In February 1972, Secretary of the Air Force Seamans placed the increase in overall engine program costs at $532 million. To circumvent the increased costs to some extent, the equipment list for the F-15 was pared back in early 1972, eliminating the planned multi-sensor display, the moving map display, the helmet-mounted sight, and the Target Identification System Electro-Optical (TISEO). The planned vertical tape-style instrumentation was also eliminated in favor of less-expensive conventional round dials. Several other items were considered for elimination, but subsequently reinstated including the bird-proof windshield. The omission of this equipment, particularly the long-range optics, would hamper the eventual operational use of the F-15.

New Radar

In August 1968, the Air Force awarded contracts to Hughes and Westinghouse for the development and testing of a new X-band pulse-Doppler radar set for the F-X fighter. During the initial analysis for the new radar system, the following configurations were considered:

1. Radar for ranging, an optical computing sight, and a dive-bombing capability utilizing a depressed reticle.
2. As above, plus a tracking radar for all-weather capability against airborne targets and semiactive guidance for Sparrow III air-to-air missiles.
3. As above, plus expansion of the tracking radar to allow detection of low flying targets and a heads-up display for aerial combat.
4. As above, with expanded radar and on-board computers to provide a limited capability against ground targets. In addition, provisions were allocated for an optical means of identifying distant airborne targets (TISEO).
5. The most complex configuration, with a multi-purpose radar suitable for blind bombing and aerial combat, as well as all the features contained in the above configurations.

In the final analysis, the fourth option was chosen, with the radar possessing a 'look-down/shoot-down' feature that would allow the detection and tracking of targets among ground clutter. The fifth option would eventually evolve into the system installed in the F-15E Strike Eagle. After the award of the F-15 contract, McAir was given the responsibility for the selection of the winning radar, subject to Air Force approval. During 1970, the two compet-

ing systems were installed in test aircraft for airborne trials, with Hughes using a Douglas WB-66D (55-391) with an F-15 radome attached to the nose. In October 1970, McAir awarded Hughes an $82 million contract for the design, development and testing of the new long range, lightweight radar.

On 12th October 1973, a 3/8th-scale model of the F-15 was dropped from the NASA NB-52 (52-0008) from 45,000 feet at 175 knots, initiating a unique flight test series. The model was controlled from a ground station at the Dryden Flight Research Center by NASA pilot Einar K Enevoldson. The flight lasted approximately eight minutes, and the model was recovered by a helicopter at approximately 15,000 feet. Alternately, skid-type landing gear could be used to land on one of Edwards' dry lakes. G P Layton was the NASA program manager for the remotely piloted research vehicle (RPRV) project which was developed to explore the F-15's stall and spin characteristics prior to the upcoming flight test program. Three models were built, the third having a more refined flight control system than the first two. The unpowered models were constructed by McAir out of aluminum, wood, and fiberglass and were 23.8 feet long, had a 16.0 foot wingspan and weighed approximately 2,425 pounds. The third model, complete with a new paint job, continued to be flown by DFRC well into the 1980s as the Spin Research Vehicle (SRV). The first F-15A-1-MC (71-0280) was rolled out

Chapter Three

The Eagle Rolls Out

The first F-15A-1-MC (17-0280) was rolled out of McAir's St. Louis plant on 26th June 1972. At that point, the program was essentially on schedule, with costs cited as below target, in contrast to the significant cost overruns and schedule slips so obvious on the F-111 and C-5A programs. Although the airframe and avionics efforts were on schedule, Pratt & Whitney was still running behind on both deliveries and testing. Total funding for the F-15 program through FY69 had amounted to $77.5 million, with $174.9 million in FY70, $349.5 million in FY71, $420.2 million in FY72, and $454.5 million in FY73 allocated to research and develop-

ment, and an additional $421.6 million in FY73 allocated for the first 30 operational aircraft.

In July 1972, allegations were made on the Senate floor that the F-15 program was concealing some significant problems, including: a tendency to spin; cross-wind landing problems; a radical yawing of the aircraft when the M61 cannon was fired; and a high failure rate of the F100 engine. Only the crosswind landing charge would find fact during flight tests, and that was easily overcome by a modification to the landing gear strut. The engine was indeed having problems completing the required testing, but the problems were documented,

understood, and modifications already underway. At least everybody thought the engine problems were understood.

After roll-out in St. Louis, the first F-15A was partially disassembled and shipped to Edwards AFB in a Lockheed C-5A transport. There it was reassembled, and following systems testing, made a 50 minute first flight beginning at 08:21 PDT on 27th July 1972 with McAir chief test pilot Irving L Burrows at the controls. During this flight the aircraft reached 12,000 feet and 320 mph. Within the first week, the aircraft had made four additional flights, totaling 4 hours and 48 minutes at speeds up to

Right: **The second F-15A (71-0281) being loaded aboard a Lockheed C-5A Galaxy transport in St Louis. After roll-out the aircraft was partially disassembled. The first five aircraft were transported to Edwards AFB in this manner.**
McDonnell Douglas via Jack D Morris

Below: **The first F-15A (71-0280) rolls out of the St Louis plant on 26th June 1972. The aircraft was finished in overall air superiority blue, with unique 'F-15' markings on the nose and vertical stabilizers. The white AIM-7s were mock-ups. Noteworthy are the open main gear doors, something rarely seen on production aircraft.**
McDonnell Douglas via Jack D Morris

Mach 1.5 and 45,000 feet. In the next two months, Irv Burrows and Peter Garrison would accumulate over 40 hours in 71-0280. Flight number 1,000 was accomplished during August 1973, by which time the F-15 had flown at speeds in excess of Mach 2.3 and altitudes above 60,000 feet.

Of the 20 test aircraft, twelve (71-0280/0291) were dedicated to Category I Contractor Development, Test and Evaluation (CDT&E) testing, and eight (72-0113/0120) were allocated to Category II Air Force Development, Test and Evaluation (AFDT&E). Category II testing began on 14th March 1974, although the Air Force had already been flying approximately 15% of the Category I flights on an unofficial basis. The Air Force test organization was known as the F-15 Joint Test Force (JTF), and its director, Col Wendall 'Wendy' H Shawler, was the first Air Force pilot to fly the F-15. The JTF was made up of 13 pilots, seven from TAC and six from the AFSC. The unit later changed its title to F-15 Combined Test Force, and as of mid-1997 supports continued F-15 flight testing. Category III was the Follow-On Test and Evaluation (FOT&E), initially conducted by the Air Force Test and Evaluation Center, and later by the 433rd FWS at Nellis AFB.

Experience from previous programs had indicated to the Air Force that some 25% (five aircraft) of the test aircraft would be lost during the flight test series. In fact, none were lost, resulting in a number of surplus airframes, four of which were later sold to Israel, and one was used for project Streak Eagle. The test aircraft were assigned McAir numbers based on their production sequence, hence the first F-15A (71-0280) was known as F1, the second aircraft (71-0281) as F2, etc.

The flight test program proceeded smoothly, and slightly ahead of schedule, during the remainder of 1972 and 1973. A wing buffeting problem in a small part of the flight envelope (30,000 feet at Mach 0.9 and 6g) was discovered early, and engineers at St. Louis tried several fixes, most notably large fences mounted mid-span on each wing of 71-0288. The final solution was found by engineers at Edwards in March 1974, who somewhat unceremoniously sawed off three square feet of each of 71-0283's wings to create the present raked wingtip. The rough edge of the wingtip was filled with wood and wood filler until metal wingtips could be fabricated, and after the fix was verified, the other test aircraft were similarly modified. It appears that the initial operational aircraft (73-0108) was the first aircraft fitted with the new wingtips at the factory.

The first three aircraft also suffered from a mild flutter condition that wind tunnel analysis revealed could be corrected by cutting a snag in the horizontal stabilizer. Therefore, a 16.5 inch wide section was removed from the inboard four feet of the leading edge of each stabilizer causing a minor shift in the center of pressure, which cured the flutter. The new stabilizer was a production feature on 71-0283,

Above and facing page: **The major exterior changes to the F-15 involved the wingtips and horizontal stabilizer. The photo above shows the original configuration with squared-off wingtips and an unbroken leading edge on the horizontal stabilizers. The photo on the facing page shows the production shapes with raked wingtips and a 'dogtooth' cut into the horizontal stabilizer. The operational aircraft (an early F-15C) carries a full war-load of four AIM-7 missiles on the air intake corners and four AIM-9s on the wing stations. The seemingly normal 610-gallon centerline fuel tank is also being carried.**
McDonnell Douglas

F-15 Test Aircraft

Serial No	McAir #	First Flight	Function
71-0280	F1	27 Jul 72	Envelope exploration; handling qualities; external stores carriage tests; Used by Air Force Recruiting Service as display; to Lackland AFB museum
71-0281	F2	26 Sep 72	F100 engine tests; to NASA; returned to USAF; to Langley AFB museum
71-0282	F3	04 Nov 72	Avionics development; first AN/APG-63 equipped a/c; calibrated airspeed tests
71-0283	F4	13 Jan 73	Structural flight test aircraft
71-0284	F5	07 Mar 73	Armament testing; stores jettison tests; first M61 equipped a/c; converted to ground systems trainer
71-0285	F6	23 May 73	Avionics testing; flight control evaluation; missile firing tests; nicknamed 'Killer'
71-0286	F7	14 Jun 73	Armament; fuel and stores testing; converted to ground systems trainer
71-0287	F8	25 Aug 73	Spin tests; high AOA evaluation; to NASA as 835
71-0288	F9	20 Oct 73	Integrated airframe/engine evaluations
71-0289	F10	16 Jan 74	Radar and avionics testbed; first a/c equipped with TEWS (ECM) equipment
71-0290	T1	07 Jul 73	Two-seat evaluation; advanced concepts demonstrator; F-15S/MTD test aircraft; NF-15B ACTIVE
71-0291	T2	18 Oct 73	Bailed to McAir as demonstrator; World tour; Strike Eagle demonstrator
72-0113	F11		Operational tests; conformal fuel tank tests; to RADC for electronic emission tests
72-0114	F12		Operational tests; sold to Israel in 1992
72-0115	F13		Operational tests
72-0116	F14		Climatic (environmental) tests; nicknamed 'Homer'; FMS to Israel in Peace Fox I
72-0117	F15		Not used in AFDT&E; FMS to Israel in Peace Fox I
72-0118	F16		Operational tests/demonstrations; FMS to Israel in Peace Fox I
72-0119	F17		Not used in AFDT&E; Project 'Streak Eagle'; to Air Force Museum
72-0120	F18		Not used in AFDT&E; FMS to Israel in Peace Fox I

All totaled, the F-15 flight test program generated 38 engineering change proposals (ECP), compared to the 135 generated by the F-4 Phantom II. All but two of these were incorporated into the first operational aircraft (73-0108), and all were incorporated into the third (73-0085). Every fighter design seems to increase in weight prior to and during production, with the original F-4 gaining 3,050 pounds between the first test aircraft and the first operational aircraft. In contrast, the F-15 only gained 188 pounds. And, in fact, between the third production aircraft and the 87th (74-0117), weight was down 283 pounds, or 95 pounds less than the first aircraft.

The F-15 was designed to be easier to produce than previous fighters, with the use of large one-piece forgings instead of building up many smaller pieces saving considerable production effort. The SPO had planned on 690,000 production hours for the first five aircraft, but McAir completed them in only 466,000. The first operational F-15 required 69,000 manufacturing hours, and an additional 11,000 hours in final assembly. By contrast, the first production F-4 (the 48th aircraft) had required 589,000 manufacturing man-hours and 35,000 man-hours in final assembly.

One of the contractual requirements was the capability that an engine be changed in less than 30 minutes. After a fair amount of practice, a highly choreographed McAir team met this requirement by changing a complete engine assembly in 18 minutes and 55 seconds on 12th February 1974. The company readily admitted that the average Air Force unit probably could not duplicate this feat (although, in fact, several have, including an ANG squadron), but the demonstration fulfilled the contract requirement, and proved the F-15 could be quickly serviced. An unintentional, but welcome, feature of the F-15 was reduced noise. As measured one mile from the departure end of a runway, the F-15 is 15 dB quieter than the F-4, and 13 dB quieter than the F-104.

During the proposal effort that led to the F-15 contract, McAir had investigated the concept of conformal packs to contain fuel and systems without taking up space on the aircraft's weapons stations. This had been in an attempt to fulfill the transatlantic ferry range required in the RFP. In early-1974 it was decided to build and demonstrate the concept, dubbed 'FAST (Fuel and Sensor Tactical) Pack', to the Air Force and other potential customers. The prototype fuel-only units were completed just 139 days after the engineering

and the first three aircraft were subsequently retrofitted. The original 20-square foot speed brake was required to extend to an almost vertical angle to create the drag required for rapid deceleration, and this caused a buffet condition at some airspeeds. The solution was to enlarge the speed brake to 31.5 square feet and change its contours so that the deployment angles remained more reasonable. The initial operational aircraft (73-0108) was the first aircraft to incorporate the new speed brake at the factory. Several of the test aircraft were modified to carry the larger speed brake, although they were not refitted with the new speed brake

well, so the speed brake could not close completely. The larger speed brake fitted to these aircraft was the type with the external stiffener.

There was another modification made early in the program that did not result in a change to the aircraft's external appearance. The aircraft, which uses comparatively narrow tracked landing gear (nine feet between the main wheels) and a high angle-of-attack (12°) for landing, was not particularly tolerant of cross-winds. An internal modification to the main landing gear struts, and several changes to the flight control system, allowed the F-15 to handle crosswinds of up to 30 knots.

Left: **71-0288 was fitted with large fences midspan on both wings in an attempt to cure a wing buffet. The final solution was to remove three square feet of the wingtip. The EROS pod being carried on the forward Sparrow mount was an early collision avoidance system used by McAir around St Louis.** McDonnell Douglas

go-ahead. The unit is designed for quick installation on the aircraft and is fitted to the fuselage of the F-15 using the standard USAF bomb lift truck with a simple adapter. Maintenance personnel raise it into position, install two bolts, and make one electrical and two fluid connections. The FAST Packs are not capable of being jettisoned, but the fuel can be dumped through the aircraft's normal dump system and the units were rated to 7g when full and 9g when empty. Each FAST Pack provides 114 cubic feet of space, is 32.5 feet long, and has a maximum cross-section of 24 by 36 inches. The Sparrow

missiles they displace can be carried on the corners of the FAST Pack itself. In addition to fuel, McAir has proposed versions containing reconnaissance equipment, Wild Weasel systems, low-level strike equipment, and even one version that incorporated a rocket engine in the back that could be used for thrust augmentation. Nevertheless, only the fuel-only version has ever been built.

The FAST Pack was successfully demonstrated on the second TF-15A (71-0291) during a flight on 27th July 1974 and was subsequently purchased by Israel for use on their aircraft.

71-0291 demonstrated the concept in September 1974 when it flew 3,063 miles from Loring AFB, Maine, to the Farnborough (England) airshow unrefueled. The aircraft lifted off at 67,000 pounds, including 33,000 pounds of fuel. Total flight time was 5.4 hours at Mach 0.85, with 4,300 pounds of fuel remaining when it landed at RAF station Bentwaters. The USAF later decided to equip most F-15C/Ds with the capability to carry type-1 conformal fuel tanks (CFT), which is a new name for the same equipment, and also specified a modified type-4 (tangential carriage) version for the F-15E.

Top: The standard early publicity shot of the F-15 showing 71-0280 during an early test flight. The day-glo markings on the air intakes differed from aircraft to aircraft. McDonnell Douglas

Left: **The first F-15A (71-0280) looking somewhat tired in September 1974. This aircraft was used for air-to-ground weapon carriage tests, and is shown here with eighteen 500-pound bombs and four AIM-7 missiles.** Dennis R Jenkins

Below, left: **After its test program was finished, 71-0280 was used by the Air Force Recruiting Service. The exhibit could be disassembled and transported by truck to various locations around the country.** Dave Begy

Below: **The first aircraft carried unique markings on the forward fuselage. This photo shows them as they existed in February 1976. The recruiting aircraft did not duplicate them correctly (compare below to the photo at left).**
Dennis R Jenkins

Above: **Aerial refueling was used extensively during the F-15 test program, the first time for an American fighter. Here the second F-15A (71-0281) takes on fuel from a KC-135 tanker. Noteworthy is the small speed brake. The aircraft was overall air superiority blue with day-glo orange trim.** McDonnell Douglas

Right, center: **71-0281 was bailed to the NASA Dryden Flight Research Center. Initially NASA could only afford to give the vertical stabilizers a new coat of white paint with the traditional NASA yellow band, plus a NASA 'meatball' on the nose.** Dennis R Jenkins

Right, lower: **By the time 71-0281 was used for test of the Space Shuttle thermal protection system tiles in 1980, it had been repainted in overall white with a royal blue strip with gold trim. This was the general paint scheme used by all NASA/Dryden aircraft at the time. This F-15A was never assigned a NASA number.** Dave Begy

Below: **The third F-15A (71-0282) taxies by the Edwards AFB control tower. Among its other duties, this aircraft was used to test various locations for the formation light strips. Noteworthy in this photo are the light strips on each vertical stabilizer, and also on top of the fuselage flanking the speed brake. Only the left side of the verticals had light strips.** Dennis R Jenkins

Top: **F4 (71-0283) was the prettiest of the test aircraft. For some unexplained reason, its dayglo markings did not fade as quickly as the other aircraft, allowing it to look new far into its career.** Mick Roth

Above: **Many of the test aircraft were fitted with mounts for cameras to observe various tests. Here is 71-0284 with a mount for three cameras on its outer wing. The cameras were positioned to observe Sparrow launches.** Dennis R Jenkins

Left, above: F5 (71-0284) had a fairly brief career. This photo shows it in 1976, already missing its rudders and speed brake to support other test aircraft. Dennis R Jenkins

Left and below: **The sixth aircraft (71-0285) was used for weapons tests. It sported the name 'KILLER' and kill markings for most of its career. The shot at below left shows the original kill markings in various shades of red. The below center shot shows revised kill markings applied in 1980. The stars are black, while the aircraft types are red.** Dennis R Jenkins

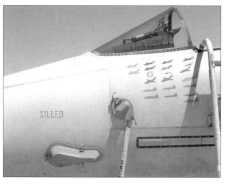

Above: **71-0286 at Edwards during December 1976. A camera is mounted on the aft fuselage boom and photo-reference markings adorn the fuselage. The outline around the national insignia is unusual.** Dennis R Jenkins

Above, right: **F7 (71-0286) was used for various asymmetrical drop tests. Here the aircraft returns from a flight with only a single external fuel tank, the other having been jettisoned during the test. Cameras are mounted outboard on each wing.** Dennis R Jenkins

Right: **The eighth F-15A (71-0287) was used for spin tests. To assist in photography, the aircraft was finished in overall gloss white with day-glo trim. Like F1 and T2, F8 carried stylized F-15 markings on the nose and wingtips.** Mick Roth

Right: **71-0287 was transferred to NASA/Dryden for various tests. The spin chute mounted on top of the fuselage between the engines is visible here. Day-glo markings were carried on the bottom of the wings, but not the top.** Dennis R Jenkins

Below: **Several of the test aircraft were fitted with the larger speed brake. Here 71-0288 shows how the speed brake did not completely retract since the larger speed brake wells were not installed. The external stiffener used on early versions of the large speed brake is also visible. It appears that the entire inside of the air intake is painted white.** Dennis R Jenkins

Left: **The last of the single-seat Cat I test aircraft, 71-0289 finished its career in a striking white and royal blue paint scheme. Several other aircraft were similarly painted after they were removed from test status and used as ground systems trainers. This photo was taken in July 1980.** Dennis R Jenkins

Below, left: **71-0289 performed most of its test duties in solid air superiority blue. This was the first aircraft with the defensive avionics suite, evidenced by AN/ALQ-135 antenna below the nose and an AN/ALQ-128 antenna on the top of the left vertical stabilizer.** Duane Kuhn

Below: **Originally, 71-0289 was painted in air superiority blue with day-glo markings. This photo from November 1974 shows that the AN/ALQ-128 antenna on the rear of the vertical stabilizer was not painted. Noteworthy is that the main gear doors are open, something seldom seen on operational aircraft.** L B Sides

Above: **Among the tests performed by 71-0290 was a series of flights to measure the environment in the cockpit without the canopy in place. A highly-instrumented dummy was placed in the rear seat for these tests.**
Dennis R Jenkins

Above, left: **The first two-seater (71-0290) in its original air superiority blue paint. T1 was assigned to the F-15 Joint Test Force, and was used for a variety of tests. The other TF-15A was used almost exclusively by McAir as a demonstrator.** Dennis R Jenkins

Left: **Like most of the other test aircraft, 71-0290 sported day-glo trim at one point during early 1974. Noteworthy is the 'T1' on the tail. T1 flew some missions with a long nose alpha/beta probe, and others without it.** Dennis R Jenkins

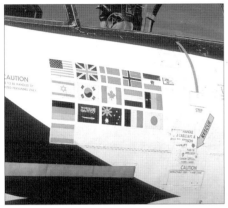

The second two-seater, 71-0291, has led the most varied life of any Eagle. Retained by McAir as a demonstrator, T2 made numerous world tours, including visits to both the Paris and Farnborough air shows. Later in life it would serve as a prototype for reconnaissance, Wild Weasel, and long-range interdiction variants.

Top, left: **Like most of the other test aircraft, T2 was delivered in air superiority blue with day-glo high-visibility markings. This photo was taken in the weight and balance hanger at Edwards AFB in March 1974.** Dave Begy

Top, right: **71-0291 was the first F-15 to leave the United States. In 1975 the aircraft visited the Paris Air Show, where it was assigned the number 65. Four white dummy Sparrow missiles were fitted during the show.** Hugh Muir

Above, left: **Whenever T2 visited a new country, its flag was painted below the front cockpit. This was true in both the air superiority blue scheme and after the bicentennial scheme was applied.** Dennis R Jenkins

Above, right: **McAir repainted 71-0291 in honor of the US Bicentennial during late 1975. Flights during this period were made both with and without the alpha/beta probe on the nose.** Dennis R Jenkins

Right, center: **In 1977 McAir modified the bicentennial scheme by replacing the 'pretzel' with a stylized globe. This 'world tour' scheme accompanied the aircraft on yet another tour of the globe in an attempt to sell the F-15 to foreign governments.** Dennis R Jenkins

Right: **The bright world tour paint scheme gave way first to a standard Compass Ghost scheme, then to this modified 'European One' paint job for 71-0291's role as the Strike Eagle demonstrator.** McDonnell Douglas

Left, top: The first of the Category II test aircraft was 72-0113. This aircraft was used to develop tactics that fighter pilots would employ when the F-15 was delivered to operational units. This was the first single-seater modified to test conformal fuel tanks. After its test program was complete, 72-0113 was retired to the storage facility at Davis-Monthan AFB, Arizona. In the early 1990s, the Rome Air Development Center would retrieve the aircraft, and mount it upside down on a large pole for electro-magnetic testing. As currently configured, the aircraft has conformal fuel tanks and dummy LANTIRN pods (see page 57). Dennis R Jenkins

Left: 72-0114 was the the first aircraft to carry all operational avionics. AN/ALQ-128 and AN/ALQ-135 antennas are clearly visible below the forward fuselage and on top of the left vertical stabilizer. Dennis R Jenkins

Below: The 49th TFW at Holloman AFB, New Mexico, received 72-0115 in late 1977 for use as a maintenance trainer. The 'HO' tail codes are noteworthy since the test aircraft seldomly sported unit markings. John Taylor

Bottom: F14 (72-0116) was named 'HOMER' and was used primarily for climatic tests. For this role, the aircraft spent considerable time in the environmental hangar at Eglin AFB, Florida. This was one of the four Cat II aircraft sold to Israel as part of 'Peace Fox I'. Dennis R Jenkins

Right, top: **Surprisingly, the 15th single-seater (F15 – 72-0117) was not used in the flight test program, and this is the only known photo of it in USAF service. The aircraft was sold to Israel as part of 'Peace Fox I'.** McDonnell Douglas

Right: **Several of the Cat II aircraft, including 72-0118 shown here, were sent to Luke AFB as maintenance trainers during the operational introduction of the F-15. There have also been reports that the aircraft were used by the 58th TFTW to train Israeli pilots at Luke prior to the aircraft's delivery to the _Heyl Ha'Avir_.** Jerry Langston

Below and bottom left: **Another aircraft that was not used in the flight test program was 72-0119. But instead of being sold to Israel, F19 was used in _Project Streak Eagle_ to set the world-class time-to-climb records in 1975.** Duane Kuhn

Bottom right: **The four Streak Eagle pilots (from left to right): McAir's Pete Garrison; Maj W R 'Mac' Macfarlane; Maj Roger Smith; and Maj Dave Peterson. Garrison was instrumental in developing the flight profiles used on the record flights flown by the three Air Force pilots.** McDonnell Douglas

Top: **The last test F-15, 72-0120, was never used during the test program, and was sold to Israel as part of 'Peace Fox I'.** Dennis R Jenkins

Left, center: **The instrument panel of 71-0280 in January 1976. A great deal of test instrumentation was installed in most of the early F-15As.** Dennis R Jenkins

Left: **Category II aircraft began to have cockpits closer to the expected production configuration. This is 72-0113 in November 1975.**
Dennis R Jenkins

Above, center: **Cameras were fitted to almost all the Category I aircraft at some point in their careers. Here, 71-0286 has cameras mounted to observe weapons release tests in September 1973.** Mick Roth

Above: **Long test booms with alpha/beta vanes were also carried by many Category I aircraft sometime during their careers.** Dennis R Jenkins

Chapter Four

The First Eagles – F-15A/B

The F-15A/B was the initial operational configuration, with 384 F-15As and 61 F-15Bs being built, including foreign military sales to Israel. The F-15B is a two-seat version of the F-15A, and was designated TF-15A until October 1978. The inclusion of the second seat and attendant systems increased the aircraft weight by approximately 800 pounds although the only external difference is a slightly-reshaped canopy that is four inches higher. The two-seater is fully mission capable with the exception of not carrying the Northrop AN/ALQ-135 ECM system, which is normally located in the area occupied by the second seat. The first operational aircraft, a TF-15A-7-MC (73-0108) was delivered to the 555th TFTS at Luke AFB on 14th November 1974.

Deliveries of the first operational F-15A/Bs to the 1st TFW at Langley AFB, began in January 1976, replacing F-4Es. Although by all accounts smooth for a new fighter, the introduction of the F-15 into service was not without its problems. The first squadrons found that they could not mount the planned number of sorties because of various minor maintenance problems, but the most serious concern was the engines. The F100 had numerous teething troubles, which should have been expected for such a new and advanced engine. The F-15

was the first of a new generation of highly-maneuverable fighters, and the Air Force had grossly underestimated the number of engine power cycles per sortie where the pilots were constantly changing throttle settings to exploit their newfound maneuverability while not over-stressing their aircraft. This caused unexpected high wear and tear on engine components, resulting in frequent failures of components such as first-stage turbine blades. But the most serious problem was with stagnation stalling.

Since the compressor blades of a jet engine are airfoil sections, they can stall if the angle at which the airflow strikes them exceeds a critical value, cutting off airflow into the combustion chamber. Stagnation stalls most often occurred during high angle-of-attack maneuvers, and they usually resulted in abrupt interruptions of the flow of air through the compressor. This caused the engine core to lose speed, and the turbine to overheat. If this condition was not quickly corrected, damage to the turbine could take place or a fire could occur. This was especially dangerous in a twin-engine aircraft like the F-15, since the pilot might not immediately notice that one of his engines had failed. To correct for this, an audible warning system was attached to the turbine temperature reading.

Stagnation stalls could also be caused by a 'hard' afterburner start, which was the afterburner failing to light when commanded to do so by the pilot. In this case, large amounts of unburnt fuel collected in the aft end of the tailpipe, which were explosively ignited by the hot gases coming from the engine core. The pressure wave from the explosion then propagated forward to the fan, causing the fan to stall and sometimes even causing the forward compressor stage to stall as well. These types of stagnation stalls usually occurred at high altitudes and at high Mach numbers. The normal recovery technique for a stagnation stall was for the pilot to shut the engine off and allow it to spool down, then attempt a restart as soon as

Below: **The F-15 was introduced to operational service in a ceremony at Luke AFB on 14th November 1974. The first operational aircraft was a TF-15A (73-0108) named 'TAC 1', and was dedicated by President Gerald Ford. The aircraft was air-superiority blue, and did not carry tail codes yet. Like most of the air-superiority blue aircraft, the refueling receptacle door was painted a dark gray. Two TF-15As actually arrived at Luke on the same day, but the second (73-0109) was not presented to the public, and did not have a name.** Dennis R Jenkins

the turbine temperature returned to a normal level. Of course, this was unacceptable in combat situations or at low altitudes.

There were frequent groundings and delays in engine deliveries while an attempt was made to fix these problems. Strikes at two major subcontractors aggravated the problem and further delayed the delivery of engines. By the end of 1979, the Air Force was forced to accept F-15 airframes and place them in storage until sufficient numbers of engines could be delivered to fly the aircraft. A massive effort by P&W helped alleviate this problem, but the F-15 suffered from an engine shortage for a long time.

Early problems with the reliability of the F100 engines were largely overcome by improvements in materials, maintenance, and operating procedures. The installation of a quartz window in the side of the afterburner assembly to enable a sensor to monitor the pilot flame of the augmentor helped to cure the problem with the 'hard' afterburner starts. Modifications to the fuel control system helped lower the frequency of stagnation stalls. During 1976 the F-15 fleet had suffered 11-12 stagnation stalls per 1,000 flying hours but by the end 1981, this rate was down to 1.5 per thousand. However, the F100 still had a reputation of being a temperamental engine under certain conditions until digital electronic engine controls were developed for the F100-PW-220.

Engine problems not withstanding, not a single F-15 was lost during the flight test program, and the F-15 is the only USAF jet fighter to complete its first 5,000 flight hours without a loss. The first F-15 loss (73-0088) occurred on 15th October 1975 after a total of 7,300 hours had been accumulated by 47 F-15s. This loss resulted from the pilot turning off both generators because he had smoke in the cockpit, resulting in a temporary loss of power to the fuel boost pumps, causing both engines to flame-out. The emergency generator came on-line, but the aircraft had been on a low level gunnery mission, and was at too low an altitude to effect an air-start, but the pilot ejected successfully. The second F-15 loss (74-0129)

This page, top to bottom:

After the arrival ceremonies, TAC 1 (73-0108) received white tail codes and markings from the 555th TFTS. All early Luke aircraft, with the exception of 73-0109, carried white tail codes. Dennis R Jenkins

This is how 73-0108 looked in June 1991 while serving with the Georgia ANG. A small 'TAC ONE' badge is on air intake, commemorating the F-15's 1975 introduction to operational service. Jeff Puzzullo via the Mick Roth Collection

The first single-seater to join the operational fleet was 73-0085. Dennis R Jenkins

A dubious distinction. 73-0088 was the first F-15 to be lost when it crashed on a low-level mission at the GIla Bend Gunnery Range in southern Arizona. Dennis R Jenkins

occurred in early 1977 after 177 Eagles had accumulated over 30,000 flight hours. The aircraft collided with an aggressor F-5E during a Red Flag exercise at Nellis AFB.

In fact, by the end of FY88, the F-15 had logged over 1 million flight hours and was averaging 3.27 major accidents per 100,000 flight hours, compared to its nearest rival, the F-16, at 6.52. By FY95, this rate was down to 1.53 major accidents per 100,000 flight hours for the F-15, with the F-16 following at 2.15. This has earned the F-15 the distinction of being the safest fighter in the history of the Air Force.

In the 15 years prior to the F-15's introduction, from 1956 to 1973, the average loss rate for twin-engine fighters was 10.5, while single-engine fighters had lost a staggering 17.1 per 100,000 flight hours (not including combat). The following illustrates some loss rates:

Aircraft Type	20,000 Hours	30,000 Hours	145,000 Hours	Notes
F-100	11	26	–	(USAF only)
F-101	10	12	–	
F-102	10	20	–	
F-104	15	24	–	(USAF only)
F-105	6	8	–	
F-106	4	6	–	
F-111	5	6	14	(USAF only)
F-4	3	9	20	(USAF only)
F-14	3	5	20	(USN only)
F-15	1	1	10	(USAF only)
F-16	4	7	22	(USAF only)

This page, top to bottom:

The first aircraft to be delivered from St Louis in the 'Compass Ghost' scheme was F-15A 73-0100, shown here in October 1975. Jerry Langston

The 1st TFW was the first operational user of the F-15. This is a 71st TFS F-15A (74-0086) from October 1976. Jack D Morris

The 110th FS of the 131st TFW makes up the Missouri ANG. Their markings included a stylized St Louis Arch when they flew 'Compass Ghost' F-15As like 76-0030. Keith Svendsen

Missouri dropped their logo when they switched to the new 'Mod Eagle' paint scheme in November 1993. Mick Roth Collection

A gaggle of Eagles from the 1st TFW line up on the ramp at Langley AFB in October 1976. Jack D Morris

During 1975, several detail changes were introduced as a result of data obtained during the Project 'Streak Eagle' record runs. These included a redesign of the ejection seat handle to accommodate pressure suit gloves more easily, the development of a new control schedule for the variable geometry inlets to improve supersonic performance, and a change in the fuel flow system to help prevent flameouts under low fuel conditions.

In April 1977, McAir proposed raising the F-15 production rate from 9 to 18 aircraft per month during FY78, and increasing the total number procured by 321. This was an attempt to achieve an economical production rate (something the F-15 never has had), thus lowering the unit cost of the Eagle to be competitive with newer, less capable aircraft (i.e.; YF-16 and YF-17). At the higher production rate, McAir offered a unit flyaway price of $8.85 million in FY78 dollars, a 28% decrease from FY77 costs. Unfortunately, the Air Force was committed to the lightweight fighter concept, and F-15 production rates actually started declining.

The air-superiority configured F-15A has an excellent thrust-to-weight ratio of over 1.45:1 with half-fuel and four Sidewinders and four Sparrows. The aircraft has a maximum speed in excess of Mach 2.5, a service ceiling of over 65,000 feet, and has demonstrated a 'zoom-climb' capability to well over 80,000 feet. The only significant shortcoming is a less than optimum fuel fraction since current thinking is that internal fuel weight expressed as a fraction of take-off weight should be about 0.30 for a modern fighter. The F-15A comes in at 0.28, and as a consequence is a bit short of the desired radius of action. This was one of the major reasons for the development of the F-15C.

This page, top to bottom:

An F-15B (76-0139) from the 123rd FS of the Oregon ANG shows their subdued markings during September 1995. The base paint is the current 'Mod Eagle' scheme. Ben Knowles via the Mick Roth Collection

An Oregon F-15A (76-0077) wearing Compass Ghost shows earlier markings that are not quite as subdued. Noteworthy in this September 1995 photo is that the aircraft does not appear to be carrying the AN/ALQ-135 ECM system, although most ANG units had been retrofitted with it by that time. Ben Knowles via the Mick Roth Collection

The Louisiana ANG (159th FW) uses F-15As (like 77-0076 shown here) with a JZ tail code and a call-sign of 'jazz'. Todd Enlund

This F-15A (75-0068) has a pair of AN/ALQ-135 antenna under its forward fuselage, and a light colored patch on the side of the fuselage covering an AN/ALQ-128 antenna. By the time this October 1994 photo was taken, most ANG squadrons had received ALQ-135 systems as the regular USAF squadrons were getting the improved AN/ALQ-135B systems. David F Brown via the Mick Roth Collection

A job that was never envisioned when the F-15 was designed was that of satellite killer. In 1979 the Air Force awarded a contract to the Vought Corporation (LTV) to develop a two-stage low-earth orbit anti-satellite (ASAT) missile. The ASM-135A used a first stage derived from the AGM-69 SRAM-A and an Altair III second stage, was 17.81 feet long, and weighed approximately 2,700 pounds. A miniature kinetic kill vehicle used an infrared seeker to home in on the target, destroying it completely by impact, and no explosive warhead was fitted.

An F-15A-17-MC (76-0086) was modified for trials with the ASM-135A which was intended to be launched against an orbiting satellite after a zoom climb to 80,000 feet. The ASM-135A was carried on the centreline station of the F-15 which was specially wired and provided with a backup battery, microprocessor, and datalink for midcourse guidance housed within a spe-cial centreline pylon. Beginning in the early 1980s, captive flights were made with the missile in place, and the first launch took place in January 1984, the missile being aimed at a pre-determined point in space. Subsequently, three launches of the ASM-135A were made against celestial infrared sources.

The first and only ASM-135A launch against an actual satellite target took place on 13th September 1985, when another F-15A-17-MC (77-0084) of the 6512th Test Squadron took off from Vandenberg AFB, zoom-climbed to 80,000 feet, then launched the ASAT against Solwind P78-1, a gamma ray spectroscopy satellite that had been launched in February 1979. Both the first and second stages fired successfully, and the miniature kinetic kill vehicle separated and homed in on the satel-lite, destroying it upon impact. However, this test enraged arms control advocates, who saw the action as a violation of a joint US/Soviet treaty forbidding the development and testing of anti-satellite weapons. Solar scientists were not happy about the test either, since although Solwind P78-1 had officially completed its mis-sion, it was still sending back useful data. A second test, this time against a dedicated tar-get satellite, was cancelled.

Initial plans were to modify 20 F-15As for the anti-satellite mission and to assign them to the 48th FIS at Langley AFB and the 318th FIS at McChord AFB. These squadrons had each received three or four of the modified F-15As before Congress became unwilling to permit any further testing of the system, and the ASAT program was officially terminated in 1988. The modifications did not affect the oper-ational usage of the F-15s although the wiring and other changes were removed as the air-craft went through the MSIP program.

This page: **76-0086** (left) **was used for much of the ASAT testing. But only 77-0084** (below) **actually used the ASM-135A to kill an orbiting satellite. The two aircraft used different tail badges during the test program.**
Right: Mick Roth Collection
All others: Dennis R Jenkins

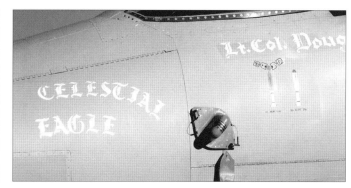

Above: **A pair of General Dynamics F-106 Delta Darts were used as dissimilar air combat opponents for a pair of F-15As (including 77-0131). By this time, most F-15s wore black tail codes, and the standard markings included a national insignia without an outline, a squadron badge on the air intake, and a TAC badge (mostly missing here) on the tail.** US Air Force

Left, upper: **F-15A (75-0020) from the 95th TFS had a blue stripe on the tail and nose, and white wingtips in December 1986.** Mick Roth Collection

Left, lower: **This particularly worn-looking F-15A (77-0079) takes subdued markings to an extreme. A close look at the vertical stabilizers shows the markings of the 199th FS of the Hawaiian Air National Guard.** Ben Knowles via the Mick Roth Collection

Below: **The F-15 is actually old enough to have taken on fuel from propeller-driven tankers. Here a 57th FWW F-15A (73-0087) from the Luke AFB Detachment takes on fuel from an Arizona Air Guard KC-97L (53-0244). At the time aircraft from both the 57th FWW and 58th TFW wore the 'LA' markings if they were based at Luke AFB instead of Nellis AFB, Nevada.** US Air Force

Chapter Five

Improved Eagles – F-15C/D

The F-15C carries 2,000 pounds more internal fuel than the F-15A, and is also equipped to carry conformal fuel tanks (CFT). The F-15C modification package was initially known as 'PEP-2000' (Production Eagle Package). An additional UHF radio, improved ECM equipment, a strengthened airframe, and a new ejection seat were also included on the F-15C. The first aircraft (78-0468) made its initial flight on 26th February 1979 at St. Louis and the F-15D (78-0561) two-seat version first flew on 19th June 1979. A total of 485 F-15Cs and 90 F-15Ds were manufactured including aircraft destined for Israel and Saudi Arabia. The 1,000th F-15 (F-15C-38-MC, 84-0030) was delivered on 3rd October 1986. The last F-15C/D airframes were ordered by the Air Force in FY86, and it is not anticipated that any future air superiority variants will be procured by the USAF. In 1989 both Israel and Saudi Arabia ordered additional F-15C/Ds. Since the basic F-15C/D airframe was out of production at the time, these aircraft used modified F-15E airframes fitted with F-15C systems.

Beginning in late-1979, the Hughes AN/APG-63 radar in early F-15C/Ds was equipped with a programmable signal processor (PSP), which enabled changes to be incorporated in the radar more easily and at less cost. An updated radar data processor increased memory from 24k to 96k words and these added features enabled the radar to operate in a high-resolution 'raid assessment' mode which could identify clustered targets individually. The PSP and other radar improvements were flight tested on an F-15A-18-MC (77-0084) during 1984 and 1985, and all F-15Cs delivered without the radar modifications were retrofitted with them.

Heavier-duty landing gear struts, wheels and tires were installed to allow for the increase

in maximum takeoff weight, which could be as high as 68,000 pounds with full internal fuel, external tanks, and CFTs. An empty F-15C is about 600 pounds heavier than the typical F-15A. The F-15C/D is equipped with an overload warning system which permits the pilot to maneuver safely to the 9g limit of the airframe at all approved gross weights, as opposed to the 7.33g restriction applied to the F-15A in certain flight regimes.

The Multi-Stage Improvement Program (MSIP) is a joint program carried out by McAir and the Warner Robins Logistics Center. A MSIP-I for the F-15A/B was developed during 1982 in conjunction with the MSIP-II program for the F-15C/D, but MSIP-I was subsequently cancelled as uneconomical. Under MSIP-II, upgrades were progressively incorporated onto the F-15C production line and then retrofitted to earlier production F-15Cs. Although MSIP-I was cancelled, as of 1996 all F-15 versions (except the E) have gone through at least portions of MSIP-II, based on the condition of the airframe and other factors.

In February 1983 the Air Force awarded McDonnell Aircraft an $86.7 million contract for initial F-15C/D MSIP-II work, with a further $274.4 million released in December 1983. This covered the introduction of the Hughes AN/APG-70 radar with PSP memory increased to 384k words, and a tripling of processor speed; upgrading the aircraft's central computer with four times the storage (128k words) and triple the speed; replacing the cockpit armament panel with a single Sperry multi-purpose color display (MPCD); new throttle grips and controls; a new video tape recorder split image control panel; and adding provisions for the Joint Tactical Information Distribution System.

Additionally, the capability to carry and launch the AIM-120A AMRAAM has been added. Other MSIP-II improvements include an enhanced ECM suite consisting of a Northrop AN/ALQ-135B internal countermeasures set (single-seat aircraft only), Loral AN/ALR-56C radar warning receiver, Tracor AN/ALE-45 chaff and flare dispensers, and an upgraded Magnavox AN/ALQ-128 warning system.

Right, above: **F-15C (81-0054) from the 54th TFS/21st TFW based at Elmendorf AFB, Alaska. This unit was one of the primary beneficiaries of the F-15's capability to carry conformal fuel tanks. This shows the unit's markings circa 1987.** Mick Roth Collection

Right: **By 8th June 1992, the 21st FW had adopted the Mod Eagle paint scheme and altered their arlier tail markings. Here a freshly painted F-15C (82-0020) is shown without the CFTs normally carried by the wing's aircraft.** J E Michaels via the Terry Panopalis Collection

The changes to the electronic systems resulted in an approximate 25% improvement in reliability, with a corresponding increase in the readiness rate. Flight testing of the new systems began in December 1984, and the first production F-15C (84-0001) to incorporate the changes was delivered on 20th June 1985.

F-15A/Bs that went through MSIP were not fitted with the APG-70 radar or conformal fuel tanks, but received most of the other changes, and are otherwise indistinguishable from MSIP-II F-15Cs. This includes the same late model main wheels that were one of the few distinguishing external features of the later F-15s. The F-15A/Bs are now equipped with the same overload warning system as the F-15C/D which permits the pilot to maneuver safely to the 9g limit of the airframe at all approved gross weights. Instead of the APG-70, a new version of the APG-63 will be fitted to the earlier aircraft, and may, in fact, replace some early versions of the APG-70. Thought was given to using a new radar based on the Navy's F/A-18E/F's APG-73 in late-model F-15C/Ds, but this was discarded due to lack of development funds. The new APG-63(V)1 radar provides improved supportability and operational capabilities.

Although the installation of TISEO on the F-15 was abandoned in 1972, the development of a new generation electro-optical sensor was initiated in 1987. Dubbed 'Eagle Eye III' by Perkin-Elmer, this sensor was to be mounted in the same left wing root space originally reserved for TISEO. The system consisted of a 23-inch-long, 10-inch-diameter lens assembly and video camera which provided an image on the armament system MPCD. Funding problems delayed, then cancelled, the system.

As a less-than-ideal solution, many F-15 units carry a Leupold high-powered rifle-scope mounted on the HUD frame as an aid for making visual identification of distant targets.

Some of the very early F-15As (mainly from FY73-75) have not been upgraded under MSIP and will be retired and made available as gate guards or donated to museums. Twenty-two of them were sold to Israel in 1992 at a very reduced cost as partial payment for policy decisions made during the Gulf War.

Although the scope of work originally defined by MSIP-II has been completed, various other modifications to the F-15 continue, and are generally considered an extension of MSIP. The most recent is a series of software updates, along with some minor hardware changes, under MSIP Suite 2M. These modifications include new software for the central computer, programmable armament control set, APG-63 radar, and JTIDS.

Although not technically part of MSIP, most F-15s will be upgraded to use improved F100-PW-220E engines, which offer better throttle response and reliability. Originally the program was to upgrade 250 engines per year and fit them into operational F-15s, but recent budget problems have reduced the rate to less than 55 engines per year. This engine change requires a minor modification to the engine compartment which is being accomplished on 280 F-15A/Bs by TCTO 1F-15-1134 beginning in December 1991 (with 77-0098 being the first aircraft modified) and 394 F-15C/Ds by TCTO 1F-15-1135 beginning in September 1991 (81-0030). The change should be complete by the end of the year 2000.

Left top: **This F-15D (82-0048) from the 325th TTW shows a new shape UHF antenna under the forward fuselage. All F-15s left the production line with three identical UHF antenna (two under the forward fuselage, one on top of the fuselage immediately behind the canopy). During the mid-1990s the new 'swept' antenna began to appear on all models of the F-15. The new antenna is functionally identical to the older antenna, and may be substituted on an as needed basis during repairs.** David F Brown via the Mick Roth Collection

Left bottom and below: **General Chuck Yeager (USAF, retired) used an F-15D (84-0046) to break the sound barrier during the 18th October 1997 Edwards AFB air show to commemorate the 50th anniversary of his first Mach 1 flight during 1947 in the Bell XS-1. Like all of Yeager's aircraft, this one was named for his wife Glennis. A close examination under 'glamorous' reveals Yeager's autograph.** Terry Panopalis

Chapter Six

The Mud Hen – F-15E

The F-15E is a two-seat dual-role fighter capable of performing long-range, deep interdiction missions in all weather, day or night. The aircraft retains its entire air-to-air capability. The prototype was funded internally by McDonnell Douglas and Hughes Aircraft as risk-sharing partners under a project known as 'Strike Eagle'. The prototype was converted from the second F-15B (71-0291) and first flew in August 1981 as part of the Advanced Fighter Capability Demonstrator (AFCD) program. The rear cockpit has been upgraded with four multi-purpose CRT displays for radar, weapons selection, and monitoring of enemy tracking systems and also contains two hand controllers for the radar, LANTIRN (Low Altitude Navigation and Targeting Infrared for Night), and FLIR (Forward Looking Infrared) units. The aft cockpit retains the flight control stick and essential flight instrumentation. A synthetic aperture radar (SAR) feature was added to the AN/APG-70 to provide almost photographic quality imagery in all weather. Front cockpit modifications include redesigned 'up-front' controls, a wide field of vision HUD, and three CRTs that provide multi-purpose displays of navigation, weapons delivery and systems operations, including moving map displays, weapons options, precision radar mapping and terrain following. For tactical target missions at night or in bad weather, the F-15E uses a wide field of vision FLIR and

Lockheed Martin LANTIRN pods. Successful integration of prototypes of all these systems was demonstrated during tests at Edwards in 1982, and subsequent testing at Eglin AFB. A digital, triple-redundant Lear Siegler Astronautics flight control system has been installed to permit coupled automatic terrain following. A Honeywell laser gyro inertial navigation system provides quick reaction capabilities, greatly reducing the five-minute alignment time required by the F-15C/D.

Some 30% of the F-15's structure was redesigned to create the F-15E, and the airframe is expected to have a 16,000 flight hour fatigue life. To accommodate the new avionics, the forward avionics bays were completely redesigned and the internal fuel capacity was reduced 51 gallons to 2,019 gallons by redesigning the forward fuel tank. The F-15E is the first two-seater to carry ALQ-135 ECM equipment, although to accomplish this the 20mm ammunition feed system had to be redesigned and the ammunition capacity cut in half to 450 rounds. A new common engine bay enables the F-15E to be powered by either the P&W F100-PW-220 or the General Electric F110-GE-100, although all aircraft produced to date have used the Pratt & Whitney engine. This commonality necessitated a complete redesign of the aft fuselage. The engine bay structure consists of large titanium sections

manufactured with superplastic forming and diffusion bonding processes, and will permit future installation of growth versions of the engines. The F-15E also incorporates digital electronic engine controls, foam-filled fuel tanks for greater survivability, higher rated electric generators, an improved environmental control system, strengthened landing gear, and larger wheels and tires.

External identifying features of the F-15E include: bulged main gear doors to accommodate the larger wheel/tire assemblies; a completely redesigned tail hook with no doors; a small bulge on the underside of the fuselage under the 20mm ammunition drum; two AN/ALQ-135B radomes on the aft fuselage booms; and a redesigned fairing between the engine exhaust nozzles.

The Air Force and McAir began flight testing the new systems for the F-15E on an F-15C (78-0468), F-15B (77-0166), and the Strike Eagle demonstrator (71-0291) at Edwards in November 1982.

A standard USAF bomb truck is used by most Air Force units to carry bombs from their storage areas to the flight line. These bombs will be loaded aboard an F-15E (90-0233) from the 90th Fighter Squadron (21st FW). David F Brown via the Mick Roth Collection

Strike Eagle carried all the production avionics and cockpit displays, but did not include any of the airframe modifications. The aircraft had previously been modified to carry FAST Packs, and had been extensively used for early air-to-ground weapons tests. The demonstration program was completed on 30th April 1983 after more than 200 flights. During these tests, 71-0291 demonstrated a take off weight of more than 75,000 pounds, a 7,000 pound increase over the F-15C/D. On this occasion the aircraft was equipped with two conformal tanks, three 610 gallon external tanks, and eight 500-pound Mk.82 bombs. The test program verified 16 different stores configurations, including the carriage of 2,000-pound Mk.84 bombs and CBU-58 weapons.

After evaluating the potential of the dual-role F-15E against the General Dynamics F-16XL SCAMP, the USAF announced on 24th February 1984 that it had selected the F-15E for continued development. The primary rationale for selecting the F-15E was its lower development costs, projected to be $270 million versus $470 million for the essentially new F-16XL. It was also believed the F-15E had more future growth potential, and was less susceptible to damage due to its twin engine configuration. Work began in April 1984 under an initial increment of a $359.4 million FPIS contract. The entire development effort and the planned procurement of 392 aircraft was estimated at $1.5 billion FY84 dollars.

Construction of three F-15Es began in July 1985, and the first aircraft (86-0183) made its initial flight on 11th December 1986 piloted by McAir test pilot Gary Jennings. The flight lasted 75 minutes and the aircraft reached Mach 0.9 and 40,000 feet. This aircraft had the redesigned forward fuselage and carried the full complement of F-15E avionics and displays, but did not have the new aft fuselage and common engine bay. The second and third aircraft are generally considered to be 'pre-production' aircraft, with 86-0184 becoming the first to receive the common engine bay ('F110 Compatible Fuselage' officially), and 86-0185 being the first aircraft to incorporate all production F-15E engineering change proposals.

Five additional aircraft were ordered in FY86, and the first production configuration F-15E (86-0186), powered by a pair of F100-PW-220 engines, was delivered to the 33rd TFW at Eglin AFB in August 1986 for in-service evaluation. Most later F-15Es would use even more reliable F100-PW-229 engines.

A total of 48 F-15Es were ordered in FY87, although six were subsequently cancelled when insufficient funds were authorized by Congress. The next year brought orders for 42 more. Thirty-six were ordered in FY89, but then cancelled when funds were not made available. However, later in the year funding was restored, and the 36 aircraft were reinstated, although with different serial numbers. Unfortunately, growing budget pressures resulted in a concerted effort to cancel procurement of the

F-15E during the early 1990s. The aircraft's performance during Operation Desert Storm brought temporary relief when Congress allowed attrition aircraft to be procured, and a limited number of new aircraft have been ordered each year throughout the 1990s. The 1997 defense spending authorization contained $275 million for six additional F-15Es, or roughly $46 million per copy, including spares and support. (This compares to $155 million for six F-16Cs in the 1997 budget, or roughly $26 million each, and a projected cost of $108 million for each F-22A). The fact that Israeli and Saudi aircraft are built on the same assembly lines means that the USAF can continue to buy F-15Es, albeit at an uneconomical rate, for the foreseeable future. The Air Force ordered five additional F-15Es in FY97, with a need for up to 40 more in future years.

Following completion of operational test and evaluation at Edwards and weapons separation tests at Eglin, production F-15Es were delivered to the 461st TFTS of the 405th TTW at Luke AFB in July 1988. The first operational F-15E unit was the 336th TFS of the 4th TFW, stationed at Seymour Johnson AFB in North Carolina, which achieved IOC in October 1989. In June 1990, the F-15E participated for the first time in the Long Rifle gunnery competition held at Davis-Monthan AFB and scored first and second place.

Below and Bottom: **The front and rear cockpits of the F-15E introduced multi-purpose CRTs. Essential flight instrumentation is still carried in case of a major problem with the electronics.** Dennis R Jenkins

Chapter Seven

Middle East and Far East Eagles

Iran was the first foreign country to take an interest in the F-15 during July 1973 when the Shah personally examined both the F-14 and the F-15 at Andrews AFB, Maryland. Iran needed an aircraft capable of shooting down the MiG-25, and thus chose the Phoenix equipped F-14, since the F-15 had not yet demonstrated this capability. Also, the F-14 was available for earlier delivery than the F-15. As late as 1975, McAir foresaw a possibility of selling 200 F-15s to Germany, 170 to Great Britain, 100 to Japan, 53 to Iran, 50 to Australia and 50 to Canada. Germany had evaluated the aircraft in March 1975, Canada in June and then again in September 1975, and Great Britain during October 1975. In fact, a sale to France seemed so certain that the second TF-15A (71-0291) spent a week painted in French Air Force markings in April 1976 while McAir was giving demonstrations to French pilots at Edwards. However, primarily due to its high cost, only three countries, Israel, Japan and Saudi Arabia, have actually purchased the aircraft to date. For the most part exported Eagles look and fly like their American counterparts. In every case the ability to carry and deliver the B61 nuclear store has been deleted, and usually the more classified pieces of the ECM systems have not been included. As late as 1997, McAir was proposing variants of the F-15E to the United Arab Emirates and South Korea.

F-15 in Israel

Israel had long been interested in the F-15 Eagle for the *Tsvah Haganah le Israel-Heyl Ha' Avir* (Israel Defense Force/Air Force, or IDF/AF)

and four Israeli pilots and one radar operator flew the first TF-15A (71-0290) at Edwards in September 1974. This was Israel's first formal evaluation of the F-15, and the aircraft was pitted against a slatted F-4E during air combat maneuvers. The F-15 won, handily. The US government offered to sell 48 F-15s to Israel, but only 25 were ordered in 1975 under the Foreign Military Sales (FMS) Peace Fox program due to budget constraints. The order caused significant controversy in Israel about procuring such an expensive fighter.

In order to accelerate deliveries to Israel, four Category II test F-15As (72-0116/0118 and 72-0120) were refurbished and delivered to Tel-Nof AB on 10th December 1976. These aircraft arrived on the Jewish Sabbath, and caused a parliamentary coalition crisis that resulted in the resignation of Prime Minister Itshak Rabin. That incident provoked the humorous claim that the F-15's first kill was the Israeli government. Although refurbished, these aircraft were not brought up to production standards prior to delivery, and retained the small speed brake characteristic of early aircraft. Israel is the only foreign country to operate the F-15A/B models.

Almost a year passed before the first of the nineteen new production F-15As (76-1505/1523), and two F-15Bs (76-1524/1525) arrived in 1977 under 'Peace Fox II'. Israel subsequently purchased eighteen additional F-15Cs (80-0122/0130 and 83-0054/0062) and eight F-15Ds (80-0131/0136, 83-0063/0064) under Peace Fox III. The first of these arrived in Israel on 26th August 1981, with deliveries completed just over a year later. Another of the Category II

test F-15As (72-0114) was supplied from USAF stocks to Israel in 1982 as an attrition aircraft.

The Israeli aircraft differ from the USAF F-15s in having AN/ARC-109 radios in place of the AN/ARC-164, and the nuclear delivery systems have been deleted. Like other non-USAF aircraft, the Israeli Eagles do not have the ALQ-128 pod on top of the left vertical stabilizer. However, the Israeli F-15s were the first to be equipped with chaff/flare dispensing units.

Israeli aircraft are capable of carrying an indigenously produced AL/L-8202 ECM pod in addition to US supplied AN/ALQ-119(V) and AN/ALQ-131 pods. All Israeli aircraft use the IC-7 ejection system instead of the ACES II used by later USAF F-15C/Ds.

All *Heyl Ha'Avir* F-15s, including the five refurbished test aircraft, are capable of carrying conformal fuel tanks, which are manufactured locally by Israeli Aircraft Industries (IAI). In addition to the normal AIM-9s, Israeli F-15s can also carry the Israeli-built Shafrir and Rafael Python 2 and Python 4 infrared homing missiles. The Israeli's have named their F-15A/Bs *Baz* (Falcon or Kestrel), F-15C/Ds *Akev* (Buzzard) and their F-15ls *Ra'am* (Thunder).

Israel purchased five additional F-15D aircraft (90-0275/0279) in early 1989 under 'Peace Fox IV' for use as attrition aircraft. No details have been released, but it is believed that these aircraft utilized the basic F-15E airframe since the original F-15C/D airframe was not in production at the time.

Seventeen early non-MSIP USAF F-15As (73-0087, 0093/0094, 0101/0102, 0104/0105, 0107, 74-0085, 0088, 0093, 0097, 0101, 0107, 0109 and 0122) along with five F-15Bs (73-0110/0113 and 74-0137) from USAF stocks were sold to Israel at a very reduced cost as a *quid pro quo* for Israel's decision not to retaliate against Iraqi Scud launches during the Gulf War. All of these aircraft were scheduled to be retired from USAF service, and will be brought up to the same standard as other Israeli air-superiority F-15s.

Left: **The first F-15I for the Israel Defense Force successfully completed its first flight on 12th September 1997. The aircraft took off at 09:42 from Lambert International Airport in St Louis with Boeing test pilot Joe Felock and weapons system operator Major Rick Junkin of the US Air Force at the controls.** Boeing

No. 133 Squadron of the IDF/AF was formed specifically to operate the F-15A/B, with No. 106 Squadron operating the F-15C/D. Both squadrons are based at Tel-Nov Air Base. There have also been reports that No. 148(R) Squadron at Tel Nov operates the F-15 in specialized roles. Since Israel jealously guards its security, few other squadron details are available. Interestingly, the IDF/AF does not have an F-15 simulator for training, and must rotate pilots back to the United States periodically for simulator training.

The IDF/AF has fitted home-built self-defense systems to their F-15s, including chaff and flare dispensers. In addition, most of the older F-15A/Bs have had their computer systems and avionics upgraded to F-15C/D standards utilizing Israeli hardware.

In January 1987 the commander of the IDF/AF stated that the USAF MSIP program should be implemented on Israel F-15s, and that the F-15E should be purchased as a long-range interdiction aircraft. During this period, McAir attempted to interest the IDF/AF in the same F-15F proposed for Saudi Arabia. In addition to the improvements made under the MSIP program, other locally-developed changes have been incorporated. These include provisions for the Elbit Display And Sight Helmet (DASH), testing of which had begun in a two-seat F-15D in October 1986. This helmet sight has been integrated with the new Rafael Python 4 short-range missile. It would take seven more years before the political and financial considerations could be worked out for the purchase of the F-15E (known as the F-15I in Israeli service).

F-15I

On 27th January 1994 the Israeli government announced the intention to purchase the F-15I, a version of the F-15E designed specifically for Israel. A $2.4 billion contract ('Peace Fox V') was signed on 12th May 1994 between the governments of the United States and Israel authorizing McAir to build 21 F-15Is "Thunder" (94-0286/0306) for the IDF/AF to be delivered at a rate of one per month beginning in early 1997. On 1st December 1995 Lockheed Martin received an FMS contract worth $74.2 million to build 23 LANTIRN targeting pods for Israel's F-15I. The aircraft will use navigation pods previously procured for IDF F-16s.

In November 1995 Israel exercised an option for four additional F-15Is (94-0307/0310) under 'Peace Fox VI', but decreased the number of targeting pods to 10. Like most Israeli F-15s, the Thunder can carry CFTs, but unlike previous F-15s, the aircraft are painted in typical IDF three-tone desert camouflage.

The No. 69 Squadron at Hetzerim AB traded their F-4Es for F-15Is to become the first operational squadron to operate the type. The first two F-15Is arrived at Hetzerim on 19th January 1998, with the remaining arriving at a rate of two per month. Unique to the F-15I is the Israeli-built Elisra SPS-2100 integrated ECM set which includes active jamming, passive radar warning, and comprehensive missile warning features. A Kaiser holographic HUD and an Elbit helmet-mounted sight are included, along with an upgraded APG-70I radar set. Secure voice radios are manufactured by Elta.

F-15J/DJ

The *Nihon Koku Jietai* (Japanese Air Self Defense Force, or JASDF) conducted two flight evaluations of the F-15 at Edwards during June and July 1975. The F-15 was one of 13 candidates being considered by the JASDF for their new fighter. After extensive review, in December 1977 Japan announced its intentions to purchase a total of 187 single-seat F-15Js and two-seat F-15DJs. These are basically similar to early F-15C/Ds, minus most of the USAF ECM and nuclear delivery systems.

A license was acquired from McAir and the US government for a group led by Mitsubishi to manufacture the F-15 in Japan. Plans called for the first two F-15Js and 12 F-15DJs to be manufactured by McAir in St. Louis, with the remainder manufactured in Japan by Mitsubishi at its plant in Komaki. A similar arrangement had been used for Japanese manufacture of the McDonnell Douglas F-4 Phantom II.

Left, from top:

This Israeli F-15A is not one of the four test aircraft that were transferred to the IDF/AF, evidenced by the large speedbrake and vertical tail pod configuration. McDonnell Douglas

A pair of IDF/AF F-15As is shown on their delivery flight from the United States to Israel. Except for the lack of ALQ-128/135 antennas, the Israeli aircraft were externally identical to their USAF counterparts. Like almost all IDF/AF aircraft, they have been extensively modified in Israel, and have capabilities that in some cases exceed those of USAF models. McDonnell Douglas

One of four test aircraft transferred to the IDF/AF as evidenced by the mass balancer configuration on the top of the vertical stabilizers. The name on the nose of #620 is 'Storm', but it is impossible to determine what its USAF serial number was. Tsahi Ben-Ami Collection

The first 14 aircraft were manufactured by McAir under project 'Peace Eagle'. The first two F-15Js (USAF 79-0280/0281, JASDF 02-8801/8802) were built in St Louis, with the first one making its initial flight on 4th June 1980. This aircraft was officially turned over to the JASDF on 15th July 1980 with the second one following on 29th July. These two F-15Js underwent 39 test flights with JASDF pilots at Edwards AFB, including weapons firing trials, and were subsequently flown to Japan in March 1981 and delivered to the Air Proving Wing at Gifu AB for further tests. The remaining 12 US-built aircraft were all two-seat F-15DJs (USAF 79-0282/0287, 81-0068/0071, and 83-0052/0053) with the first of these flying on 26th August 1981, and subsequent delivery on 11th December. The next eight F-15Js (JASDF 12-8803, 22-8804/8810) were assembled by Mitsubishi Heavy Industries from knock-down kits supplied by McAir and the first Japanese-assembled F-15J (12-8803) flew at Komaki on 26th August 1981.

The JASDF has a complicated six-digit serial system with the first digit corresponding to the last digit in the procurement year (0 = 1980, 1 = 1981, etc.), the second the basic class of aircraft (2 = multi-engined), the third the basic role (8 = all-weather fighter), and the last three digits the individual aircraft number in sequence. The Japanese also do not use the normal USAF 'block' number system for Mitsubishi aircraft. Instead, logical groups of aircraft are designated with a '(C-#)' system where the # is replaced by a sequential number (similar in concept to block numbers). In 1990, the unit cost of the F-15J was estimated at US$55.2 million, representing a significant premium over the cost of USAF F-15Cs (or F-15Es). As of 1996, the F-15J/DJ continues in low-rate production, and new two-seat aircraft are projected through the turn of the century.

For the aircraft manufactured in Japan, Mitsubishi builds the forward and center-fuselages, and is also responsible for final assembly and flight testing. Fuji Heavy Industries builds the landing gear doors, Kawasaki is

Right, from top:

An F-15J (92-8913) from the 203rd squadron of the 2nd Air Wing during a gunnery meeting in July 1992. Masahiro 'Scotch' Koizumi

An exceptionally clean F-15J (32-8827) from the 202nd Squadron, 5th Air Wing.
Masahiro 'Scotch' Koizumi

The commander's aircraft from the 304th Squadron, 8th Air Wing, was this F-15J (12-8924) in May 1995.
Masahiro 'Scotch' Koizumi

This F-15DJ (32-8060) has orange wing and tail tips for use as an aggressor in November 1991.
Masahiro 'Scotch' Koizumi

November 1986 saw this F-15DJ (22-8055) assigned to the 303rd Squadron, 6th Air Wing.
Masahiro 'Scotch' Koizumi Collection

responsible for the wings and tail assemblies, Sumitomo builds the landing gear, and IHI builds the F100 engine. Other participants include Shin Meiwa (drop tanks) and Nippi (pylons and missile launchers). The ECM system is also of Japanese manufacture.

The ECM system, which is generally comparable to the Northrop AN/ALQ-135, is designated J/ALQ-8, while the J/APR-4 radar warning receiver is less sophisticated than the Loral AN/ALR-56. As of the mid 1990s, Japanese aircraft have been seen with antennas under the forward fuselage that look remarkably similar to the ALQ-135 antennas on USAF F-15s, along with small cooling scoops on the fuselage next to the bottom of the air intakes. A data link for interfacing with the Japanese GCI (ground control intercept) network is also fitted. JASDF Eagles were initially powered by F100-PW-100 turbofans, but beginning in 1991, these were replaced by F100-PW-220s, and by improved F100-PW-220Es in 1996.

The F-15J's service evaluation was carried out by the *Koku Jikkendan* (Air Proving Wing) at Gifu AB on Honshu. The first operational squadron was 202 Hikotai (Squadron) of 5 Kokudan (Air Wing), which began receiving Eagles in 1981, replacing F-104J Starfighters. In 1986/87, Eagles began to replace the F-4EJ in JASDF service, the first unit to convert being 303 Hikotai at Komatsu. In addition, six F-15DJs are assigned to the Hiko Kyodotai, an aggressor squadron based at Nyutabaru. Problems with the Mitsubishi T-2's low power

and excessively-high accident rate led to a decision to adopt the F-15DJ for the aggressor squadron. Like other aggressor squadrons around the world, the Hiko Kyodotai aircraft have received very unusual paint schemes to assist them in their role as adversaries.

F-15 in Saudi Arabia

The *Al Quwwat al Jawwiya as Saudiya* (Royal Saudi Air Force, or RSAF) obtained 46 F-15Cs (80-0062/0106 and 81-0002) and 16 F-15Ds (80-0107/0121 and 81-0003) under the FMS Peace Sun program to replace their aging BAC Lightnings. The original Saudi order was for 47 F-15Cs and 15 F-15Ds, but on the production line a USAF F-15D (81-0066) was swapped for an RSAF F-15C (81-0003) which became USAF F-15C 81-0056, with the new Saudi two-seater carrying the same serial number as the single-seater it replaced (81-0003). All of the Saudi F-15C/Ds are externally identical to USAF versions except for the lack of an AN/ALQ-128 pod on the top of the left vertical stabilizer and the lack of ALQ-135 antennas on the fuselage booms and under the forward fuselage.

The delivery of F-15s to Saudi Arabia has always been controversial, with Israel and its supporters in the US Congress being unhappy about such an advanced warplane being in the hands of a potential adversary. Although the US Congress eventually did approve the sale, a limit was imposed in 1980 which restricted Saudi Arabia to having no more than 60 Eagles in the country at any one time. Consequently

the last two F-15Cs were retained by McAir as attrition aircraft. There were also restrictions placed on the delivery of the associated conformal fuel tanks to Saudi Arabia, which would have brought Israel within range. It should be noted however, that all Saudi Eagles are CFT-capable, and that at least a limited number of CFTs were transferred to the RSAF during the Gulf war.

Some of the early RSAF F-15s, wearing USAF markings, were used at Luke AFB to train a cadre of Saudi air and ground crews. The first F-15C/Ds arrived in Saudi Arabia on 11th August 1981, and have since been supplied to No. 5 Squadron at King Fahad AFB at Taif, No. 6 at King Khaled AFB at Khamis Mushayt, and No. 13 at King Abdul Aziz AFB at Dhahran. On 5th June 1984 two Iranian F-4Es were shot down over the Gulf by Saudi F-15s after receiving intercept instructions from an orbiting E-3A AWACS. This marked the first (and so far only) encounter in which McDonnell-built aircraft fought each other.

US Congressional opposition to the delivery of further combat aircraft to Saudi Arabia and the Kingdom's desire to diversify its supply of military hardware led to a decision to order Panavia Tornados from Britain. However, in a move to ensure the continued availability of attrition aircraft, Saudi Arabia ordered 12 additional F-15C/Ds in early 1989. Opposition within Congress and the White House delayed any work on this order for almost two years.

The Iraqi invasion of Kuwait on 2nd August 1990 changed everything. The limit of only 60 F-15s in country at any one time was quickly dropped, and 20 additional F-15Cs (79-0015, 0017/0019, 0023/0024, 0028, 0031/0033, 0038/0039, 0043, 0045, 0051/0052, and 0055) and four F-15Ds (79-0004/0006 and 0010) were rushed to the RSAF from USAF stocks. These aircraft retain an ECM pod on top of the left vertical stabilizer, although the AN/ALQ-128 equipment itself was deleted prior to delivery. During Operation 'Desert Shield', the USAF released ALQ-135 ECM systems to the Saudis, and most RSAF F-15Cs were retrofitted.

During mid-1991, McAir began filling the 1989 order for nine additional F-15Cs (90-0263/0271) and three F-15Ds (90-0272/0274) that had been placed before the Gulf war began. As with an Israeli order placed around the same time, these aircraft used the basic F-15E airframe since the original F-15C/D was no longer in production. The aircraft were to be

Above left: **A fully armed Saudi F-15C takes off for a combat air patrol during Operation Desert Shield. The use of three tanks is unusual. The RSAF would claim two air-to-air kills during the Gulf War.** McDonnell Douglas

Left: **One of the Saudi F-15S (94-0867) was sent to Edwards AFB for follow-on operational testing. While at Edwards it wore US markings on the wings and forward fuselage. It is shown here on 18th October 1997 at the Edwards air show.** Terry Panopalis

stored in St Louis, and dispatched to Saudi Arabia as needed to replace lost aircraft.

During 'Desert Shield/Storm', RSAF F-15s flew combat air patrols and on 24th January 1991, Capt Ayehd Salah al-Shamrani from No. 13 Squadron used an F-15C (80-0058) and a pair of AIM-9L Sidewinders to shoot down two Iraqi Mirage F.1EQs that were flying along the Persian Gulf coast. An orbiting E-3A AWACS had detected the Iraqi aircraft 80 miles away on an apparent anti-ship missile attack profile when the F-15 was vectored in for the kill.

F-15S

In 1992, Saudi Arabia requested 24 F-15Fs, which were basically single-seat F-15Es without some of the more advanced avionics deemed too sensitive for export. The sale was rejected by the US Congress. Later in 1992, McAir proposed selling F-15H models, basically F-15Es lacking some of the more specialized capabilities, to Saudi Arabia. Again, the sale was rejected by the US Congress. Finally, on 10th May 1993, the RSAF was given permission to purchase 72 F-15XPs (93-0852/0923), slightly downgraded versions of the F-15E, currently known as the F-15S. The contract is estimated to be worth $9 billion, including training, ground equipment, maintenance, and support. This makes the F-15S the largest foreign military sales (FMS) program in US history.

The F-15S is substantially similar to the F-15E, with an APG-70S radar, F100-PW-229 engines, Have Quick II radios, and a full complement of ECM equipment. Forty-eight of the aircraft will be optimized for air-to-ground missions and will be equipped with LANTIRN pods, with the remainder being optimized for the interception role. The aircraft are capable of carrying AGM-65D/G Maverick missiles, as well as CBU-87, GBU-10, GBU-15, and GBU-24 bombs. The most readily apparent external difference is that the F-15S is painted in the new 'Mod Eagle' paint scheme instead of the monotone gunship grey typical of the F-15E.

Initially production was to be at a rate of two per month but budgetary pressures within the

Kingdom have forced this to be halved to approximately one aircraft per month. The first F-15S made its initial flight on 19th June 1995, and was delivered to the RSAF in a ceremony at St Louis on 12th September 1995. The remaining 71 aircraft are to be delivered by the end of 1999, along with conformal fuel tanks and LANTIRN systems for the 48 air-to-ground versions. The sale also includes 154 -229 engines and ground support equipment.

F-15U / F-15U(Plus)

This proposed version was designed to satisfy a requirement from the United Arab Emirates for 20-80 long-range interdiction aircraft. The F-15 was competing with the F-16, Dassault Rafale, Eurofighter 2000, and the Sukhoi Su-37MK. The original F-15U was basically an F-15E with systems tailored for the Emirates,

including final assembly in the UAE. The F-15U(Plus) was a significantly upgraded aircraft, housing an additional 5,665 pounds of fuel in a thicker clipped-delta 50° leading-edge sweep wing, more weapon stations on the wings, and an internal LANTIRN installation. Typical ordnance loads included nine Mk 84 2,000-pound bombs, or seven laser-guided GBU-24s. The F-15 did not make the downselect, and a decision is expected in 1998.

A version of the F-15U(Plus) has also been proposed to South Korea, which is expected to place an order in 1999 for up to 120 new fighters. The 'F-15K' (if the current designation strategy is maintained) would be co-produced in South Korea much like the F-16 (KFP-1). The F-15 is considered a likely winner in this competition if the 1998 Asian money crisis does not postpone or cancel the procurement.

Top: **A fully-armed Saudi F-15C maneuvers during Operation 'Desert Storm'.** McDonnell Douglas

Middle: **The first Royal Saudi Air Force F-15D (80-0107) was initially used at Luke AFB as a trainer for Saudi pilots, complete with USAF markings. The aircraft is readily identifiable by its lack of an ALQ-128 antenna on the left vertical stabilizer. The aircraft was later ferried to Saudi Arabia.** Dennis R Jenkins

Right: **This F-15D (79-0010) is easily identifiable as one of the F-15s hurriedly transferred from USAF stocks to the Royal Saudi Air Force at the beginning of the Gulf War. The ALQ-128 antenna on the left vertical stabilizer was not included on any foreign F-15C/Ds except the 24 ex-USAF Eagles transferred in August 1990. These markings are typical of those found on all Saudi F-15C/Ds, with 'Royal Saudi Air Force' written in Arabic and English on the nose, and a Saudi flag on the vertical stabilizer.** Department of Defense

JASDF F-15J/DJ Serial Numbers

Serial No(s)	Qty	Block Number	Notes
02-8801 - 8802	2	F-15J-24-MC	Built by McAir as 79-0280/0281
12-8803	1	F-15J-24-MC	Built by McAir: Assembled by Mitsubishi
12-8051 - 8054	4	F-15DJ-26-MC	Built by McAir as 79-0282/0285
22-8804 - 8806	3	F-15J-24-MC	Built by McAir: Assembled by Mitsubishi
22-8807 - 8810	4	F-15J-25-MC	Built by McAir: Assembled by Mitsubishi
22-8811 - 8815	5	F-15J (C-1)	Built by Mitsubishi
22-8055 - 8056	2	F-15DJ-29-MC	Built by McAir as 79-0286/0287
32-8816 - 8817	2	F-15J (C-1)	Built by Mitsubishi
32-8818 - 8827	10	F-15J (C-2)	Built by Mitsubishi
32-8057 - 8058	2	F-15DJ-32-MC	Built by McAir as 81-0068/0069
42-8828 - 8844	17	F-15J (C-2)	Built by Mitsubishi
42-8059 - 8060	2	F-15DJ-33-MC	Built by McAir as 81-0070/0071
52-8845 - 8847	3	F-15J (C-2)	Built by Mitsubishi
52-8848 - 8863	16	F-15J (C-3)	Built by Mitsubishi
52-8061 - 8062	2	F-15DJ-36-MC	Built by McAir as 83-0052/0053
62-8864 - 8868	5	F-15J (C-3)	Built by Mitsubishi
62-8869 - 8878	10	F-15J (C-4)	Built by Mitsubishi
72-8879 - 8881	3	F-15J (C-4)	Built by Mitsubishi
72-8882 - 8895	14	F-15J (C-5)	Built by Mitsubishi
82-8896 - 8998	3	F-15J (C-5)	Built by Mitsubishi
82-8899 - 8905	7	F-15J (C-6)	Built by Mitsubishi
82-8063 - 8066	4	F-15DJ (C-6)	Built by Mitsubishi
92-8906 - 8908	3	F-15J (C-6)	Built by Mitsubishi
92-8909 - 8913	5	F-15J (C-7)	Built by Mitsubishi
92-8067 - 8070	4	F-15DJ (C-7)	Built by Mitsubishi
02-8914 - 8916	3	F-15J (C-7)	Built by Mitsubishi
02-8917 - 8922	6	F-15J (C-8)	Built by Mitsubishi
02-8071 - 8073	3	F-15DJ (C-8)	Built by Mitsubishi
12-8923 - 8928	6	F-15J (C-9)	Built by Mitsubishi
12-8074 - 8076	3	F-15DJ (C-8)	Built by Mitsubishi
12-8077 - 8079	3	F-15DJ (C-9)	Built by Mitsubishi
22-8929 - 8931	3	F-15J (C-9)	Built by Mitsubishi
22-8932 - 8940	9	F-15J (C-10)	Built by Mitsubishi
32-8941	1	F-15J (C-10)	Built by Mitsubishi
32-8942 - 8943	2	F-15J (C-11)	Built by Mitsubishi
32-8080	1	F-15DJ (C-10)	Built by Mitsubishi
32-8081 - 8087	7	F-15DJ (C-11)	Built by Mitsubishi
42-8944	1	F-15J (C-11)	Built by Mitsubishi
42-8945 - 8950	6	F-15J (C-12)	Built by Mitsubishi
52-8951 - 8952	2	F-15J (C-12)	Built by Mitsubishi
52-8953 - 8957	5	F-15J (C-13)	Built by Mitsubishi
52-8088	1	F-15DJ (C-13)	Built by Mitsubishi
62-8958 - 8960	3	F-15J (C-14)	Built by Mitsubishi
62-8089	1	F-15DJ (C-13)	Built by Mitsubishi
72-8961 - 8963	3	F-15J (C-15)	Built by Mitsubishi
72-8090	1	F-15DJ (C-14)	Built by Mitsubishi
82-8964 - 8965	2	F-15J (C-16)	Built by Mitsubishi (Planned)
82-8091	1	F-15DJ (C-15)	Built by Mitsubishi (Planned)
82-8092 - 8093	2	F-15DJ (C-16)	Built by Mitsubishi (Planned)
92-8094	1	F-15DJ (C-16)	Built by Mitsubishi (Planned)
92-8095 - 8097	3	F-15DJ (C-17)	Built by Mitsubishi (Planned)
02-8098	1	F-15DJ (C-17)	Built by Mitsubishi (Planned)

Mitsubishi-Built F-15s: 199   Total JASDF F-15s: 213

USAF Serial Numbers Delivered to Saudi Arabia

Serial No(s)	Qty	Block Number	Notes
79-0004 - 0006	3	F-15D-24-MC	Transferred to Saudi Arabia in August 1990
79-0010	1	F-15D-24-MC	Transferred to Saudi Arabia in August 1990
79-0015	1	F-15C-24-MC	Transferred to Saudi Arabia in August 1990
79-0017 - 0019	3	F-15C-24-MC	Transferred to Saudi Arabia in August 1990
79-0023 - 0024	2	F-15C-24-MC	Transferred to Saudi Arabia in August 1990
79-0028	1	F-15C-24-MC	Transferred to Saudi Arabia in August 1990
79-0031 - 0033	3	F-15C-24-MC	Transferred to Saudi Arabia in August 1990
79-0038 - 0039	2	F-15C-25-MC	Transferred to Saudi Arabia in August 1990
79-0043	1	F-15C-25-MC	Transferred to Saudi Arabia in August 1990
79-0045	1	F-15C-25-MC	Transferred to Saudi Arabia in August 1990
79-0051 - 0052	2	F-15C-25-MC	Transferred to Saudi Arabia in August 1990
79-0055	1	F-15C-25-MC	Transferred to Saudi Arabia in August 1990
79-0060	1	F-15C-26-MC	Transferred to Saudi Arabia in August 1990
79-0062 - 0063	2	F-15C-26-MC	Transferred to Saudi Arabia in August 1990
80-0062 - 0067	6	F-15C-28-MC	FMS for Saudi Arabia, 'Peace Sun'
80-0068 - 0074	7	F-15C-29-MC	FMS for Saudi Arabia, 'Peace Sun'
80-0075 - 0085	11	F-15C-30-MC	FMS for Saudi Arabia, 'Peace Sun'
80-0086 - 0099	14	F-15C-31-MC	FMS for Saudi Arabia, 'Peace Sun'
80-0100 - 0106	7	F-15C-32-MC	FMS for Saudi Arabia, 'Peace Sun'
80-0107 - 0110	4	F-15D-27-MC	FMS for Saudi Arabia, 'Peace Sun'
80-0111 - 0112	2	F-15D-28-MC	FMS for Saudi Arabia, 'Peace Sun'
80-0113 - 0114	2	F-15D-29-MC	FMS for Saudi Arabia, 'Peace Sun'
80-0115 - 0117	3	F-15D-30-MC	FMS for Saudi Arabia, 'Peace Sun'
80-0118 - 0119	2	F-15D-31-MC	FMS for Saudi Arabia, 'Peace Sun'
80-0120 - 0121	2	F-15D-32-MC	FMS for Saudi Arabia, 'Peace Sun'
81-0002	1	F-15C-32-MC	FMS for Saudi Arabia, 'Peace Sun'
81-0003	1	F-15D-32-MC	FMS for Saudi Arabia, 'Peace Sun'
90-0263 - 0267	5	F-15C-49-MC	Sold to Saudi Arabia in 1989
90-0268 - 0271	4	F-15C-50-MC	Sold to Saudi Arabia in 1989
90-0272 - 0274	3	F-15D-50-MC	Sold to Saudi Arabia in 1989
93-0852 - 0863	12	F-15S-54-MC	FMS for Saudi Arabia, 'Peace Sun IX'
93-0864 - 0875	12	F-15S-55-MC	FMS for Saudi Arabia, 'Peace Sun IX'
93-0876 - 0887	12	F-15S-56-MC	FMS for Saudi Arabia, 'Peace Sun IX'
93-0888 - 0899	12	F-15S-57-MC	FMS for Saudi Arabia, 'Peace Sun IX'
93-0900 - 0911	12	F-15S-58-MC	FMS for Saudi Arabia, 'Peace Sun IX'
93-0912 - 0923	12	F-15S-59-MC	FMS for Saudi Arabia, 'Peace Sun IX'

Total to Saudi Arabia: 170

USAF Serial Numbers Delivered to Israel

Serial No(s)	Qty	Block Number	Notes
72-0114	1	F-15A-5-MC	Sold to Israel in 1992
72-0116	1	F-15A-5-MC	FMS for Israel, 'Peace Fox I'
72-0117 - 0118	2	F-15A-6-MC	FMS for Israel, 'Peace Fox I'
72-0120	1	F-15A-6-MC	FMS for Israel, 'Peace Fox I'
73-0087	1	F-15A-7-MC	Sold to Israel in 1992
73-0093 - 0094	2	F-15A-8-MC	Sold to Israel in 1992
73-0101 - 0102	2	F-15A-9-MC	Sold to Israel in 1992
73-0104 - 0105	2	F-15A-9-MC	Sold to Israel in 1992
73-0107	1	F-15A-9-MC	Sold to Israel in 1992
73-0110	1	F-15B-7-MC	Sold to Israel in 1992
73-0111 - 0112	2	F-15B-8-MC	Sold to Israel in 1992
73-0113	1	F-15B-9-MC	Sold to Israel in 1992
74-0085	1	F-15A-10-MC	Sold to Israel in 1992
74-0088	1	F-15A-10-MC	Sold to Israel in 1992
74-0093	1	F-15A-10-MC	Sold to Israel in 1992
74-0097	1	F-15A-11-MC	Sold to Israel in 1992
74-0101	1	F-15A-11-MC	Sold to Israel in 1992
74-0107	1	F-15A-11-MC	Sold to Israel in 1992
74-0109	1	F-15A-11-MC	Sold to Israel in 1992
74-0122	1	F-15A-12-MC	Sold to Israel in 1992
74-0125	1	F-15A-12-MC	Sold to Israel in 1992
74-0137	1	F-15B-10-MC	Sold to Israel in 1992
76-1505 - 1514	10	F-15A-17-MC	FMS for Israel, 'Peace Fox II'
76-1515 - 1523	9	F-15A-18-MC	FMS for Israel, 'Peace Fox II'
76-1524 - 1525	2	F-15B-16-MC	FMS for Israel, 'Peace Fox II'
80-0122 - 0124	3	F-15C-27-MC	FMS for Israel, 'Peace Fox III'
80-0125 - 0127	3	F-15C-28-MC	FMS for Israel, 'Peace Fox III'
80-0128 - 0130	3	F-15C-29-MC	FMS for Israel, 'Peace Fox III'
80-0131 - 0132	2	F-15D-27-MC	FMS for Israel, 'Peace Fox III'
80-0133 - 0136	4	F-15D-28-MC	FMS for Israel, 'Peace Fox III'
83-0054 - 0055	2	F-15C-35-MC	FMS for Israel, 'Peace Fox III'
83-0056 - 0062	7	F-15C-36-MC	FMS for Israel, 'Peace Fox III'
83-0063 - 0064	2	F-15D-35-MC	FMS for Israel, 'Peace Fox III'
90-0275 - 0279	5	F-15D-50-MC	Sold to Israel in 1989
94-0286 - 0294	9	F-15I-56-MC	FMS for Israel, 'Peace Fox V'
94-0295 - 0306	12	F-15I-57-MC	FMS for Israel, 'Peace Fox V'
94-0500 - 0503	4	F-15I-57-MC	FMS for Israel, 'Peace Fox VI'

Total to Israel: 104

Chapter Eight

The Eagle Goes to War

The first operational aircraft, TF-15A-7-MC 73-0108 (named TAC-1) was formally accepted during ceremonies at Luke AFB, Arizona, on 14th November 1974 and was assigned to the 555th TFTS, 58th TFTW. President Gerald R Ford presided over the ceremonies that were watched by some 22,000 spectators. Two additional 58th squadrons, the 461st and 550th, received F-15s, and all were used to train pilots, flight instructors, and ground crews. As part of an operational readiness test in 1976, an F-15 from Luke intercepted a Bomarc missile flying at 68,000 feet and a speed of Mach 2.7, and destroyed the drone with an AIM-7F Sparrow III. Although this success was widely reported in the press, this test series and others showed that the Sparrow still has considerable difficulty intercepting maneuvering targets, or targets located in ground clutter.

In 1976, the second TF-15A (71-0291) conducted a world tour to celebrate the American Bicentennial and to promote the F-15 overseas. Painted in a bicentennial red, white, and blue paint scheme, the aircraft flew over 34,000 miles during a two and one-half month period. During this trip, the F-15 logged more than 100 flight hours, and averaged more than one flight per day. In the course of this journey, the aircraft became the first fighter to fly un-refueled across the Australian continent. The trip also included stops in: Alconbury, England; Bitburg, Germany; Yokota, Japan; Osan and Kunsan, Korea; Kadena, Okinawa; Clark AB in the Philippines; Guam; Hawaii; and Luke AFB.

The first operational wing to receive the Eagle was the 1st TFW at Langley AFB, Virginia, beginning on 9th January 1976, with the first aircraft (74-0083) named *Peninsula Patriot*. About the same time the 1st TFW was getting their aircraft, problems began to surface at Luke. The F-15 had been fielded with an advertised capability of 1.13 sorties per day, but in real-life was averaging about 0.61. There were several factors involved in this failing, primarily that the mean-time-between-failure (MTBF) rate was less than half of what had been predicted. It took longer to diagnose problems than originally thought, and there was a lack of spare parts in the logistics system to repair the failures once found. The engines placed the largest demands on the maintenance effort, with about 15 maintenance man-hours per flight hour (MMH/FH), or almost half of the 31 MMH/FH required for the entire aircraft. This was over twice the powerplant maintenance (per engine) required on the F-16A, which uses the same engine. The complex fire-control system was also producing its share of headaches, although these were eased as more capable automated diagnostic equipment was fielded and the avionics configuration stabilized.

By January 1977, 143 aircraft had been delivered, accumulating 25,031 flight hours during 19,626 flights. Fifty-one aircraft were at Luke (58th TFTW), 63 at Langley (1st TFW), and 2 at Nellis (57th FWW). The St Louis factory was producing new aircraft at the rate of nine per month. The F-15 was introduced to Europe with a mass deployment in June 1977 when 23 Eagles from the 36th TFW departed Langley and flew 3,600 miles in seven and one-half hours to Bitburg AB, Germany. Led by General Fred C Kyler, commander of the 36th, the F-15s cruised at 38,000 feet and 500 miles per hour, refueling several times from Air Force KC-135 tankers while en-route.

During March 1977. the commander of AFSC, General Alton D Slay, spent several days in front of the Senate Armed Services Committee explaining the reasons for the dismal F-15 readiness rates, most of which centered around engine problems. In April 1977, the Air Force raised the allowable operating time for the P&W F100 from 500 to 750 hours after several engines in the 'Pacer Century' program successfully passed the 500 hour mark with no problems revealed during subsequent tear-down inspections. 'Pacer Century' was a program conducted in which 12 production engines were flown at accelerated rates to gain reliability and maintainability data. The program involved six engines with the 58th TFTW at Luke and six engines with the 1st TFW at Langley. With the engine problems at least partially cured, the readiness rates for the F-15 climbed to an acceptable level, and would increase further as the new electronic systems became more reliable.

The 57th Fighter Weapons Wing (FWW) at Nellis AFB also received 14 Eagles during 1977, with all of them being assigned to the 433rd FWS. The 57th's job was to continue FOT&E and also develop tactics for the use of the F-15. As of 30th September 1977, 245 Eagles had been delivered, flying 58,800 hours in 43,900 flights. The 58th TTW had 50 aircraft, the 1st TFW had 76, the 57th FWW had 14, and the 36th TFW at Bitburg was up to full strength with 73 aircraft. Also during 1977, the 57th FWW's F-15s participated in the AIMVAL/ACEVAL (Air Intercept Missile Evaluation/Air

Right: Lt Robert W Henemann used this F-15C (84-0019) to score against two Iraqi Su-25s on 6th February 1991. At the time the 53rd TFS was assigned to the 36th TFW at Bitburg AB, Germany. However, by the time this photo was taken the 53rd had been transferred to the 52nd FW at Spangdahlem AB, Germany. The two Iraqi flags still adorn the forward fuselage just under the windscreen. Noteworthy is the tiger stripe tail marking in place of the assigned yellow stripe. Terry Panopalis Collection

Combat Evaluation) test program. This was a joint Air Force/Navy program to evaluate current and future air-to-air missiles on the air combat maneuvering range located at Nellis AFB. The tests also evaluated the impact of differing numbers of combatants on each side during air-to-air combat. The program lasted approximately 10 months and involved F-15s and F-14s of the Blue force, versus F-5Es and T-38s of the Red force.

Engine problems continued to plague the F-15, with afterburner failures and engine stagnation being factors in five of the nine crashes as of April 1979. The Air Force and industry teams modified the aircraft's jet fuel starter to facilitate in-flight restarts, restricted afterburner use and modified engine maintenance procedures. In trying to find a common cause for five engine-related accidents incurred by the 36th TFW alone, afterburner hard-starts were blamed for more than three-quarters of all F100 stagnation stalls. In a November 1979 report, Gen Slay described 755 stall stagnations in 1,385 operational engines. It is interesting to note that P&W identified three modifications to the F100-PW-100 engine, but due to budgetary restrictions only two were incorporated into engines destined for the F-15. The third was approved only for F-16 engines with the rationale being the F-15 has two engines, and hence an extra margin of safety.

In spite of these problems, by the end of 1979 the F-15's loss rate was less than half that of any other fighter in USAF history at the same point operationally. 1978 and 1979 were the first years that the F-15s were deployed globally, with F-15s based at 10 locations in four countries deploying to 12 other countries: Greece; the UK; Spain; Denmark; Pakistan; Norway; Belgium; Italy; Korea; Japan; the Philippines; and Canada.

Maintenance man-hours per flight hour (MMH/FH) is the measure of how much maintenance it takes to keep an aircraft flying. The P-51 in 1944 averaged about 8 MMH/FH, while the F-5A in 1965 averaged about 16. The highest recorded to date for an operational weapons system is 52 MMH/FH for the early F-111D. The F-15s designers spent considerable effort in designing the F-15 to be easily maintained, with an estimate of between 8 and

Top left: **F-15s were amongst the first Coalition aircraft to arrive in Saudi Arabia, and the F-15Es would take the war into Iraq. Aerial refueling was critical to the success of the initial deployment to the Middle East and also when the air war began. Noteworthy here is the blending of the speed brake into the top of the fuselage, something that changed during the course of production.** McDonnell Douglas

Left: **The 49th TFW at Holloman AFB was the only regular Air Force unit not to transition into the newer F-15C/D, and operated their original F-15A/Bs until 1991. The markings here are typical of early operational F-15A/B units.** Dennis R Jenkins

10 MMH/FH. By the time the Category II testing was complete, the figure was down to 19, but engine problems forced this number back up to about 32 during 1979.

Fortunately, the introduction of the improved electronics on the F-15C, as well as the continued improvement in the F-15A's systems, has increased the operational readiness rate to an acceptable level. The introduction of the F100-PW-220 engine, with its digital electronic engine controls, has greatly reduced the number and frequency of stall/stagnations, and has also dropped the MMH/FH for the F-15 down to around 14, the second lowest for any operational fighter (the F-16, by virtue of its single engine, is averaging about 10 MMH/FH). Additionally, the increased engine reliability has further lowered the F-15 loss rate, and at one million flight hours it is the safest fighter in the history of the Air Force.

The Fighting Baz

In 1983, McAir released a report that claimed the F-15 was credited with 54.5 confirmed air-to-air kills, including: 23 MiG-21s, 3 MiG-23s, 3.5 MiG-25s, 24 MiGs of unspecified types, and a single helicopter. Another two MiG-21s were claimed as probable kills. Not mentioned in this report, but clearly evident to any interested observer, was that all of these kills were credited to the Israeli Air Force.

By late 1978, the IDF/AF had received its original order for 25 F-15A/Bs, and the No. 133 squadron was considered operational with the type. The first IDF/AF action using F-15s took place on 27th June 1979 when a mixed force of F-15s and IAI Kfirs provided top cover for other IDF/AF aircraft carrying out an attack on terrorist bases near Sidon in southern Lebanon. A number of Syrian MiG-21s attempted to intercept the attacking force, but Israeli Grumman E-2 Hawkeye AWACS aircraft directed the top cover against them. The F-15s launched AIM-7 missiles against a group of Syrian MiG-21s in a well planned ambush. The Sparrows proved to be ineffective and in the dogfight that followed the F-15s killed four MiG-21s, while a Kfir C2 claimed a fifth, all with Sidewinder or Shafrir short-range missiles.

Another seven Syrian MiG-21s were shot down over Lebanon by December 1980, including four on 24th September 1979, one on 24th August 1980, and two on 31st December 1980. The F-15's twelfth confirmed kill was of more significance since it was the first ever of a MiG-25. On 13th February 1981, a pair of IDF/AF RF-4Es penetrated Lebanon at 40,000 feet flying at more than Mach 1. Syrian MiG-25s were scrambled to intercept, and a few minutes later the RF-4Es released chaff and turned away from the Foxbats. A single F-15 had been flying below the RF-4s, and in a planned maneuver, zoom-climbed to 30,000 feet and fired an AIM-7F against a MiG-25 that was 10,000 feet above and moving towards the F-15. The MiG-25 was destroyed, and the other MiG-25 broke off the engagement and retreated at high speed. A second MiG-25 was shot down by an F-15 on 29th July 1981.

The war in Lebanon in June 1982 brought more victories for the IDF/AF F-15s. By sheer coincidence, No. 106 squadron was formed on 6th June 1982 to operate the new F-15C/Ds that were beginning to arrive. The war began the same day, and the F-15C/Ds were in actuality operated by No. 133 squadron along with their F-15A/Bs. During this conflict, the F-15s claimed a reported 36.5 kills. These included a pair of MiG-23MFs on 25th June, and a MiG-25 downed over Beirut on 31st August after it was first damaged by a MIM-23B Improved Hawk surface-to-air missile (hence, only a half kill for the F-15). None of the F-15s were lost during this conflict, although one was severely damaged on 9th June, probably by a surface to air missile, but its pilot managed to limp it to a landing at Ramat-David AB, demonstrating the excellent behavior of the F-15 after suffering battle damage, or any other type of in-flight damage for that matter.

A year earlier, on 19th March 1981, an IDF/AF F-15 flew into a flock of storks immediately after take-off, ingesting one of the birds into the left engine, and hitting several more. Nevertheless, the burning F-15 was landed in one piece by its pilot, although it was considered a write-off. The ultimate demonstration of the F-15's ability to survive an amazing amount of damage came on 1st May 1983 when a simulated dogfight took place between two IDF/AF F-15Ds and four A-4N Skyhawks in the skies over the Negev. One of the F-15Ds (#957, nicknamed Markia Shchakm, four kill marks) collided with one of the A-4s. The A-4 crashed, and the Eagle lost its right wing just outboard of the manufacturing joint where it attached to the fuselage. Although the F-15 initially entered a spin downward and to the right, the pilot quickly discovered that applying full afterburner provided sufficient thrust to keep the aircraft in the air and relatively stable. The tail hook was used to snatch an arresting cable, slowing the F-15 from its touch-down speed of 260 knots to 100 knots. An emergency arresting net had been erected at the far end of the runway, but the pilot managed to stop the aircraft before impacting the net. McDonnell Douglas attributes the saving of this aircraft to the amount of lift generated by the engine intake/body and '… a hell of a good pilot.' Two months later, the F-15 had been repaired and was returned to service, later scoring a fifth MiG kill.

No. 106 squadron, finally operational after the Lebanese War, demonstrated the long-range attack capability of the F-15 on 1st October 1985. The target of the eight F-15Ds was the PLO headquarters at Khamam al-Shat, Tunis, a round trip of over 2,500 miles. The F-15s refueled in the air twice on the three hour outbound leg from a Boeing 707 tanker which they met west of Crete. After the first refueling, a pair of spare F-15Bs returned home while the eight remaining aircraft pressed the attack with unspecified precision guided weapons. The three hour return trip was uneventful, and all aircraft returned home safely. The IDF/AF F-15s claimed a pair of MiG-23s shot down over Syria with AIM-7s on 19th November 1985.

Right: **Israeli F-15D #957 shows the damage caused by a mid-air collision with an A-4N during dissimilar air combat training. The F-15 was repaired and returned to service two months later.** McDonnell Douglas

The next five years was fairly uneventful for the F-15 apart from the interception of a Libyan Gulfstream IV on 4th February 1986, and the escort to Ben-Gurion Airport of a hijacked Aeroflot Il-76T on 2nd December 1988.

At least four IDF/AF F-15s have been lost in accidents. One was lost in August 1981 after flying through a flock of storks, and the second was lost on 2nd April 1987 when an F-15C inadvertently went into a spin during an air combat training mission. The pilot waited until the last minute to attempt to eject, and his ejection seat malfunctioned, killing the pilot. On 15th August 1988, two F-15As collided during an air combat training mission. The Israelis have since modified their air combat instrumentation system to include a warning of collision courses on the pilot's HUD.

During the Gulf War, IDF/AF F-15s were maintained at a high degree of readiness, including around-the-clock combat air patrols from August 1990 until February 1991. Although the Israeli F-15s were not directly involved in the Gulf War, they indirectly benefited from the conflict. Since 1986, when the advanced MiG-29 entered service in Syria, the

Below: **Israeli F-15C #840, named** *Commando* **(in Hebrew on the radome), shows six kill marks on the forward fuselage. Other than the adapters on the wing pylons for Python air-to-air missiles, the aircraft is generally similar to its USAF counterparts.** Tsahi Ben-Ami

Israelis had a sense of uncertainty about the outcome of an air combat between the F-15 and the MiG-29. The USAF F-15 kills of five MiG-29s during 'Desert Storm' eased these concerns considerably, resulting in part for the 1994 order for 25 F-15Is.

American Eagles Join the Fray
The first 15 years of the Eagle's service in the USAF proved peaceful. Then, on 1st August 1990, Iraqi forces invaded Kuwait and five days later a multi-national coalition led by the United States launched Operation 'Desert Shield' to defend against any Iraqi moves southward against Saudi Arabia. The 1st TFW at Langley deployed its F-15C/Ds to Dhahran in Saudi Arabia and on 12th August F-15Es from the 336th TFS at Seymour Johnson left for the Gulf.

The F-15C/Ds soon began to fly combat air patrols in co-operation with Saudi F-15Cs and British and Saudi Tornado F.Mk.3s, whereas the F-15Es began to train for the strike mission against Iraq should that become necessary. During such a training mission, a 4th FW F-15E (87-0203) crashed on 30th September 1990, killing both crewmen.

A second round of 'Desert Shield' buildups took place in November 1990 when the F-15C-equipped 58th TFS, deployed to Tabuk in western Saudi Arabia. The 53rd TFS also deployed to Tabuk. Aircraft of the 7440th Composite Wing joined the 525th TFS and 32nd TFS based at Incirlik in Turkey. A second F-15E

squadron, the 335th TFS from Seymour Johnson, moved to Al Kharj.

During Operations 'Desert Shield' and 'Desert Storm', 120 F-15C/Ds deployed to the Persian Gulf and flew more than 5,900 sorties. Forty-eight F-15Es were deployed to the Gulf and flew more than 2,200 sorties.

Desert Storm began on the morning of 17th January 1991, and 31 enemy aircraft were destroyed by USAF F-15s during the Gulf War, mostly by pilots of the 58th TFS, against zero losses. Most of the kills were made at long range by the AIM-7 Sparrow, which had performed so poorly in Vietnam but which turned in an outstanding performance in the Gulf War. Six kills were made by the F-15C with AIM-9 Sidewinders, and one was credited to an F-15C pilot who maneuvered his opponent into flying his MiG-29 into the ground. The single kill by an F-15E, against an unidentified helicopter on 14th February, used a laser-guided bomb. The F-15's 20mm cannon was never fired in anger during 'Desert Storm', nor was the AIM-120 missile, although there were more than 1,000 'captive carries' of the AIM-120A during combat missions in the last few days of the war. The only other coalition fighters to score air-to-air victories were a pair of Navy F/A-18Cs which downed two F-7As (MiG-21) on 17th January.

No F-15C/D Eagles were lost in combat, although two F-15Es were shot down by ground fire, one on 18th January (88-1689) and one (88-1692) on 20th January. The crew of the

first plane were killed, the crew of the second were taken prisoner, but released on 4th March 1991. Both aircraft were lost on low-level night interdiction missions, presumably to small arms or AAA fire.

After the war was officially over F-15Cs continued to carry out patrols to enforce the 'no-fly' zone imposed under the terms of the cease-fire. On 20th March 1991, an F-15C (84-0014) shot down an Iraqi Su-22M with an AIM-9L. On 22nd March, an F-15C (84-0010) from the 53rd TFS shot down another Su-20/22 violating the no-fly order. Another F-15C (84-0015) was able to claim a Pilatus PC-9 trainer which was flying in close vicinity of the downed Su-22 when its pilot bailed out without a shot being fired.

On 14th April 1994, there was a tragic 'friendly fire' incident over northern Iraq, when a pair of F-15Cs of the 52nd Fighter Wing enforcing the 'no-fly' rule mistakenly shot down two UH-60 Blackhawk helicopters, killing 26 American and United Nations personnel who were carrying out humanitarian aid to Kurdish areas of Iraq. One of the helicopters was destroyed by an AIM-120, the other by an AIM-9.

Interestingly, the Gulf War provided the impetus for the F-15 to increase its readiness rate from 88% before the conflict to 96% during the war.

Right, top and center: **Triple-killer F-15C (85-0102). Capt David G Rose scored against a MiG-23 on 29th January 1991, and Capt Anthony R Murphy scored two Su-20/22 on 7th February 1991. The single green star next to Col Rick Parson's name symbolizes his kill of a Su-20/22 on 7th February 1991 flying a different F-15C (85-0124).** Kenneth Kula via the Mick Roth Collection

Below: **An F-15C (83-0017) from the 71st FS of the 1st FW. This aircraft was used by Capt Steve Tate on 17th January 1991 to down an Iraqi Mirage F.1EQ. This was the only confirmed kill by the 1st FW. Photographed in August 1995.** Pat Martin via the Mick Roth Collection

Above: **An F-15E maneuvers over the Saudi desert during Operation 'Desert Shield'. The light colored rectangles ahead of the main wheel doors are AN/ALE-45 flare and chaff dispensers. The AN/ALE-45 dispensers are not ideally located since one-quarter of the flare load cannot be carried when the LANTIRN targeting pod (on the lower air intake) is installed. The bulged wheel well unique to the F-15E show up well in this view. The rear fuselage on all F-15s is left unpainted because the engine heat causes paint to peel prematurely.**
McDonnell Douglas

Right: **The Strike Eagle Demonstrator (71-0291) poses with a display of air-to-ground weapons on the dry lake at Edwards AFB, California, in February 1976. Even at this early date, when the air-superiority F-15s were just beginning to enter service, McDonnell Douglas was proposing the F-15 as a strike aircraft to replace the F-4E. At this point the concept of LANTIRN pods had not been developed, and the aircraft was frequently seen carrying Pave Knife pods.**
McDonnell Douglas via the Terry Panopalis Collection

Above: **The fourth test F-15A (71-0283) displays its brand new day-glo orange markings at the NASA/Dryden open house in May 1973. The orange generally faded in the intense desert sun, and seldom did the early aircraft look this good. The horizontal black stripes on the vertical stabilizers were unique to this aircraft. The large cylinder on the nose boom protects the instrumentation from the general public (and vice versa).** Dennis R Jenkins

Right: **The view of an F-15 from a KC-135. This was an early test aircraft which still has the original (unclipped) wing tips. The dog-toothed horizontal stabilizer has already been added however. This was the day-glo pattern on top of most of the early test aircraft. Noteworthy is the small speedbrake in its partially deployed position.** Don Logan

Below: **Streak Eagle (72-0119) at Grand Forks AFB, North Dakota. Besides the obvious lack of paint, other external changes include modified mass balancers on top of each vertical stabilizer, and a long instrumentation boom. Note the large UHF antenna under the rear of the canopy.** Doug Slowiak via the Jay Miller Collection

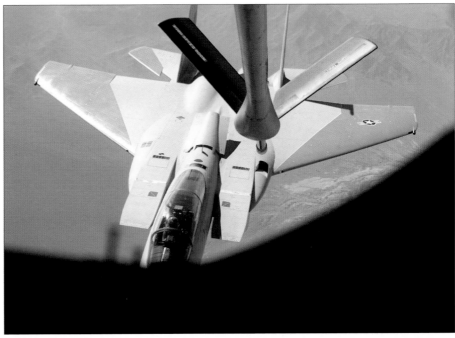

Left: **Second TF-15A (71-0291) in its world tour markings, a variation of the bicentennial markings applied during 1976, which itself was based on the scheme developed for (but never used by) the Thunderbirds demonstration team.** Jack D Morris

Below: **For four days in April 1976, the second TF-15A (71-0291) was painted in** *Armée de l'Air* **(French Air Force) markings for demonstration flights. Unfortunately, the French decided against purchasing the Eagle for cost reasons, leaving this as the only 'French' F-15.** Dennis R Jenkins

Bottom: **A cutaway of the F-15I shows the basic configuration of the two-seat strike variants (F-15E and F-15S). Except for some electronic equipment, the three variants are substantially identical.** Boeing

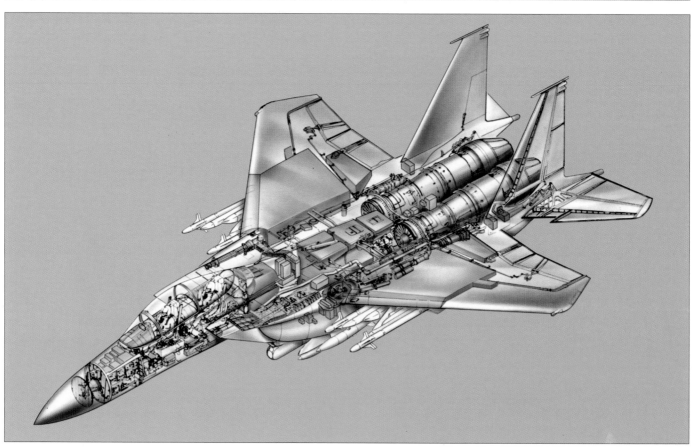

Above and right: **The eighth test aircraft (71-0287) was used extensively for research into the digital engine controls that eventually solved most of the F-15's engine problems. The Digital Electronic Engine Control program was an attempt to cure the persistent stall/stagnation problem the F-15 was experiencing. The results of these tests were used to finalize the electronic engine controls introduced on the F100-PW-220 engine. Two distinct test programs, DEEC and HIDEC, were undertaken by NASA, each exploring a different mechanism for adding electronic controls to high-performance engines. This pioneering work is now standard equipment on almost all modern jet engines.** NASA/DFRC

Right: **While being used as the 'Peep Eagle' reconnaissance demonstrator, 71-0291 wore a USAF-standard Compass Ghost scheme. The reconnaissance equipment was normally carried in a conformal centerline pod that is not shown here.** Daniel Soulaine via the Mick Roth Collection

Below: **The well-traveled second two-seater (71-0291) wore a standard Mod Eagle paint scheme in July 1992. Even at this late date the pods on top of the vertical stabilizers have not been updated to production standards.**
Dennis R Jenkins

Above: **The NF-15B ACTIVE (71-0290) shows the canards that are made from F/A-18 stabilators. The fairings that cover the actuators for the canards can be seen on top of the engine intakes. Despite the number of modifications made to this aircraft, it still retains the original small speed brake on top of the fuselage.** NASA / DFRC

Below: **ACTIVE is prepared for an engine test on the hard stand near Dryden. The wheels and tires have been removed, and the aircraft securely fastened to the ground to permit full-thrust runs without fear of the aircraft moving. The thrust-vectoring nozzles do not look terribly different than normal production F100 nozzles.** NASA / DFRC

The early days at Luke AFB, Arizona, presented some of the most colorful paint schemes used by the F-15 in USAF service. The early air superiority blue aircraft were hard to see in the clear desert sky, so three aircraft were painted with high-visibility stripes, although two of the aircraft finally selected were 'Compass Ghost'. And noted aviation artist Keith Ferris developed an 'attitude deceptive' paint scheme that was tried on the F-15 (as well as an F-4, F-14, and T-38) for a short period of time.

This page, top to bottom:

In mid-1976, four F-15s (including 74-0089) were painted in Ferris attitude deceptive paint schemes. Each aircraft was slightly different, using various shades of gray and different geometric patterns. Although the scheme proved fairly successful in initially confusing the opposing pilots, it also allowed the aircraft to be spotted at longer ranges. Bill Malerba

This F-15A (73-0103) at Luke was painted in high-visibility red and white 'invasion stripes' as a test during early 1976 to find a more visible paint scheme for the Eagle during transition training at Luke. Note that the fuselage stripes sweep back, unlike the black and white scheme where the stripes were vertical. The ALQ-128 antenna on the forward fuselage were not painted. This scheme, like the others tested, was not adopted for use. Mick Roth

The Commander of the 12th Air Force used this TF-15A (73-0112) which during early 1976 was painted with black and white invasion stripes. Notice the differences between this aircraft and the one with red stripes above. Mick Roth

The third high-visibility test aircraft from Luke in April 1976 used yellow bands on the tails and wings. This F-15A (73-0100) was the first aircraft delivered in the definitive 'Compass Ghost' scheme instead of air-superiority blue. Overall the visual effect of the yellow bands was very pleasing, and it is unfortunate that the scheme was not adapted for operational use. Note the early pod configuration on the top of the vertical stabilizers. Dave Begy

The ex-ADC fighter interceptor squadrons provided an all too brief glimpse of colorful markings for the Eagle. Each squadron brought the traditional markings they had used on their F-106s, but unfortunately, the air defense role was quickly passed to F-16s and the ADTAC F-15s were reassigned to Air National Guard units where they lost their distinctive markings.

Opposite page, top to bottom:

The commander's aircraft (76-0111) from the 318th Fighter Interceptor Squadron on 9th August 1986. Doug Remington via the Mick Roth Collection

The commander's aircraft (76-0100) from the 48th FIS in July 1987. David F Brown via the Mick Roth Collection

The commander's aircraft (76-0015) from the 5th FIS was photographed at Peterson AFB, Colorado, in September 1987. Robert B Greby via the Mick Roth Collection

Above: **Special 'NO STEP' markings were developed for use on the composite honeycomb surfaces on the F-15. Although normally seen early in the F-15's career, these markings are beginning to disappear in the late-1990s as composite technology becomes more widely used. The markings are grey instead of yellow on 'Compass Ghost' and 'Mod Eagle' aircraft .** Dennis R Jenkins

This page, top: **The July 1981 Tiger Meet at Bitburg AB, Germany, was hosted by the 53rd TFS, which also provided this F-15C. For years the Tiger Meet provided an excuse for squadrons in the USAFE and other European air forces to paint aircraft in unusual markings. The mid-1980s saw the end of this tradition, with most aircraft simply using a tiger head or a small tiger stripe on the tail. The late 1990s have begun to see a resurgence of the colorful markings.** Jay Miller Collection

This page, above: **Excellent portrait of a current 1st FW F-15C (83-0033). The 'Mod Eagle' paint scheme is typical of mid-1990s practice, although the tail codes are unusually bright (and slightly crooked) to highlight a commander's aircraft. A full complement of air-to-air missiles are loaded, with an AIM-7 on the forward air intake position, and AIM-120s on the aft fuselage and also on the outboard wing rail, and, mostly hidden, and AIM-9 on the inboard wing rail. The standard 610-gallon fuel tank is hung on the centerline.** Don Logan

Right: **An Israeli two-seater (No. 733, probably an F-15B) flies formation with a restored IDF/AF Mk IX Spitfire. Interestingly, this F-15 shows two ECM antennas on the rear fuselage booms that appear the same as the USAF AN/ALQ-135B antennas on early USAF F-15Es, although it is relatively certain the ALQ-135 was not exported to Israel this early.** IAF Magazine via Tsahi Ben-Ami

Below: **The 18th FW at Kadena AB has slightly modified the standard Mod Eagle paint scheme's lines on the vertical stabilizer in order to accommodate single-color tail codes. This simplifies painting the aircraft and is becoming more common with a significant number of squadrons adopting it. This F-15C (78-0531) is representative of the wing's aircraft.** David F Brown via the Mick Roth Collection

Bottom: **A single MiG kill adorns this F-15C (85-0122) from the 33rd FW in October 1994. This aircraft has the forward-facing band-3 AN/ALQ-135B antennas on top and bottom of nose, just aft of the radome.** David F Brown via the Mick Roth Collection

Top: **This Category II F-15A (72-0113) had been delivered to the USAF on 3rd March 1974, transferred to MASDC on 17th April 1978, dropped from the inventory as salvage on 21st June 1978, and mounted on a pedestal for electromagnetic testing at Newport Irish Hill, NY in early 1979.** Later that year antennas for the Joint Tactical Information Distribution System (JTIDS) were evaluated using the aircraft. It was modified in 1983 to accept type-1 CFTs. During the late 1980s the AN/ALQ-135 ECM system antennas were tested. In 1994 type-3 CFTs were installed, but these were soon modified to type-4 configuration to allow testing as an F-15E. LANTIRN pods were also added at this point. During 1994-95 the aircraft was tested as a possible next-generation Wild Weasel. Interestingly, the closest horizontal stabilizer (borrowed from a 'Compass Ghost' aircraft) is mounted on the wrong side (the walkway markings are normally on the top). This demonstrates the symmetrical nature of these stabilizers and that they can be swapped between sides as necessary.
USAF Rome Laboratory

Right center: **72-0113 at Rome Laboratory during F-15E testing. The aircraft received a dark paint scheme, finally replacing the air superiority blue it had spent the previous 15 years in.**
USAF Rome Laboratory

Bottom: **Several Eagles are maintained at Edwards AFB for continued testing, including this F-15B (76-0132) assigned to the 415th Test Squadron. Most of the Edwards aircraft are painted white with red trim, but a few retain their operational grey paint schemes.** Craig Kaston

Top: **The commander's aircraft from the 4th FW at Seymour Johnson while it was at Nellis AFB. A SUU-10 training store, two 500lb low-drag bombs, and an ACMI pod (on the Sidewinder rail) and LANTIRN are clearly evident. All 'Mud Hens' are painted in a monotone Gunship Grey, and usually carried subdued markings in black. The radomes are generally a shade or two darker than the rest of the aircraft.** Mick Roth

Above, center: **This F-15E was painted up for the 422nd TES at Nellis during July 1990. The orange markings on the bombs are unusual. The yellow and black checkerboard tail stripes are a long standing Nellis tradition.** Ben Knowles
via the Mick Roth Collection

Right: **As of 1st January 1998 there were 102 F-15As and 9 F-15Bs in AMARC at Davis-Monthan AFB, Arizona. Some of these aircraft are in flyable storage awaiting reassignment, while others are being used for spare parts to support aircraft in operational squadrons. These F-15As are missing their radomes, intake ramps, and rudders. The white overcoat is a protective sealant.** Teresa Vanden-Heuvel/US Air Force/AMARC

Three 57th FWW F-15Cs were used to evaluate a possible Strike Eagle paint schemes in late 1986 and early 1987. All courtesy of Paul Minert via the Mick Roth Collection

Opposite page, top: **Here F-15C (82-0028) shows a distinctive three-tone grey camouflage similar to the one used by the F-16XL.**

Opposite page, center: **F-15C (82-0029) in a two-tone grey that was later modified for use as the 'Mod Eagle' scheme used by almost all the air-superiority F-15s.**

Opposite page, bottom: **F-15C (82-0022) in the overall gunship grey that was ultimately selected for use on the F-15E.**

58

Above: **A later F-15S shows slight variation in the national markings. Interestingly, this aircraft has an AN/ALQ-128 pod on the left vertical stabilizer, and appears to have the flush ALQ-128 antennas on the forward fuselage also. Note the configuration of weapons pylons on the type-4 conformal fuel tanks.** McDonnell Douglas

Left: **The first F-15S (93-0852) poses for a publicity shot in front of the St Louis production plant. Contrary to many published reports, the F-15S is capable of carrying conformal fuel tanks, as shown here. The markings shown here are different than earlier Saudi F-15C/Ds, and also different than later F-15S models.** McDonnell Douglas

Below: **The first Israeli F-15I on the assembly line in St Louis. The production rate for the F-15 has declined dramatically, with only a handful of F-15E, F-15I, and F-15S aircraft coming off the line per year. This particular aircraft made its first flight on 12th September 1997, still wearing its chromate yellow-green instead of its final desert camouflage. Twenty-four additional F-15Is will be delivered by 1999.** Boeing

This page: **The first F-15I for the Israeli Air Force (94-0286 made its first flight on 12th September 1997 with Boeing test pilot Joe Felock at the controls. The F-15I is the first production F-15 to use a camouflage other than shades of grey. The F-15I and F-15S are arguably the most advanced F-15s, powered by F100-PW-229 engines and including revised AN/APG-70 radar sets. The first F-15I was officially rolled-out at St Louis on 6th November 1997. Noteworthy are the 'turkey feathers' on the F100 engines, and the Python 4 and AIM-120 missiles on the wing pylons.** Boeing

This page, top to bottom:

Each of the *Hiko Kyodotai* aggressors is painted differently in order to provide dissimilar air combat training for the JASDF. Here F-15DJ (02-8071) wears brown and green paint over the standard Compass Ghost scheme during September 1991. Masahiro 'Scotch' Koizumi

This aggressor F-15DJ (02-8073) wore brown paint over the standard 'Compass Ghost' scheme in September 1991. The aggressors, like the other Japanese F-15s, do not have an AN/ALQ-128 antenna on the left vertical stabilizer. Masahiro 'Scotch' Koizumi

A different paint scheme for an aggressor. In October 1992 this F-15DJ (02-8072) had a liberal application of blue over the standard 'Compass Ghost' paint. Since all of the aggressor aircraft retained their full combat capability, the radomes were not painted. Masahiro 'Scotch' Koizumi

Tsuiki Air Base celebrated their 50th anniversary in 1992, and this F-15J (72-8888) from the 304th Squadron/8th Air Wing was painted to mark the occasion. Unusually, this F-15J's forward UHF antenna is the same as its USAF counterparts. Most F-15J/DJs have a larger antenna in this location as part of the Japanese-unique radio set. Masahiro 'Scotch' Koizumi

This page, top to bottom:

The 204th Squadron, 7th Air Wing celebrated their 30th anniversary in 1995, coinciding with the 10th anniversary of the squadron receiving the Eagle. So F-15J 32-8826 was painted in elaborate markings to commemorate the occasion. Note two small J/ALQ-8 antennas under the nose in roughly the same location as the USAF ALQ-135s. It was quite a while after the F-15J's introduction to JASDF service before these antennas began to appear on the aircraft; perhaps the Japanese had as many problems developing their ECM system as Northrop did the ALQ-135. Masahiro 'Scotch' Koizumi Collection

During 1991, the 204th Squadron celebrated the 10th anniversary of the F-15's introduction into JASDF service (with the 202nd Squadron, 5th Air Wing). Masahiro 'Scotch' Koizumi Collection

This aggressor F-15DJ (02-8065) used a black pattern over its 'Compass Ghost' in September 1991. Masahiro 'Scotch' Koizumi Collection

F-15DJ (92-8068) is also assigned to the aggressor squadron, and used a green overspray during late 1991. All Japanese aggressors carry full national insignia on the fuselage and both sides of each wing, unlike some of their American counterparts which either carry no insignia or use foreign insignia to provide additional realism. Masahiro 'Scotch' Koizumi Collection

The 'Eagle Driver (left) and 'Eagle Keeper' (right) patches are used by some pilots and ground crew, respectively.

The F-15 Test Force is an alternate patch occasionally used by the F-15 test forces at Eglin and Edwards. Sometimes this patch reads 'Combined Test Force' which is technically more correct.

All patches courtesy of Dennis R Jenkins

A variety of different patches and decals have been used by the Eagle community within the USAF. The large Eagle decal (right) is the basis for most of the designs.

The patch below was the result of the F-14 versus F-15 competition. Note the Eagle flying away from the somewhat battered Tomcat.

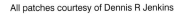

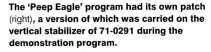

The original blue 'F-15 Joint Test Force' patch (above) used the stylized F-15 emblem first seen painted on the nose of 71-0280 when it was rolled out.

A favorite of pilots in the early years was the 'F-15 Eagle' patch (below) that also used the stylized F-15 emblem.

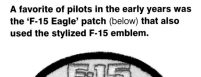

The 'Peep Eagle' program had its own patch (right), a version of which was carried on the vertical stabilizer of 71-0291 during the demonstration program.

The F-15E introduced its own insignia (bottom left) when it was rolled out.

The F-15 ASAT program spawned two patches (below center), although the left one was the most popular.

The AIMVAL/ACEVAL demonstration early in the F-15's career created the patch at bottom right.

Chapter Nine

Eagles of a Different Feather

In May 1971 McAir received a contract to develop a composite wing for the F-15 consisting of boron and graphite filaments embedded in epoxy resin. The wing was to be 500 pounds lighter with a longer fatigue life than the metal wing used in production aircraft. Structural test articles were completed and flight tests were scheduled for late-1975. Unfortunately the project was cancelled in February 1975, but the technology found uses in the F/A-18A and AV-8B projects. A subsequent project did result in the first F-15B (71-0290) flying with aluminum-lithium (Al-Li) wing panels which are 5% stronger and 9% lighter then the conventional aluminum panels they replace. Flight tests started in the summer of 1986 and continued aboard 71-0290 in its role as the F-15S/MTD demonstrator and as the NF-15B ACTIVE. Aluminum-lithium alloy was also tested on the left wing root fairing on 71-0291 during its 'Peep Eagle' demonstration tour. Although never adopted for production on the F-15, these tests did prove the worth of this new lightweight metal for use on high performance aircraft.

In 1974 McAir received a $6 million contract from the Air Force Flight Dynamics Laboratory at Wright-Patterson AFB, Ohio, to design and build an advanced environmental control system (AECS) for use in the F-15. The Air Force had evaluated aircraft electronic system failures and found that 52% of them were directly related to temperature, humidity, or dust. Chief engineer for McAir was Virgil M Marti, who led a team to develop a high-capacity cooling system, complete with dust separators and a dehumidifier. In addition to maintaining lower temperatures in the electronics, the system reduced windscreen fog, and provided a more comfortable cockpit, since the cockpit shares the same environmental unit. The system was

flight tested aboard an F-15A-2-MC (71-0282) at Edwards during the spring of 1978, and at NAS Dallas in September 1978. Lessons learned from this test program were incorporated into production F-15s.

In February 1982 McAir was awarded a 15 month contract by the Flight Dynamics Laboratory (FDL) to demonstrate an advanced integrated flight control/fire control system under the 'Integrated Flight Fire-Control (IFFC)' program, also known as 'Firefly III'. The program involved extensive simulation at the FDL and McAir, and then flight tests in a modified F-15A at both Edwards and Nellis. The IFFC allowed a sensor locked on a target to effectively fly the aircraft to weapons release or gunfiring position. Development flights began in April 1982 on F-15B-20-MC (77-0166) equipped with IFFC and an Automatic Tracking Laser Illumination System (ALTIS II) pod on the forward port-side AIM-7 station. During these trials, air-to-air weapons were fired at simulated targets while the F-15 was maneuvered at high offset angles, demonstrating its ability to employ weapons accurately while in three-dimensional flight. This allowed the F-15 an earlier opportunity to fire, and also extended the time available for fir-

ing during a dogfight. Many of the lessons learned were used during the integration of LANTIRN on the F-15E.

Another attempt at decreasing the structural weight of the aircraft was made beginning 11th October 1985 when McAir received a contract from ASD for the construction of two composite horizontal stabilizers. The program started in February 1986 and was completed in September 1986. Two complete horizontal stabilizers were produced, with one being used for static tests and the other undergoing ground vibration tests after installation in the first F-15B (71-0290). Each torque box consisted of a substructure made of superplastically formed and diffusion bonded titanium with the skins consisting of boron fiber composite coated with boron carbide. The coating allowed the fiber to retain strength during the manufacturing process. The leading and trailing edges were made of superplastically formed aluminum to avoid corrosion. The project demonstrated a 50% cost reduction over the current machined titanium substructure, and also yielded a 17% weight reduction. Many of the techniques learned were subsequently applied to the F-15E program.

Right: **The third test aircraft (71-0282) sported a shark mouth in November 1977 while it was testing the Advanced Environmental Control System. An AECS logo is barely visible on the air intake behind the drop tank, and an Eagle logo is on the tail. Also unusual are the extra formation light strips on the vertical stabilizers. The lights were on the left side of both tails, but there were none on the right side of either tail. There were also additional formation light strips on the upper wing surfaces.** Dennis R Jenkins

F-15S/MTD (NF-15B)

In October 1984 McDonnell Douglas was awarded a $117.8 million cost-sharing contract to develop and flight test an advanced technology version of the F-15. The contract had an eventual value of $272 million, with industry contributing slightly less than half the costs. The industry team included prime contractor McDonnell Douglas and major subcontractors Pratt & Whitney (engines and nozzles), General Electric (flight control computer and software implementation), Cleveland Pneumatic (landing gear), and National Water Lift (hydraulic actuators). Program manager for McAir was Ken Token, while Lt Col Felix Sanchez filled the role for the Air Force.

This aircraft, commonly called the F-15S/MTD (STOL/Maneuvering Technology Demonstrator), investigated four specific technologies: two-dimensional (2-D) thrust vectoring/reversing jet nozzles; integrated flight and propulsion controls; rough/soft field landing gear; and advanced vehicle/pilot interfaces. It was intended primarily as a flight test vehicle for emerging technologies that had potential application to the Air Force Advanced Tactical Fighter (YF-22/YF-23). The aircraft was largely patterned after a concept proposed by McAir for the AFTI demonstrator program that was eventually awarded to General Dynamics using a modified F-16.

McDonnell Douglas modified the first F-15B (71-0290) for the flight test program, with the aircraft being redesignated NF-15B. The changes included controllable foreplanes, modified from F/A-18A Hornet tailplanes,

mounted above the engine inlet trunks forward of the wings. The foreplanes were mounted at a dihedral angle of 20°, and could operate symmetrically or asymmetrically to provide pitch and roll moments, and were used as stability maintaining surfaces instead of for primary flight control. In theory they permitted the NF-15B's maximum allowable load factor to be increased above 9g without additional structural reinforcement. The aircraft was also fitted with F-15E style rough/soft-field landing gear and a cockpit basically similar to the F-15E. Provisions for an AN/APG-70 radar unit with synthetic aperture and ground mapping features, and LANTIRN navigation pods were also incorporated into the aircraft. The actual installation of this equipment necessitated the removal of the test boom initially fitted to the air-

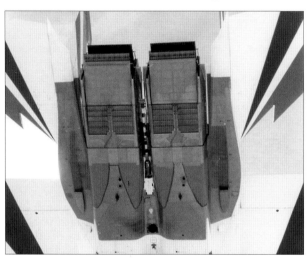

Above and below: **The F-15S/MTD (71-0290) showing off its unusual two-dimensional exhaust nozzles. These nozzles could deflect thrust upwards or downwards as much as 20°. Louvers ahead of the nozzles allowed thrust reversing, a technique reduced the F-15's landing distance to as little as 1,366 feet. These two-dimensional nozzles pioneered much of the technology being used by the F-22's nozzles, although the F-15 ACTIVE's nozzles probably represent a better thrust-vectoring system. The canards are modified F/A-18 stabilators.** AFFTC History Office

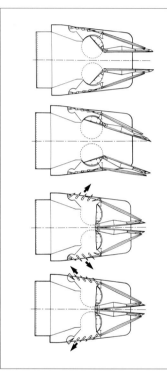

In their neutral position, the nozzles function much like normal convergent-divergent exhaust nozzles found on most high-performance fighters.

To gain greater lift during take-off, or to improve maneuverability in-flight, the nozzles could vector thrust as much as ± 20 degrees vertically.

The main nozzle could be closed and louvers above and below the engine opened to provide a small amount of braking thrust as required.

The main nozzle could be closed and louvers above and below the engine directed forward to provide a significant measure of reverse thrust, shortening landing distances considerably.

craft's nose, and was accomplished fairly late in the test program.

Rectangular, two-dimensional vectoring nozzles manufactured from titanium and carbon-fiber were installed at the rear of modified F100-PW-220 engines, replacing the F-15's standard afterburner ducts. The nozzles could vector engine thrust ±20° from the longitudinal axis to enhance take-off performance and maneuverability, and were also designed to provide any level of reverse thrust throughout the flight envelope, including approach and landing. The engine's fan ducts were modified to withstand the pitch vectoring loads that develop when the 2-D nozzles were vectored. Four 2-D engine/nozzle units were constructed by P&W, two for ground tests, which totalled about 350 hours, and two for flight tests. The 2-D nozzle provided an exhaust area roughly equivalent to that of a standard F100-PW-220 axisymmetric nozzle. The engine/nozzle could be vectored from +20° to –20° in approximately 0.5 seconds, and could go from full afterburner to full reverse thrust in about 1.5 seconds. The modified propulsion plants were said to be '... slightly heavier ...' than standard engines.

Initial test flights with the new foreplanes and conventional axisymmetric exhaust nozzles began on 7th September 1988 and continued until January 1989. These flights were originally scheduled to include the two-dimensional nozzles, but development problems delayed the delivery of some components until early 1989. During these flights the aircraft reached a maximum altitude of 48,000 feet and a speed of Mach 1.7 during 41 flight hours accumulated in 43 flights. The two-dimensional nozzles were fitted to the aircraft during the spring 1989, and McAir pilot Larry Walker took the modified aircraft for its first flight on 10th May 1989. During this flight the aircraft reached 20,000 feet and Mach 0.9 and the aircraft's exhaust nozzles were used in a conventional mode, with thrust vectoring and reversing not attempted. An additional four flights conducted from the Lambert-St. Louis International Airport and a speed of Mach 1.85 at 48,000 feet was reached during these flights. The aircraft was ferried to Edwards on 16th June for a flight test program that ran through January 1990. Early ground tests of the engine/nozzle revealed several small problems, including a convergent flap liner that limited the use of afterburner to a few seconds.

A four channel digital fly-by-wire system integrated the flight control system and controlled all functions of the foreplanes, ailerons,

horizontal tail surfaces, and vectoring nozzles to provide high precision control of the aircraft. A key capability demonstrated during the flight test series was called 'auto-guidance' and allowed accurate landings without the use of ground navigational aids. During these tests, the pilot identified a distant landing strip using the AN/APG-70 SAR and LANTIRN, and designated a landing point using a high-resolution ground map displayed on a cockpit CRT. Aircraft systems then provided the pilot with azimuth and elevation steering commands on the HUD, allowing the pilot to fly a glideslope for touchdown at the previously designated landing point.

Performance parameters specified for the F-15S/MTD included take-off and landing runs of 1,500 feet on a 50-foot-wide hard, wet, rough surface runway at night and in adverse weather, with full internal fuel and 6,000 pounds of ordnance. The F-15S/MTD demonstrated a take-off run of just over 1,000 feet and a landing run of 1,250 feet on a wet runway with crosswinds gusting to 30 knots. A 10,000 pound increase in payload when operating from a 1,500 foot runway was also demonstrated.

Air combat maneuvering was enhanced by a 53% improvement in roll rate with up to a 33% improvement in pitch rate. The additional weight and drag of the modifications decreased the aircraft's cruising radius by 4%. A total of 10 test flights were allocated to demonstrate in-flight thrust vectoring/reversal in combat situations. Other benefits to future programs from two-dimensional exhaust nozzles include smaller vertical fins (since the nozzles can provide some pitch and yaw control), and eliminating the need for a speed brake.

The program ended on 15th August 1991 after accomplishing all of its flight objectives. The vectored thrust nozzles were returned to

Pratt & Whitney, although the aircraft itself would be called upon for further flight tests of yet another vectored thrust system as the F-15 ACTIVE. In preparation for these tests, the aircraft was sent to NASA's Dryden Flight Research Center to receive a new set of engines and control systems.

NF-15B ACTIVE

The NF-15B ACTIVE (Advanced Control Technology for Integrated Vehicles) project uses the same NF-15B (71-0290) previously modified by the S/MTD program. ACTIVE is intended to develop and demonstrate flight control technologies that will significantly enhance the operational characteristics for the next generation of high performance aircraft. ACTIVE is a joint NASA, Air Force, McDonnell Douglas Aerospace, and P&W program. The flight test program will encompass approximately 60 flights totaling 100 hours.

Externally, the aircraft is configured much like the S/MTD demonstrator, except that the two-dimensional thrust vectoring engine nozzles have been replaced by two F100-PW-229 engines that were modified with multi-directional thrust vectoring nozzles. The engines have modified fan duct cases to provide the additional strength required to withstand the vectoring forces. Installation of the nozzles also required modifications to the aircraft's rear fuselage and main engine mounts.

The new nozzles are officially known as pitch-yaw balance beam nozzles, and can be vectored up to ±20° in any direction. The nozzle features a fail-safe, dual-redundant actuation system, making it compatible with single-engine, as well as twin-engine, applications. Unlike the earlier two-dimension nozzles fitted to S/MTD, these nozzles are not fitted with thrust reversers. A similar pitch-yaw vectoring

Right: **The thrust-vectoring capabilities of the ACTIVE's special F100-PW-229 engines are shown here. The left engine is deflected downward, while the right engine is in a neutral position. The small speed brake is again evident, shown here in its fully extended position. Compare the tail markings with the same aircraft shown on page 52.** NASA / Dryden

nozzle has been selected for integration into a modified F-16D in the Variable-stability In-flight Simulator Test Aircraft (VISTA) program.

Initial test flights centered on defining normal aircraft operations with the new nozzles and flight software. Slow-speed thrust vectoring tests were then accomplished, and on 24th April 1996 the NF-15B ACTIVE achieved its first supersonic yaw vectoring flight at Dryden. The first thrust vectoring at Mach 2 occurred on 31st October 1996, and was accomplished by NASA test pilot Jim Smolka at 45,000 feet. This was the first known Mach 2 thrust vectoring by any aircraft, and effectively completed opening the flight envelope for ACTIVE. In December 1996, ACTIVE was removed from flight status for modifications to various systems, particularly the computerized flight control system. Testing is scheduled to continue in mid-1998, including additional supersonic vectoring demonstrations.

NASA

The second F-15A (71-0281) was acquired by the NASA Dryden Flight Research Center on 17th December 1975, and was used for the aerodynamic testing of the Space Shuttle's thermal protection tiles by mounting them on the inner wing leading edge. The tiles attached to the starboard wing simulated those on the leading edge of the orbiter's wing, whereas those on the port wing simulated those on the junction of the orbiter's wing and fuselage. The tiles attached to the F-15A's wing were ultimately subjected to almost 1.5 times the dynamic pressure which the Shuttle experiences during launch. The aircraft was returned to the USAF on 28th October 1983 without ever being assigned a NASA number and is now on display at Langley AFB in Virginia.

Beginning in 1994, NASA started flying an F-15B (74-0141) as the Aerodynamic Flight Facility designated NASA 836. The Flight Test Fixture-II (FTF-II) is installed on the centerline pylon in a manner similar to the normal centerline tank. The FTF-II is a low-aspect-ratio structure that is 107 inches long, 32 inches high, and 8 inches wide with a 12° elliptical nose section and blunt trailing edge. Built primarily of carbon/epoxy materials, the fixture consists of a pylon with replaceable side panels, nose section, and vertical test article. The modular configuration allows the FTF-II to be modified to satisfy a variety of flight test requirements. The upper 19 inches of the FTF is the permanent pylon that houses avionics, research instrumentation systems, and other support equipment common to most flight experiments. The lower 13 inches is the vertical test article that, in the current configuration, matches the contour of the upper avionics pylon. The vertical test article is removable and may be replaced by other shapes.

In 1996 DFRC completed flight testing of the X-33 thermal protection system using the F-15B/FTF-II. These tests provided information on the material's durability at flight velocities through adverse weather, much like the tests conducted for Shuttle tiles 11 years earlier.

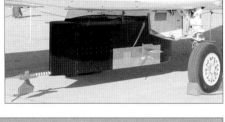

Right and below: **NASA operates an F-15B (74-0141) as an Aerodynamic Flight Facility. The black Flight Test Facility (FTF-II) attached to the centerline can accommodate a variety of experiments. One of the first programs to use this aircraft was the X-33 reusable launch vehicle demonstrator, which tested thermal protection system concepts on the FTF-II.**
Dennis R Jenkins

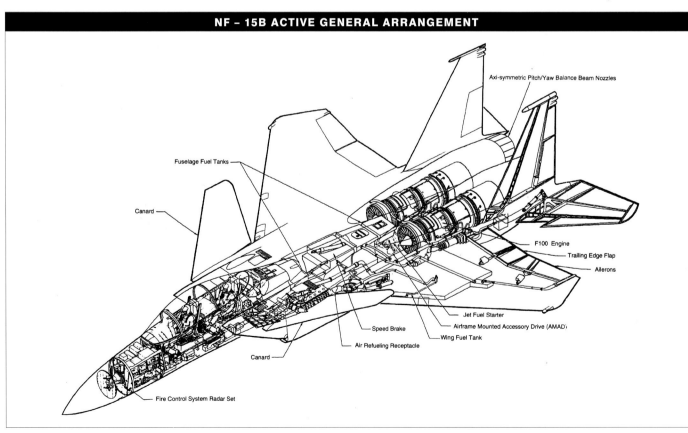

NF – 15B ACTIVE GENERAL ARRANGEMENT

Axi-symmetric Pitch/Yaw Balance Beam Nozzles

Fuselage Fuel Tanks

Canard

F100 Engine

Trailing Edge Flap

Ailerons

Jet Fuel Starter

Airframe Mounted Accessory Drive (AMAD)

Speed Brake

Wing Fuel Tank

Air Refuelling Receptacle

Canard

Fire Control System Radar Set

NASA F-15 Flight Research Facility

The eighth F-15A (71-0287) was acquired by DFRC on 5th January 1976 and received NASA number 835, although it was more commonly known as the F-15 Flight Research Facility. It was highly instrumented and equipped with an integrated digital propulsion and flight control system. Flight research carried out by NASA with this modified F-15 evaluated advanced integrated flight and propulsion control system technologies during more than 25 advanced research projects involving aerodynamics, performance, propulsion control, control integration, instrumentation development, human factors, and flight test techniques. The NASA F-15 was the first aircraft to demonstrate a fully integrated inlet-engine-flight control system, a self-repairing flight control system, and a propulsion-only flight control system. It was also used as a testbed to evaluate aerodynamic pressures on Space Shuttle thermal protection tiles at specific altitudes and speeds.

DEEC. In 1982 and early-1983 NASA tested an advanced digital electronic engine control (DEEC) fuel management system in support of the F100-PW-220 development aboard 71-0287. The system was based on a 16-bit microprocessor which controlled the gas generator and afterburner control units. During the summer of 1983, 71-0287 was used in a further series of demonstrations for the Engine Model Derivative (EMD, now called the Improved Performance Engine – IPE).

These tests demonstrated that relatively modest engine improvements could drastically improve performance: acceleration from Mach 0.8 to Mach 2.0 was improved 41% at 35,000 feet, as well as improved air-start capabilities and better specific fuel consumption figures.

ADECS. The Advanced Digital Engine Control System traded excess engine stall margin for improved performance. This was achieved through integrated computer-based flight and engine control systems. The engine stall margin, the amount that engine operating pressures must be reduced to avoid an engine stall, was continually monitored and adjusted by the integrated system, based on the flight profile and real-time performance needs. Using this information, ADECS freed up engine performance that would otherwise be held in reserve to meet the stall margin requirement. Improved engine performance obtained through ADECS could take the form of increased thrust, reduced fuel flow, or lower engine operating temperatures because peak thrust was not always needed.

Initial ADECS engineering work began in 1983. Research and demonstration flights with the ADECS system, which began in 1986, displayed increases in engine thrust of 10.5%, and up to 15% lower fuel flow at constant thrust. The increased engine thrust observed with ADECS improved the rate of climb 14% at 40,000 feet and its time-to-climb from 10,000 feet to 40,000 feet was reduced 13%. Increases of 14-24% in acceleration were also experienced at intermediate and maximum power settings. No stalls were encountered during even aggressive maneuvering, although intentional stalls were induced to validate ADECS methodology.

HIDEC. Later, the F-15 participated in the testing of the NASA/USAF Highly Integrated Digital Electronic Control (HIDEC) program which involved a flight control system that was capable of detecting in-flight failures and automatically reconfiguring the aircraft's control surfaces to compensate for them. During May 1989, special equipment aboard 71-0287 correctly identified and isolated a simulated flight control system failure while in flight. Other elements of this project included failure detection and identification, followed by automatic reconfiguration of the flight control system. This involved the system automatically reconfiguring itself to redistribute a failed (or missing) flight control surface's functions to the other flight control surfaces, a much more advanced version of a rudimentary capability the F-15 already has. As conceived, the system would alert the pilot, identify the problem, display the revised aircraft configuration, and define a new allowable flight envelope.

Top: **71-0281 was used for various research programs, including evaluating Space Shuttle thermal protection system tiles. Tiles were mounted on the starboard wing and the port wing extension, with a smooth surface being achieved with the liberal use of body putty. Surprisingly, the wingtip had not been modified to the raked configuration.** NASA / Dryden

Center: **The second test aircraft (71-0281) during a 1976 research flight for the NASA Dryden Flight Research Center. The aircraft still has the original wingtips.** NASA Dryden

Bottom: **The F100 afterburning turbofan was a pacing item in the F-15's development. This second-generation turbofan engine was meant to correct the multitude of problems encountered with the TF30 engine used in the F-111, but never truly lived up to its promise until the advent of digital electronic engine controls. Here, the NASA HIDEC testbed (71-0287) shows why the danger area extends over 200 feet behind the aircraft during engine run-ups.** NASA / Dryden

SRFCS. During late 1989 and early 1990, the F-15 FTF investigated what could become a major breakthrough in airborne flight control capability. It was the first aircraft to demonstrate a Self-Repairing Flight Control System (SRFCS). The USAF program demonstrated the ability of a flight control system to identify a component failure, isolate the failure, and reconfigure other control devices such as ailerons, rudders, elevators, and flaps to continue the aircraft's mission or be landed safely. For example, if a horizontal stabilizer on the aircraft was damaged or failed in flight, the SRFCS immediately diagnosed the failure and determined how the remaining flight control surfaces could be repositioned to compensate for the damaged or inoperable stabilizer.

A display in the cockpit also informed the pilot of the control surface reconfiguration, and information displayed by the SRFCS showed the pilot what operational limitations he must observe as a result of the damaged or failed component. These limitations included reduced g-loading, reduced angle of attack maneuvering, or reduced air speed and altitude margins, depending upon the damage.

The SRFCS also had the capability of identifying failures in electrical, hydraulic, and mechanical systems. When a failure in a normal flight control system occurred, ground maintenance diagnostic tests were conducted to identify the origin of the failure so that appropriate corrective actions were taken. Ground maintenance crews often spend up to 60% of their time attempting to duplicate flight failures and correcting them. In many cases, the failure cannot be identified on the ground because actual flight conditions cannot be duplicated. System malfunctions on an aircraft equipped with a SRFCS can be identified and isolated at the time they occur, and repaired as soon as the aircraft is on the ground.

PSC. Research flights with the F-15 FTF began in the summer of 1990 on a program called Performance Seeking Control (PSC) with the goal of optimizing total aircraft engine performance during steady-state engine operation. Utilizing digital flight control, inlet control, and engine control systems, PSC used integrated control laws to assure that peak engine and maneuvering performance was available to the pilot at all times, regardless of the mission or immediate needs. Among the functions

of PSC were a reduction of fuel usage at cruise conditions, maximized thrust during accelerations, climbs, and dash, and extended engine life by reducing the turbine inlet temperature.

The program also included developing methods within the digital engine control system to detect degradation of components. This type of information, coupled with normal preventive maintenance, could help assure failsafe propulsion systems in high performance aircraft of the future.

PCA. Several accidents in which part or all of an aircraft's flight control system was lost prompted Dryden and NASA's Ames Research Center to establish a research program to investigate the capabilities of a Propulsion Controlled Aircraft (PCA), using only engine thrust for flight control. The eighth test F-15A (71-0287) was to serve as the first aircraft to intentionally demonstrate this capability.

Initial flight studies with the pilot manually controlling the throttles and all F-15 flight controls locked showed that it was possible to maintain gross control. Altitude could be maintained within a few hundred feet using both throttles together. To climb, thrust would be added; to descend, thrust would be reduced. Heading could be controlled to within a few degrees, using differential throttle to generate yaw, which results in roll. These initial flights also showed there was not adequate precision flight control capability to land on a runway. This was due to the small control forces and moments of engine thrust, difficulty in controlling the airplane's shallow dive and climb motion, and difficulty in compensating for the lag in engine response.

Simulation studies at Dryden and McAir duplicated the flight results, and control research and simulation studies also established the feasibility of using feedback of parameters such as flight path angle, pitch rate, bank angle, roll rate, and yaw rate to augment the throttle control capability and to stabilize the aircraft. The only equipment added to the aircraft was a control panel containing two thumbwheels, one for the pilot's flight path command, and the other for bank angle command. All of the needed sensors and actuators were available from various integrated flight/propulsion control research projects that had previously used the F-15 FTF.

Tests of the PCA-configured F-15 were

accomplished at speeds of 150 knots with the flaps down and at 170-190 knots with the flaps up. Initial flights tested the 'up and away' control capability, with landing approaches down to less than 10 feet above the ground. Flight tests of PCA concluded with successful 'hands-off' landings at Edwards AFB, California.

NASA 835, in a beautiful white and blue paint scheme, is currently (1997) being used for spare parts to keep NASA 836 and the F-15/ACTIVE flying. The USAF has requested that NASA return the aircraft for further disposition (most probably scrapping), but Dryden has resisted due to potential impacts to the other NASA F-15 programs.

Proposals and Other Dreams

The first derivative study of the F-15 was during 1971-72; an interceptor to work in conjunction with the new Airborne Warning and Control System (AWACS) E-3A. The Air Force instituted a series of studies (Advanced Manned Interceptor, CONUS Interceptor, etc.) for a new interceptor and had considered a wide variety of possibilities, including the Lockheed F-12B, an improved General Dynamics F-106, and the Grumman F-14. The YF-12 and F-106 were dropped from consideration in late-1971, and the F-14 was generally rated at par or slightly better than the F-15 in the interceptor role. The studies also included a stretched, F100 powered F-111 (designated F-111X-7), and a modified North American RA-5C (NR-349) powered by three J79s. Initial funding consisted of $5 million in FY73 money for continued engineering studies, but the program was cancelled shortly thereafter, the existing ADC F-106s continuing to serve until they were replaced by F-15As beginning in the early-1980s.

Another variant that has been proposed since the beginning of the F-15 project is the RF-15 reconnaissance aircraft. There have been several variations to this theme, one involving a special nose with camera ports, similar in concept to that employed on the RF-4B/C. This version also employed a TV camera, a multi-spectral scanner, and side-looking radar in a modified lower fuselage. However, in most concepts the modifications were limited to data processing equipment, with all sensor equipment to be contained in FAST Packs. The Air Force has never enthusiastically supported the idea of an RF-15, mainly because of its potential cost. As a private venture McAir also developed a conformal reconnaissance pod designed to be carried instead of the centerline stores station of two-seat F-15s under the company-funded F-15(R) 'Peep Eagle' program. The Reconnaissance Technology Demonstrator (RTD) pod could carry a full range of current Air Force camera

Left : **This ex-123rd FS F-15A (76-0059) is in flyable storage in AMARC at Davis-Monthan AFB, Arizona. The white 'spraylat' is a latex sealant used to preserve the aircraft.**
Teresa Vanden-Heuvel/US Air Force/AMARC

and imaging equipment. Optionally, it is capable of transmitting imagery data to ground stations directly. Flight tests of the RTD pod were conducted by 71-0291 in the summer of 1987.

F-15G Wild Weasel

McAir has periodically proposed a version of the two-seat F-15 as the heir-apparent to the F-4G Advanced Wild Weasel defense suppression aircraft. The McAir demonstrator F-15B (71-0291) was flight tested with an aerodynamic pod under its nose, vaguely reminiscent of the F-4G chin pod, that was intended to hold the AN/APR-38 Wild Weasel system. While generally endorsed by the USAF, the cost of the aircraft made its adoption for this role unlikely. Nevertheless, in May 1986, McAir received a $500,000 ten-month study contract for continued development under the internal 'Wild Weasel VII' nomenclature, although no production contract was forthcoming. McAir assigned the unofficial F-15G designation to this study, continuing the traditional use of 'G' for Wild Weasels (F-105G and F-4G).

In 1994, the USAF awarded yet another contract ($21 million in FY94, $37.4 million in FY95) to McAir to explore the feasibility of adapting the F-15C to the Suppression of Enemy Air Defenses (SEAD) role, replacing the F-4G. As part of the program, it was proposed to modify F-15Cs to fire the AGM-88 HARM anti-radiation missile with additional avionics for the SEAD role housed in distinctive 'cheek' fairings. However, based mainly on its lower cost, specially modified F-16Cs were chosen as the SEAD platform, and the F-15 Wild Weasel never made it past a paper study. The Air Force continues to be interested in the concept however, and it could make a return at a later date if the F-16 SEAD capability proves to be inadequate.

F-15(N) and F-15(N-PHX)

McAir spent considerable time and effort from 1970 to 1974 to define several versions of the F-15 for naval service. An unofficial (and perhaps, unwelcome) title of 'Seagle' was applied by various organizations involved. The first presentation to the Navy occurred in July 1971. McAir's position was that due to its excellent thrust-to-weight ratio and good visibility, the F-15 could easily be adapted for carrier operations. The only modifications required to enable it to operate off of CVA-19 class (or larger) carriers were: strengthened landing gear; an extendible front landing gear strut to produce the proper angle of attack upon catapult launch; installation of a nose-tow catapult system; folding wings; and a beefed-up arresting hook and associated structure. Both the nose and main landing gear wells would have to be enlarged to accommodate the increased

stroke of the new gear. These modifications would add approximately 2,300 pounds to the basic F-15A.

The Navy was not overly impressed with this proposal, so McAir further modified the design. Two McAir models (199-A-11A and 199-A-12) were then presented to the Navy. Model 199-A-12 featured a bridle catapult attachment, while 199-A-11A had a nose-tow catapult attachment, otherwise they were identical.

The design also featured a dual nose wheel arrangement, increased fuselage structural strength, a Navy-type refueling probe, and most important, an improved high-lift system, in addition to all the originally proposed modifications. The high-lift system was composed of full-span leading edge flaps, BLC trailing edge flaps, and a slotted aileron, all of which contributed 632 pounds to the projected 3,055 pound increase (to 42,824 pounds) over the USAF F-15A. An additional 71.9 pounds would be added for Navy avionics, including: AN/APN-15(V) radar beacon set; AN/ASW-27B digital data communications set; AN/ALQ-91A countermeasures set; AN/ASN-54(V) approach power compensator set; AN/ALQ-100 deceptive countermeasures set; AN/ARA-63 receiver decoding group; and an AN/APN-194 radar altimeter. The standard TEWS ECM system would be deleted.

These versions of the F-15(N) were still armed the same as the USAF F-15A (M61A1, AIM-7, and AIM-9), and were deemed roughly equal to the F-14B in overall performance, except for range. The radius of action in a fighter-escort configuration was 271 nm on internal fuel, compared to 481 nm for the F-14B and 319 for the F-4J. With external tanks, this increased to 516 nm versus 685 for the F-14B and 485 for the F-4J. No data was generated for FAST Pack equipped aircraft. A total of $403.5 million was

projected for non-recurring engineering costs, with a flyaway price of $7.6 million based on a 313 aircraft production run.

The F-15N then became the focus of Navy Fighter Study Group III. This group disregarded the McAir data, enlarged the nose to carry the AN/AWG-9 radar, and added Phoenix missiles, resulting in an aircraft that weighed 10,000 pounds more than the basic F-15A. This weight increase, along with the associated drag, greatly decreased the performance of the F-15, negating any advantage it had over the F-14A. There was also considerable concern over the 12° angle-of-attack used by the F-15 (compared to 10.2° for the F-14A) during approaches, and the relatively narrow landing gear track.

McAir and Hughes countered the study group's criticisms with a further modified version known as F-15(N-PHX), which added a rudimentary AIM-54 Phoenix missile capability. This version (model 199-A-19B) took the model 199-A-11A and modified the AN/APG-63 radar set into an AN/APG-64. These modifications involved increasing the transmit power to 7 kW (compared to 10 kW in the AN/AWG-9 and 5.2 kW in the AN/APG-63), a command link, a track-while-scan capability, and a Phoenix test feature. The radar antenna was also modified to effect a slight frequency shift. The central computer had its load changed to support the new track-while-scan modes, as well as adding additional memory and Phoenix unique software. Some cockpit controls and displays were also modified. The aircraft could carry up to eight AIM-54s: one on each fuselage AIM-7 station, one on each inboard wing pylon, and two (in tandem) on a special centerline pylon. The appropriate missile cooling systems were added to each station. Take-off gross weight was up to 46,009 pounds. The high-lift devices

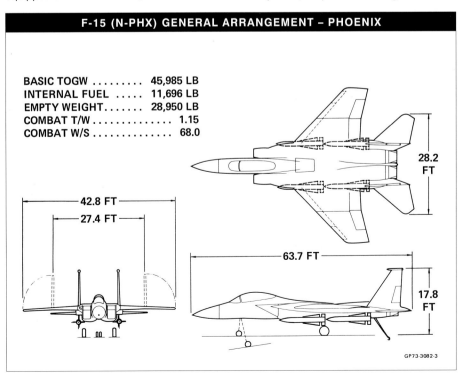

F-15 (N-PHX) GENERAL ARRANGEMENT – PHOENIX

BASIC TOGW . . . . 45,985 LB
INTERNAL FUEL . . . . . 11,696 LB
EMPTY WEIGHT. . . . . . . 28,950 LB
COMBAT T/W 1.15
COMBAT W/S 68.0

28.2 FT

42.8 FT
27.4 FT

63.7 FT

17.8 FT

GP73-3082-3

Right: **The Model 199-A-19B Navy F-15(N-PHX) proposed adding a rudimentary AIM-54 Phoenix missile capability to a navalized F-15, complete with folding wings and a reinforced tail hook.**
McDonnell Douglas

STREAK EAGLE

THIS CERTIFICATE WAS ABOARD F-15A,
SERIAL NUMBER 72119, ON ITS SUCCESSFUL ASSAULT
ON THE WORLD CLASS TIME TO CLIMB RECORDS
AT GRAND FORKS AIR FORCE BASE, NORTH DAKOTA.

FLOWN BY: PILOT   *Rog Smith*   MAJ, USAF
             PILOT   *W. R. Macfarlane*   MAJ, USAF
             PILOT   *Dave Peterson*   MAJ, USAF

MCDONNELL DOUGLAS

RECORD	DATE	TIME
3,000 Meters	January 16, 1975	27.57 Sec.
6,000 Meters	January 16, 1975	39.33 Sec.
9,000 Meters	January 16, 1975	48.86 Sec.
12,000 Meters	January 16, 1975	59.38 Sec.
15,000 Meters	January 16, 1975	77.02 Sec.
20,000 Meters	January 19, 1975	122.94 Sec.
25,000 Meters	January 26, 1975	161.02 Sec.
30,000 Meters	February 1, 1975	207.80 Sec.

were changed to include full-span Krueger leading edge flaps, BLC trailing edge flaps, and single-slotted ailerons. Approach speed to a carrier was estimated at 136 knots.

Another proposal was also presented, one essentially echoing the results of Navy Fighter Study Group III. The aircraft was equipped with the Hughes AN/AWG-9 weapons system from the F-14A, but otherwise resembled the earlier F-15(N-PHX). Estimated non-recurring R&D costs were $1.173 billion in FY72 dollars. Based on a 313 unit production run, the flyaway cost was $11.5 million per aircraft.

On 30th March 1973, the Senate Armed Services Committee's ad hoc Tactical Air Power subcommittee started new discussions on the possibilities of modifying the F-15 for the Navy mission. At this point the F-14 program was having difficulties, and the subcommittee wanted to look at possible alternatives, namely lower-cost (stripped) F-14s, F-15Ns, and improved F-4s. There were even proposals by Senator Eagleton for a 'fly-off' between the F-14 and F-15, but this never transpired. These discussions, along with some other considerations, led to the forming of Navy Fighter Study Group IV, out of which the aircraft ultimately known as the F/A-18A was born.

The Day the Eagle Streaked

For two weeks beginning on 16th January 1975, three Air Force pilots and a modified F-15A-6-MC (72-119) made an assault on the world class time-to-climb for aircraft powered by jet engines. The three pilots, Maj Roger Smith, Maj W R 'Mac' Macfarlane, and Maj Dave Peterson were all members of the F-15 Joint Test Force at Edwards. Pete Garrison, a McAir pilot, was instrumental in the develop-

ment of the flight profiles used for the records. Project 'Streak Eagle' had three objectives:

- To enhance Air Force esprit de corps and morale, and to foster the attractiveness of an Air Force career,
- To establish the credibility of USAF forces as an integral element of the United States' overall military posture,
- To provide data on the F-15's capabilities at extremes of altitudes and performance under controlled test conditions.

On 1st April 1974, the Air Force awarded McAir a $2.1 million dollar contract for aircraft modifications and general support, with configuration approval on 18th May 1974. All test aircraft then in inventory were evaluated, and the choice narrowed between F5 (71-0284) and F17 (72-0119). Several items led the choice of 72-0119: it was 800 pounds lighter than F5; it was an Air Force (Cat II) aircraft as opposed to a contractor (Cat I) aircraft and its absence would have less of an impact on the test program (in fact, it was an unneeded attrition aircraft); and since F17 was just rolling down the production line fewer things would have to be 'undone'. The aircraft was modified by McAir between 27th April and 11th June 1974 for the tests by deleting all non-mission critical systems including: the flap and speed brake actuators; internal armament; the radar and fire-control system; non-critical cockpit displays and radios; one of the generators; the utility hydraulic system; the landing and taxi lights; and, of course, the 50 pounds of paint (hence it's name). Additions included: a revised oxygen system; support equipment for the full pressure suit worn by the pilots; extra batteries;

a long pitot boom with alpha and beta vanes; an over-the-shoulder video camera; a battery powered radio; sensitive g meters; a standby attitude gyro; a large VHF antenna under the canopy behind the pilot; and a special 'hold-down' device in place of the tail hook. The final result was an aircraft that weighed 1,800 pounds less than the other block-6 aircraft. Fully fueled in preparation for a 30,000 meter run (on the 37th test flight), 72-0119 weighed 36,799 pounds. Simulations, primarily of the high altitude profiles, were run 3rd May – 30th September and the application to the Federation Aeronautique Internationale (FAI) was made on 15th September 1974. The profile for the 30,000 meter (98,425 feet) record was:

- Release from the hold-down at full afterburner with 7,000 pounds of fuel,
- Gear up and rotate at 70 knots (three seconds after release !),
- At 420 knots, rotate vertically into an Immelmann and hold 2.65g,
- Expect to arrive level, upside down, at 32,000 feet and Mach 1.1,
- Rotate to right side up, accelerate to Mach 1.5 while climbing to 36,000 feet,
- Accelerate to Mach 2.25 and pull 4.0g to a 60° climb angle,
- Hold 60° climb,
- Shut down the afterburners and the engines when they flame-out,
- Ride ballistically over the top at 55 knots and 103,000 feet,
- Descend at a 55° dive angle,
- When below 55,000 feet, try to start the engines, and
- Go Home.

The record runs were accomplished at Grand Forks AFB, North Dakota, where the cold atmospheric conditions were ideal. Six different record flights were flown (there were several unsuccessful ones in between), and margins of 15-33% were achieved over the previous records. For the record attempts the aircraft was physically held down to the runway while full power was applied.

A highly modified MiG-25 (E-266) later recaptured several of the higher altitude records, and also set one to 35,000 meters, although it is still a matter of some controversy over whether it was rocket assisted. All of these records have since been broken by the P-42 prototype for the Sukhoi Su-27 interceptor. There was consideration given to further modifying 'Streak Eagle', including using more powerful production engines, and making another attempt, but this never materialized. Streak Eagle has since been turned over to the Air Force Museum at Wright-Patterson AFB where, to protect it from corrosion, it has been painted in a modified 'Compass Ghost' scheme utilizing two tones of blue instead of the normal grey. The Museum's plans for the aircraft are uncertain, management preferring to obtain a MiG killer F-15C and discard 'Streak Eagle'.

Chapter Ten

Eagle Operators

The McDonnell Douglas F-15 Eagle has been in US Air Force squadron service for over 20 years. Fortunately, the US has needed to call upon it to serve in only one major war, Desert Storm, although the Saudi's and Israeli's have had to use it operationally numerous times. The aircraft has proven itself well in combat, scoring over 100 air-to-air victories without a single loss to enemy aircraft.

During its 20 years, the F-15 has seen major changes in the structure of the US Air Force. The Tactical Air Command (TAC), once the mainstay of the fighter world, has been disbanded and a new Air Combat Command (ACC) created. A short career as a continental defense interceptor ended when the Aerospace Defense Command (ADC) was disbanded, and most interceptor duties have since been assumed by the smaller Lockheed F-16 Fighting Falcon.

The F-15 has been assigned to eight Air National Guard squadrons, seven of which continue to operate the type. Unlike many aircraft, where the ANG units operate obsolete or less capable variants, the F-15s operated by the Air Guard units are equal in every important way to the newer active duty aircraft.

Air Combat Command

The creation of Air Combat Command (ACC) on 1st June 1992 resulted largely from dramatic changes in the international arena. The collapse of the former Soviet Union, and the resultant end of the Cold War, led senior US defense planners to conclude that the structure of the military establishment which had evolved during the Cold War years was not well suited to the new world situation. The likelihood of a large-scale nuclear conflict seemed thankfully remote, but US military forces would increasingly be called upon to participate in smaller-scale regional contingencies and humanitarian operations.

Consequently, the Air Force began to reconsider the long-standing distinction between the Strategic Air Command (SAC) and the Tactical Air Command (TAC). The term 'strategic'

had become almost totally linked to the notion of nuclear deterrence, while the focus of 'tactical' operations was a cooperative mission with the Air Force working in tandem with ground and naval forces. The distinction, however, did not lend itself to a limited conflict. During the war in Southeast Asia, 'strategic' B-52 bombers performed 'tactical' missions, while 'tactical' fighter aircraft carried out 'strategic' bombing deep into enemy territory. Operation 'Desert Storm' in early 1991 further blurred the distinction between the two terms. Consequently, as senior Air Force officials sought to reexamine roles and missions, the redundancy of this former division came under their scrutiny.

General Merrill A McPeak, Air Force Chief of Staff, envisioned eliminating superfluous organizational layers. The Vice Chief of Staff, General John M Loh, had pondered the strategic and tactical distinction for some time and discussed with the Chief of Staff and Air Force Secretary Donald B Rice the need to restructure major commands in the face of the blurring of this distinction. General Loh continued to examine this matter after assuming command of Tactical Air Command on 26th March 1991. General George L Butler, Commander-in-Chief, SAC, also supported change. These three general officers spearheaded the drive to integrate the assets of SAC and TAC into a single operational command.

Another significant change resulted from an overhaul of flying training responsibilities. Following its activation, ACC was responsible for aircraft-specific aircrew training, including initial weapon system and continuation training. On 1st July 1993, the 58th and 325th Fighter Wings – the F-16 and F-15 training units – were transferred from ACC to the Air Education and Training Command (AETC). Concurrently, the unit's home bases, Luke AFB and Tyndall AFB, also moved from ACC to AETC ownership.

The participation of ACC units and personnel in a variety of operations throughout the world has consistently illustrated the command's motto: 'Global Power for America.' In Southwest Asia, ACC provided active duty and reserve component forces for Operation 'Desert Storm' and Operation 'Southern Watch' to deter Iraqi aggression. In October 1994 the ACC demonstrated its ability to react quickly to the buildup of Iraqi troops near the border of Kuwait. In addition, ACC, from its inception, has provided support for counter-drug operations in the form of Airborne Warning and Control Systems (AWACS) and fighter aircraft.

1st Fighter Wing

On 14th March 1974, the Air Force announced plans to station the first operational F-15 wing at Langley AFB, Virginia. Langley was chosen due to its heritage and ideal location for TAC's

Right: **An early F-15A from the 555th TFS banks towards the desert near Luke AFB, Arizona. The ECM system has not been installed, evidenced by the lack of antennas.** Roger Smith

secondary air defense mission. On 6th June 1975, Tactical Air Command directed 9th Air Force to move the 1st FW, and its associate squadrons, from MacDill AFB to Langley. Although the designation of the unit moved, the majority of MacDill personnel remained in place, and served under the newly designated 56th TFW. The next six months was spent preparing for the arrival of the F-15, and on 18th December 1975 the wing's first F-15B arrived. Official welcoming ceremonies were held on 9th January 1976, when the first F-15A arrived. The wing's first squadron to equip with the F-15 was the 27th FS, which can lay claim to being the oldest fighter squadron in the Air Force, with a continuous history dating to 15th June 1917. The 94th FS was the second squadron to receive F-15s, and had been made famous by Captain Eddie Rickenbacker in the First World War as the 'Hat in the Ring' squadron. The 94th is the second oldest fighter squadron in the Air Force. The wing uses non-standard 'FF' tailcodes to signify 'First Fighter.'

After achieving their Initial Operational Capability (IOC), the 1st FW embarked on Operation 'Ready Eagle' to help prepare the 36th TFW at Bitburg AB for their reception of the F-15. By 23rd September 1977, the wing provided Bitburg with 88 operational ready pilots, 522 maintenance specialists, and later trained an additional 1,100 maintenance personnel at Bitburg. After show-casing the new fighter across the United States, and participating in numerous training exercises, the Wing undertook several overseas deployments. The 94th TFS deployed eight aircraft to Japan, Korea, and the Philippines in the spring of 1978, and the 94th and 71st deployed 18 Eagles to the Netherlands in the fall of the same year. Unknowingly forecasting the future, in early 1979 the 94th TFS deployed 12 aircraft to Operation Prized Eagle, a short-notice exercise to Saudi Arabia.

Beginning on 7th August 1990, the 27th and 71st Tactical Fighter Squadrons deployed 48 aircraft to Saudi Arabia in support of Operation Desert Shield. By 16th January 1991 the wing had amassed 4,207 sorties. On 17th January 1991, 16 1st TFW F-15s departed King Abdul-Aziz Air Base and headed toward Iraq to participate in the opening round of Operation 'Desert Storm'. During this first night of the operation, Captain Steve Tate of the 71st TFS shot down an Iraqi F.1EQ Mirage, using a single AIM-7M Sparrow. It would be the 1st FW's only kill in 'Desert Storm', during which the wing flew 2,564 combat sorties. On 8th March 1991, the 1st TFW returned to Langley from Saudi Arabia. The end of the Gulf War did not bring an end to 1st FW support in Southwest Asia, however, and the 1st FW provides aircraft six months per year to monitor the southern no-fly zone under Operation 'Southern Watch'. In October 1994, when Saddam Hussein tested the world's resolve by again placing forces near the Kuwaiti border, the wing participated in a short-notice deployment, Operation 'Vigilant Warrior'. When Iraqi troop movements began again in September 1996, the wing was prepared to deploy under Operation 'Desert Focus'.

On 1st October 1991, the 1st Tactical Fighter Wing was redesignated 1st Fighter Wing. Marking the end of the Cold War, the wing hosted the first leg of a Russian-American fighter exchange in July 1992. Thirty-seven members of the Russian Air Force, two Su-27 fighters, and one IL-76 transport deployed to Langley AFB for demonstrations and joint exercises. Two months later, two F-15Cs and 40 support personnel visited the RussianAir Force at Lipetsk Air Base, Russia.

3rd Wing

Originally established at Elmendorf AFB, Alaska, in 1966 and assigned to the Alaskan Air Command as the 21st Composite Wing, the unit was assigned the air defense of Alaska and adjoining parts of Canada. The Alaskan Air Command became the Alaska Command of PACAF on 7th July 1989, and then was redesignated the 11th AF on 9th August 1990. The 21st CW was redesignated as a Tactical Fighter Wing in 1990, and subsequently on 26th September 1991 became a Fighter Wing. This designation was short-lived, and the unit was redesignated as the 3rd Wing on 19th December 1991. The 3rd Wing had previously been based at Clark AFB in the Phillipines, and was moved when a lease agreement could not be reached with the island government. The Wing uses 'AK' tailcodes, signifying 'Alaska'.

The 43rd TFS received their first F-15A/B on 21st June 1982, but transitioned into F-15C/Ds previously used by the 1st TFW at Langley beginning on 23rd May 1987. The 43rd TFS was disbanded and operationally replaced by the 19th Fighter Squadron on 1st January 1994

Left top: **The commander's aircraft (86-0164) from the 493rd FS at Lakenheath is fairly typical of MSIP F-15Cs serving in Europe. A mixed load of AIM-7 and AIM-120 missiles is shown. The tail strip is black with a yellow border.**
Terry Panopalis Collection

Left: **The 48th FW frequently deploys to Aviano, Italy, in support of the United Nations operations in Bosnia. Here an F-15E (90-0248) is shown with a load of iron bombs and an AIM-120 AMRAAM. Unusually, the covers over the pitot and alpha probes are gloss black, perhaps because this aircraft is flown by the commander of the 48th FW at Lakenheath. The tail strip (front to back) is blue/yellow/red bordered in white.**
Terry Panopalis Collection

when F-15C/Ds replaced the 19th's F-16s. The 19th FS flew 160 sorties during Operation 'Provide Comfort'. The squadron has never lost an aircraft or pilot in air-to-air combat, yet has managed 70 confirmed kills (none of these in the F-15). Appropriately, considering their home base, Captain Hugh Elmendorf was the squadron's Commanding Officer in 1923.

On 8 May 1987 the wing activated the 54th TFS flying F-15A/Bs for a short while before receiving F-15C/Ds in 1988. The 54th TFS had been disbanded for 27 years, having last flown F-89Js in 1960. The squadron participated in Operation Provide Comfort from April through June 1995, although significant support was provided by personnel from the 19th FS. On 29th May 1990 the Wing acquired the 90th TFS from Clark AFB in the Phillipines and equipped it with the F-15E. The Squadron was subsequently designated as a Fighter Squadron, and currently operates 20 F-15Es.

While the wing's air superiority aircraft were painted in 'Compass Ghost' they had a 'Big Dipper' and 'North Star' painted on a dark field inside each vertical stabilizer. The dark field has disappeared from the aircraft as they have been repainted into the 'Mod Eagle' scheme. Currently the inside of the verticals have a black 'Big Dipper' and 'North Star' painted over their standard camouflage.

4th Wing
'Fourth but First' is the motto of the 4th Wing based at Seymour Johnson, North Carolina., and the first user of the Mud Hen. The unit transitioned from the F-4E to the F-15E beginning on 29th December 1988 when the 'Spirit of Goldsboro' arrived. The 336th Tactical Fighter Squadron became the first operational F-15E squadron on 1st October 1989, and the transition from F-4E to the F-15E was completed on 1st July 1991, making the 4th FW the first operational F-15E wing in the Air Force. On 22nd April 22 1991, the 4th Tactical Fighter Wing was redesignated the 4th Fighter Wing and incorporated the assets of the 68th Air Refueling Wing, a former Strategic Air Command unit flying the KC-10 tanker. The 4th Fighter Wing began another force structure change in 1994. All but six KC-10s were reassigned to the Air Mobility Command, and the 333rd FS returned to Seymour Johnson to perform type conversion training for all F-15E units, a function previously performed by the 550th FS of the 56th FW at Luke. Fittingly, the Wing uses 'SJ' tailcodes.

The 333rd TFS was moved from Davis-Monthan AFB, Arizona, to Seymour Johnson without personnel or equipment, effective 1st October 1994 to conduct formal training for all Air Force F-I5E aircrew members. To accomplish this mission, the squadron operates 18 F-15Es and has 280 permanent personnel. Training consists of four courses: basic, transition, instructors, and senior officer checkout. The basic course lasts seven months and trains new pilots and weapon systems officers to fly the F-15E. The four month transition course is for experienced fighter crews who are changing to the F-15E from another first line fighter type. The instructors' course lasts 2.5 months

and involves training experienced F-15E aircrews how to become instructors. The senior officer checkout is a one month course intended to familiarize senior officers who have been assigned to a base with F-15Es.

The 334th TFS flew its first F-15E sortie on 1st January 1991 and subsequently served as the host unit for several units deploying to Operation 'Desert Shield' and 'Desert Storm'. Aircrews and support personnel from the 334th deployed to Operation 'Desert Storm' to augment other wing squadrons as required. The squadron became operational in the F-15E on 18th June 18 1991, and deployed to Saudi Arabia the next day to relieve remaining elements

Top right: **An F-15C from the 19th FS climbing vertically. A single training AIM-7 is carried on the fuselage and an ACMI pod is on one of the Sidewinder rails.** US Air Force

Right: **Since they frequently need long range, the 57th FIS operated F-15Cs (80-0050 shown here) equipped with CFTs, although this example is carrying two external fuel tanks instead. The checkerboard pattern on the vertical stabilizer is black and white.** Mick Roth Collection

combat sorties, logging 3,200 hours, and dropping 6.5 million pounds of ordnance. During the conflict, the squadron lost two aircraft, with one crew killed, and the other imprisoned by the Iraqis until the end of the war.

Since the end of the Gulf War, the 336th has participated in exercises such as Maple Flag, Gunsmoke, Combat Hammer, Red Flag, Ocean Venture, Combat Anchor, and Quick force. The squadron also rotates back to Southwest Asia to enforce the United Nation's 'no-fly' zone under Operation Southern Watch.

At the time the 4th Wing's squadrons deployed to the Middle East, the AN/ALQ-135B ECM system was not completely operational (there were software integration problems), and the squadron did not have sufficient LANTIRN targeting pods to equip all of its aircraft. This limited the types effectiveness early in the war, and probably contributed to the loss of two 336th aircraft. By the end of the war, however, there was little doubt the F-15E was one of the premier strike aircraft in any air force.

4th Tactical Fighter Wing (Provisional)

When Operation 'Desert Shield' began on 6th August 1990, the F-15 was one of the primary weapons chosen to defend Saudi Arabia. The 336th FS from the 4th Wing was the only operational F-15E squadron in the Air Force, and its aircraft began arriving at Thumrait, Oman on 12th August 1990. The aircraft were subsequently moved to Al Kharj, Saudi Arabia when the 4th TFW(P) was established under the 14th Air Division (Provisional). Subsequently, the 335th FS arrived in-theater, and by the time Operation 'Desert Storm' began on 17th January 1991 there were 48 F-15Es in Saudi Arabia. One aircraft (87-0203) was lost in a pre-war training accident on 30th September, claiming the lives of Major Peter S Hook and Captain James Poulet. Combat operations claimed two additional 336th FS aircraft: 88-1689 on 18 January, with the loss of Major Thomas F Koritz and Major Donnie R Holland; and 88-1692 on 20th January. The crew of the latter, Colonel David W Eberly and Major Thomas E Griffith, Jr were captured by the Iraqis and interned until 4th March.

In addition to the two F-15E squadrons, 4th TFW(P) also controlled the F-15C-equipped 53rd TFS from the 36th TFW at Bitburg, and two Air National Guard F-16 squadrons (138th TFS/New York, and 157th TFS/South Carolina). The 336th returned home shortly after the end of hostilities, and the 335th a couple of months later. Subsequently, the 4th TFW(P) formed the basis for the formation of the 4404th TFW(P) at Al Kharj Air Base.

of the 335th, providing combat air patrol for withdrawing ground forces. Appropriately, this squadron is named the 'Eagles,' a name they had long before they transitioned to the F-15.

The 335th TFS achieved IOC on 1st October 1990, and on 28-29th December 1990 deployed 24 F-15Es along with support personnel and equipment to Al Kharj Air Base in central Saudi Arabia. On the night of 17th January the squadron participated in the initial assault on Iraq, hitting communications facilities, power networks, and airfields around Baghdad. Given the mission of finding and destroying Iraq's SCUD missile launchers, the 335th FS brought Iraq's use of this terror weapon to a virtual halt, earning the squadron the nickname 'Scud Busters'. During the war, the squadron flew 1,097 combat missions over

Iraq and occupied Kuwait, dropping over 4.8 million pounds of ordnance. The squadron remained in-theater until the end of hostilities, returning home on 27th February 1991. The 335th scored the F-15E's only air-to-air kill in Operation 'Desert Storm', when Capt Richard Bennett and Daniel Bakke (WSO) dropped a GBU-10 into a flying Iraqi Hughes 500 helicopter. The squadron still periodically deploys to Saudi Arabia to enforce the UN sanctions against Iraq.

The 336th TFS was the first operational F-15E squadron when it achieved IOC on 1st October 1989. The squadron deployed on 9th August 1990 in support of Operation 'Desert Shield'. On 17th January 1991, the 336th launched 24 aircraft against targets in Iraq, and by the end of 'Desert Storm' had flown 1,100

4404th Wing (Provisional)

Although the 4404th Wing (Provisional) was officially activated on 2nd June 1992, its predecessors date to 13th March, 1991. On that date, Headquarters TAC activated the 4404th TFW(P) at Al Kharj Air Base. The original assets of the 4404th TFW(P) came from the 4th TFW(P), which had operated during the Gulf War. In June 1992 the wing relocated to King Abdul Aziz Air Base, Dhahran, where it was officially reactivated as the 4404th Wing (Provisional) on 2nd August 1991.

On 27th August 1992, the United Nations restricted the Iraqi flight operations south of the 32nd parallel in response to Iraqi attacks on Shiite minorities in southern Iraq. Coalition forces from the US Navy, the British Royal Air Force, and the French Air Force joined the wing in Operation 'Southern Watch', monitoring Iraqi compliance with the UN mandate. At the beginning of 1998, the Coalition continues to fly Southern Watch missions around the clock. Beyond the 'Southern Watch' mission, the wing also supported Operation Restore Hope in December 1992 and evacuated over 600 US and foreign citizens from Yemen in May 1994. US Air Force aircraft, particularly F-15E squadrons, deploy to the 4404th as required to support operational needs.

As fate had it, the 4404th Wing would not remain at Dhahran. After a terrorist truck bomb killed 19 airmen, the wing was ordered to move to a safer location within the Kingdom of Saudi Arabia. Prince Sultan Air Base was chosen as the relocation site, which meant that the 4404th was returning home to Al Kharj where it first originated. The morning of 5th August, the first of five C-5s landed and over a 45 day period, the wing moved aircraft, personnel, and equipment from Riyadh and Dhahran to its new home at Prince Sultan Air Base.

Since the wing's activation, it has employed 16 different types of aircraft. Currently, the wing employs a diversified fleet consisting of F-15C, F-15E, F-16, KC-135, KC-10, RC-135, E-3, U-2, C-130, HC-130, and C-21 aircraft which provide fighter, electronic combat, reconnaissance, command and control, air refueling, search and rescue, and cargo/troop transport capabilities. The 4404th Wing (Provisional) has over

4,500 personnel assigned to six geographically separated locations, in three countries in the Southwest Asia area of responsibility.

18th Fighter Wing

The 18th FW is based at Kadena AB in Okinawa, Japan, and consists of the 12th FS, 44th FS, and 67th FS. The wing is under the control of the Pacific Air Forces (PACAF), 5th Air Force. The wing received their first F-15C/D on 26th September 1979, replacing F-4Ds. The F-15s had previously been operated by the 33rd FW at Eglin AFB prior to reaching Kadena. Due to their remote operating location, most depot-level maintenance is performed under contract by Korean Air Lines in Pusan, Korea. On a rotating basis, the 18th FW provides aircraft to stand alert on the Korean peninsula. In a slight variation of the standard Air Force tail stripes, every aircraft in the 18th FW carries all three squadron colors. The outermost color denotes the squadron the aircraft is assigned to. Most aircraft have carried a stylized shogun warrior on the inside of each tail, and the 'ZZ' tailcodes do not represent anything in particular.

32nd Fighter Squadron

One of the more interesting squadrons in the Air Force was the 32nd FS based at Camp New Amsterdam, Soesterberg, The Netherlands. This squadron was under operational control of

NATO through the Royal Netherlands Air Force, and their 'CR' tailcode was short for 'Crown,' a theme also represented on their unit crest. All squadron aircraft had an orange stripe outlined in green on the vertical stabilizers, although this squadron (and most of the Air Materiel Command units) usually wore the stripe about a foot lower than other Air Force units. As part of Operation 'Coronet Sandpiper', the 32nd received its first F-15A/B on 13th December 1978, replacing F-4Es.

During Operation 'Desert Storm', the squadron was deployed to Incirlik, Turkey, where Captain Donald Watrous scored an air-to-air victory over an Iraqi MiG-23. During 1990, some of the squadrons F-15C/Ds were supplied to the Royal Saudi Air Force. These were replaced by MSIP F-15A/Bs (which are equally as capable as F-15C/Ds) before the squadron was disbanded in 1994.

33rd Fighter Wing

The 33rd Fighter Wing received its first F-15B (77-0156) for maintenance training on 21st September 1978. The wing uses 'EG' tailcodes, representing their home base at Eglin AFB, Florida. The official F-15 arrival ceremony was held on 15th December 1978, with the final F-15A/B arriving on 21st June 1979. The wing began receiving F-15C/Ds on 3rd July 1979 with the delivery of the first 'production' F-15C

Right: **The 33rd Fighter Wing scored most of the air-to-air kills in the Gulf War. Here an F-15C (85-0102) shows three MiG-kill stars on the forward fuselage. These are kills accredited to the F-15, opposed to ones credited to individual pilots. Captain David Rose made a single kill in 85-102 on 29th January 1991, and Capt Anthony Murphy added two more on 7th February 1991.** Mick Roth Collection

Right, lower: **Several two-seat F-15Bs (such as 77-0158) were operated by the 32nd FS based at Camp New Amsterdam, Soesterberg, Netherlands. The squadron would later transition to the F-15C/D.** Mick Roth Collection

Above: **Fortunately, this is a configuration the F-15E has never had to carry into combat – two B61 nuclear stores, one under each CFT. Actually, these are BDU-38 training stores. The B61 (or Mk 61) can be tailored to yield between 10 and 500 kilotons of explosive power. The weapon is 13.4 inches in diameter, 11.75 feet long, and weighs between 695 and 716 pounds.** Department of Defense

(78-0470). However, the wing was simply acting as a staging area for the 18th TFW at Kadena, and was not considered operationally capable. After the F-15C/Ds were sent to Kadena under Operation 'Ready Eagle III', the 33rd began receiving F-15A/Bs from the 32nd TFS at Soesterberg, The Netherlands. The wing finally began receiving its won F-15C/Ds on 23rd February 1983.

In October 1986 the 33rd became the only fighter wing to date to win the William Tell air-to-air weapons meet two consecutive times. In November 1987, the wing won the first Long Arrow, which is an ACC no-notice, air-to-air competition. During late 1988 and early 1989 the 33rd conducted operational testing of the AIM-120A AMRAAM, with the 58th TFS becoming operational with the weapon in February 1991. The wing currently has more than 2,000 active duty military and 14 civilian members assigned, and the FY95 payroll was more than $53 million. The 33rd FW uses an Eagle head on a dark background on the inside of the vertical stabilizer as a unit marking.

The 58th TFS received their first F-15A on 15th March 1979, achieving their IOC on 23rd May 1979. In late 1979, the squadron deployed to Europe with 18 aircraft and flew 1,001 sorties in less than three weeks. The unit repeated this deployment in 1982 with 24 aircraft, making this the first full F-15 squadron deployment. In December 1989, the squadron was called upon to lead the way for Operation 'Just Cause' by flying initial force protection sorties for invasion missions. The squadron converted to the F-15C/D prior to deploying to Tabuk Air Base, Saudi Arabia, in August 1990 as part of 'Desert Shield'. The 58th scored 13 air-to-air kills during the Gulf War, the highest total from any single squadron. Beginning in February 1991 the squadron became operational with the AIM-120, and although several hundred sorties were flown with the weapon during the war, none were fired in anger.

On 16th March 1970 the 59th FIS was redesignated the 59th TFS, and was assigned to the 33rd TFW on 1st September 1970. During 1979,

the squadron began transitioning from the F-4 to the F-15C/D. The 59th TFS also deployed to Operation 'Desert Storm', scoring two air-to-air kills during the conflict. Like the other 33rd FW squadrons, the 59th FS was based at Tabuk, Saudi Arabia.

Between 15th June 1979 and 16 April 1980 the 60th TFW trained 55 pilots and processed 54 F-15C/Ds for the 18th TFW as part of the Kadena 'Ready Eagle' program. The squadron converted back to the F-15A/B before receiving their own F-15C/Ds. The 60th made its first combat deployment since World War II when it sent ten F-15s to Grenada in support of Operation 'Urgent Fury', the rescue of American medical students held in Grenada. The unit flew support missions for Operation 'Just Cause', the removal of Panamanian dictator Manuel Noriega from Panama. The squadron scored a single air-to-air kill during Operation 'Desert Storm'.

36th Fighter Wing

The USAFE's 36th FW was the first European user of the F-15, reaching its full strength on 30th September 1977. The wing was assigned the air defense of NATO's central front, and expected to be the first unit in combat should a European war have broken out. The Wing used 'BT' tailcodes in reference to Bitburg AB, where the wing was based. The 36th periodically hosted the NATO 'Tiger' meet, and usually painted one aircraft in 'tiger' motif to participate.

The 22nd FS did not deploy aircraft during Operation 'Desert Storm', although both pilots and maintenance personnel flew with the other two squadrons during the conflict. The squadron was deactivated in 1994. The 53rd FS deployed to Tabuk, Saudi Arabia during Operation 'Desert Storm'. The squadron scored 11 air-to-air kills during and immediately after the Gulf War. The squadron was deactivated in late 1994, although the aircraft and personnel were reactivated under the 52nd Wing at Spangdahlem on 25th February 1995. Officially the squadron was assigned a yellow stripe on the vertical stabilizer, but its aircraft generally flew with yellow and black 'tiger' stripe to cele-

brate the squadron's name. The 525th FS deployed to Incirlik, Turkey during Operation 'Desert Storm' and scored five air-to-air kills during the Gulf War. The squadron was deactivated in 1992 as the situation in Europe improved.

48th Fighter Wing

A late-comer to the F-15 was the 48th Fighter Wing at RAF Lakenheath, England, who finally traded their General Dynamics F-111s for F-15Es beginning on 21st February 1992. The wing has been based at Lakenheath since 1960, and is assigned to USAFE, 3rd Air Force. The Wing makes regular deployments to Aviano, Italy, to provide muscle for Operation 'Deny Flight' over Bosnia, and was involved in a UN-authorized strike against a Serbian airfield at Uḍbina, Croatia, on 21st November 1994. A second strike was carried out a few days later against a surface-to-air missile site near Bihac. During August-September 1995 48th Wing aircraft flew strikes against Bosnia-Serb ground forces as part of Operation 'Deliberate Force', marking the first time F-15Es employed GBU-15 optically-guided 2,000 pound bombs against hostile targets. The wing also provided aircraft to Operation 'Provide Comfort' when it sent a detachment to Incirlik, Turkey. The 492nd FS achieved IOC with the F-15E on 20th April 1992. The 493rd FS began converting to the F-15C/D in December 1992. The 494th FS achieved IOC on 13th August 1992.

49th Fighter Wing

The 49th FW became a user of late-production F-15A/Bs beginning on 20th December 1977, replacing F-4Es at Holloman AFB, New Mexico.

IOC was achieved on 4th June 1978. History was made during February 1980, when two pilots from the 49th flew their F-15s 6,200 miles in just over 14 hours, and established a record for the longest flight of a single-seat fighter aircraft. The flight required six aerial refuelings and proved that a deployment could be made to an overseas area on short notice. In July 1980, the wing was tasked to support the Rapid Deployment Force, requiring the wing to be ready to deploy its aircraft, crews, and support personnel on short notice. The wing served with the Rapid Deployment Force until July 1981, when the tasking was transferred to the 1st TFW at Langley AFB. The Wing's won top honors at the 1988 William Tell competition, including the coveted 'Top Gun' trophy for the best fighter pilot.

The 7th FS was the first of the Wing's squadrons to receive the F-15, and also the first to be deactivated, on 30th September 1990. The 8th FS was deactivated on 30th September 1992. The 9th FS deployed to Tabuk, Saudi Arabia, after the end of hostilities to relieve elements of the 33rd FW. The squadron was deactivated on 30th September 1992 shortly after its return from Saudi Arabia.

The Wing was the last regular Air Force operator of the F-15A/B, and the only original user not to convert to the newer F-15C/D. The last F-15 departed Holloman on 5th June 1992, ending 14 years of Eagle operations. The 49th subsequently became the Air Force's only operator of the F-117 stealth fighter. The 'HO' tailcodes reflect their home base, and most aircraft carried a subdued Eagle motif on the inside of the vertical stabilizers.

52nd Wing
When the 36th FW at Bitburg AB was closed down, one of its F-15C/D fighter squadrons was transferred to nearby Spangdahlem Air Base. The 53rd FS was reactivated as part of the 52nd Wing at Spangdahlem on 25th February 1995 and is equipped with 18 F-15C/D aircraft. The 52nd Wing is the largest fighter operation and most versatile wing in the US Air Forces, Europe, with four fighter squadrons and an air control squadron. In addition to the 53rd FS, both the 22nd and 23rd Fighter Squadrons fly F-16s, while the 81st FS employs the A/OA-10. Since July 1993, the wing has had F-15, A-10, and F-16 aircraft deployed to Aviano Air Base, Italy, in support of Operation Deny Flight.

56th Fighter Wing
The 56th FW is part of the 19th Air Force, Air Education and Training Command. On 1st October 1991 the F-15E squadrons of the 405th TTW joined the 58th FW to consolidate the training assets at Luke AFB under a single command. On 1st April 1994 the 58th FW was redesignated the 56th Fighter Wing, adopting the number from the deactivating F-16 training unit at McDill AFB, Florida. The 58th number was then assigned to the 542nd CTW at Kirkland AFB, New Mexico.

The 461st TFTS was redesignated a Fighter Squadron on 1st April 1994, only to be deactivated on 4th August 1994, leaving a single F-15E training squadron. The 550th FS (having been redesignated from TFTS along with the 461st) was the last remaining F-15E Replacement Training Unit (RTU) at Luke when it was decided it was more economical to transfer the training function to the operational F-15E wing at Seymour Johnson AFB. The transfer began in the latter part of 1994 following the activation of the 333rd FS under the 4th FW. The last class at Luke graduated in February 1995, and the last F-15E left a month later. The 555th TFTS was disbanded on 1st April 1994, then reactivated in Italy as an F-16 squadron within the 31st FW.

Below: **Some of the weapons that can be carried on the F-15E Strike Eagle. A B61 'special' (nuclear) store is in the foreground. Many others have been certified for the F-15E, and this represents only a small cross-section of weapons available for use on the 'Mud Hen'.**
McDonnell Douglas

57th Wing

The 57th in its present form was created from the 4525th FWW on 15th October 1969. On 1st April 1977 the unit was redesignated 57th TTW, and subsequently has returned to being a FWW, a FW, and since 1994 simply a Wing. The 57th FWW was one of the first users of the F-15. This unit was TAC's test and evaluation unit for fighter weapons and tactics, and traditionally has used 'WA' tailcodes, reportedly standing for 'Weapons Acquisition.' The wing received their first F-15A/Bs during 1977, and actually operated several of the original 20 test aircraft for short periods while awaiting their production aircraft. Currently the wing operates 10-12 F-15Es, equally divided between the 422nd and the WSN. A further 6-8 F-15Cs serve the F-15C Weapons School.

The 422nd Test Evaluation Squadron (TES) was originally designated the 422nd Fighter Weapons Squadron (FWS). The squadron provides the continual refinement of combat tech-

niques and tactics, including weapon release profiles, maneuvering, and electronic warfare tactics. The squadron also validates all F-15 technical orders. The 433rd FWS used the F-15 on and off since 1978, but all the functions of this unit were transferred to the WSN and WSE. The F-15E Weapons School, Night (WSN) and F-15C Weapons School (WSE) provide operational assessment of the tactics and procedures developed by the 422nd. Other Weapons Schools exist for the A-10 (WST) and F-16 (WSF). Each FWS operates as an advanced 'college' where tactics and weapons employments are taught to a cadre of experienced flight crews. These crews then return to their operational units to pass on the information.

58th Tactical Training Wing

The 58th TTW had been designated the 58th Tactical Fighter Training Wing until 1st April 1977. The 'LA' tailcode is representative of

'Luke, Arizona.' The wing was the RTU for the F-15 at the outset of the type's service career. On 29th August 1979 the 58th TTW terminated its F-15 training program and transferred its F-15s to the 405th TTW, activated at Luke on the same date. All three F-15 squadrons transitioned to the 405th at the same time. The 58th was subsequently redesignated a Fighter Wing and became the RTU for the F-16. When the 405th TTW was disbanded, the 58th again received F-15s, and was subsequently redesignated the 56th FW.

The 461st TFTS received its first F-15 on 1st July 1977. The 550th TFTS received its first F-15 on 25th August 1977. The 555th TFTS 'Triple Nickel' was the first operational squadron to receive an Eagle when it received a TF-15A (73-0108) christened 'TAC 1' after being accepted by President Gerald Ford on 14th November 1974.

325th Fighter Wing

The 325th Fighter Weapons Wing (FWW) began operations on 1st July 1981 as part of the Air Defense Weapons Center at Tyndall AFB, Florida. The 325th accomplished the operations, test and evaluation, and maintenance portions of the weapons center's mission which was directly related to combat readiness training for air defense. On 15th October 1983 it was redesignated the 325th TTW, and assumed its air superiority training responsibilities as part of the United States Air Defense Weapons Center. The wing was established to serve as the Replacement Training Unit (RTU) for Air National Guard F-15 units, and was also responsible for all F-15 maintenance training. The wing's first F-15A was received on 7th December 1983, and training of the first F-15A/B class began in August 1984. On 1st July 1993 the wing was transferred to the Air Education and Training Command and the 19th Air Force. The wing usually acted as the 'host' for the biannual William Tell air-to-air weapons competition held at Tyndall. When the RTU at Luke AFB was disbanded, the 325th assumed RTU duties for all F-15 air-to-air training. In August 1991 the 325th was redesignated a Fighter Wing.

In January 1984, the 1st FS was reactivated as the 1st Tactical Fighter Training Squadron to train pilots in the F-15. The squadron was redesignated the 1st FS on 17th September

Left, top: **Laser-guided bombs (LGB) have become the favorite weapon for the Mud Hen. The back-seater uses the LANTIRN targeting pod to guide the bombs precisely to a target - in many cases hitting within inches of the aim point. An F-15E from the 244nd TES at Nellis drops four 500lb LGBs, with four more still on the CFTs for another salvo.** US Air Force

Left: **One of the 422nd TES F-15Es is shown here with LANTIRN pods and a travel pod on the conformal fuel tank. The checkerboard tail stripe is black and yellow, long a tradition at Nellis.**
J E Michaels via the Mick Roth Collection

1991. The 2nd FS also began life as a TFTS, and began converting from the F-106A Delta Dart to the F-15A/B in January 1984. The squadron was redesignated 2nd FS on 1st November 1991, and has a secondary role of augmenting the continental air defenses as an interceptor squadron if required. The 95th FS had previously been designated a Fighter Interceptor Training Squadron (FITS), but was redesignated shortly after it began receiving F-15A/Bs in April 1988.

366th Wing

In early 1991, the Air Force announced that the 366th Tactical Fighter Wing at Mountain Home AFB would become the first 'air intervention' composite wing. The wing would grow from a single-squadron of EF-111As to a five squadron wing with the ability to deploy rapidly and deliver integrated combat airpower. The air intervention composite wing's rapid transition from concept to reality began in October of 1991 when Air Force redesignated the wing as the 366th Wing. The wing's newly reactivated fighter squadrons became part of the composite wing on 11th March 1992. The 389th FS began flying the F-16C, while the 391st FS was equipped with the F-15E. In July 1992 the 366th gained the 34th Bomb Squadron equipped with B-1Bs. On 25th September 1992, the 390th Electronic Combat Squadron was redesignated the 390th FS, and equipped with F-15Cs. During October 1992, the composite

wing gained its final flying squadron when the 22nd Air Refueling Squadron was activated and equipped with the KC-135R Stratotankers.

During 1993, and again in 1995, the 366th served as the lead unit for Operation Bright Star, a large combined exercise held in Egypt. In July 1995, the wing verified its combat capability in the largest operational readiness inspection in Air Force history when it deployed a composite strike force to Cold Bay, Canada, and proved they could deliver effective composite airpower. In 1996, the wing also deployed a composite force in support of Operation 'Provide Comfort' in Turkey, and in 1997 launched another composite force to support Operation 'Southern Watch' in Saudi Arabia.

Right, top: A pair of F-15As from the 36th TFW at Bitburg show the standard configuration flown by the Wing while defending Europe. McDonnell Douglas via the Terry Panopalis Collection

Right, middle: One of the few in-flight shots to show an F-15 with an AN/ALQ-119(V) pod. This pod can only be carried on the centerline station, and is generally only used on two-seaters. Ford Aerospace via the Terry Panopalis Collection

Right, lower: A Mountain Home F-15C (86-0158) shows the new forward fuselage ALQ-135 antenna. Noteworthy is that the radome does not match the rest of the paint scheme, something that has become more prevalent in the mid-1990s. The radomes are replaced more frequently than the aircraft go through depot, so the paint on the radome is usually fresher. Interestingly, the rubberized portion at the tip is not painted, and they are all molded in either 'Compass Ghost' or Gunship Gray and therefore none of them match the so-called 'Mod Eagle' scheme. Recently, de-lamination of the composite radome, and even more so the speed brake, has become a problem. Mick Roth

Right: An F-15C (86-0157) from Mountain Home's 390th FS shows the new shape of the ALQ-135 radome on the rear fuselage boom. Previously this radome was round, while on this aircraft (and several others) it has taken a more rectangular cross-section. There is nothing in documentation that explains why the shape was changed, other than the obvious conclusion that the shape, and perhaps function, of the antenna inside has changed. Mick Roth

405th Tactical Training Wing

The 405th TTW was activated at Luke AFB on 29th August 1979, becoming the RTU for all Air Force F-15A/Bs. The 405th took control of all three Luke F-15 squadrons at the same time. In 1988 the wing began transitioning to the Strike Eagle, becoming the RTU for all Air Force F-15Es. Interesting, it appears that no F-15C aircraft have ever been assigned to Luke, although all other variants (A, B, D, and E) have been. The 461st TFTS received their first F-15E on 1st August 1987, converting from air-superiority variants. The squadron was disbanded in 1992. The 550th TFTS received their first F-15E on 12th May 1989, converting from the F-15A/B. The 555th TFTS received their first F-15E during late 1992. On 1st January 1981 the 426th TFTS was assigned to the 405th TTW as an F-15 squadron. The 426th was deactivated on 29th November 1990.

1st Air Force

The 1st AF was responsible for the air defense of the continental United States and Canada. It was a descendant of the Air Defense Command (ADC) which was disbanded on 1st October 1979 and its responsibilities transferred to TAC. On that date TAC formed the Air Defense Tactical Air Command (ADTAC) at the former ADC headquarters in Colorado Springs, Colorado. The headquarters was subsequently transferred to Langley AFB, Virginia, on 1st June 1981. On 6th December 1985 the organization was redesignated the 1st AF.

Since 1st October 1986 the 1st Air Force has performed an operational air defense role as the CONUS NORAD Region. The 1st Air Force commander serves as the commander Continental NORAD Air Defense Region. A Canadian Forces general officer serves as the deputy commander. First Air Force resources include operations control centers, radar warning systems, and fighter aircraft used to conduct peacetime air sovereignty and wartime air defense missions.

Aircraft assigned are the F-15 and the air defense version of the F-16. Since 1989, the 1st Air Force has supported the US Customs Service and a variety law enforcement agencies in their efforts to track and identify air traffic suspected of carrying illegal drugs into the United States.

Four F-15-equipped Fighter Interceptor Squadrons (FIS) were originally assigned to the 1st AF, each using early F-15A/B models in the air interceptor role. The air defense role was subsequently transferred to the F-16, and the F-15s were redistributed to ANG squadrons. The ANG squadrons would later be transferred to the operational control of the 1st Air Force.

The 5th Fighter Interceptor Squadron (FIS) received its first F-15A/B in April 1985, replacing the General Dynamics F-106 Delta Dart. The Minot AFB-based unit retained the colorful yellow lightning bolt tail motif used on their F-106s. The unit operated F-15s for barely three years, being inactivated on 1st July 1988. The defense mission for the northern border is now accomplished by F-16s of the 119th FIG at Fargo, North Dakota.

The 48th FIS received their first F-15A/B on 14th August 1981, transitioning from the F-106. The unit retained their blue and white strip and echelon tail markings for a while, but later reverted to standard TAC-style tailcodes using 'LY' for Langley AFB where they are based. The squadron officially stood-up with the F-15A/B on 5th April 1982, and was deactivated on 30 September 1991. The squadron's F-15s were transferred to the 131st FW of the Missouri ANG. This squadron, along with the 318th FIS, received three or four F-15As modified to carry the ASM-135A anti-satellite (ASAT) missile, although the missile itself never entered production.

The most photographed of the interceptor squadrons, the 57th FIS at Keflavik, Iceland, routinely intercepted Soviet bombers and reconnaissance aircraft in the area known as the 'GIUK (Greenland, Iceland, United Kingdom) gap.' This squadron converted from F-4Es to the F-15C/D in November 1985, and is the only FIS still operating the F-15. The C/D model was chosen instead of the A/B since the squadron needed the extra range provided by the conformal fuel tanks. Unlike the other FIS units, the 57th did not use colorful markings on their F-15s. For most of their careers, these F-15s have had a map of Iceland with an Eagle's head in the center on the inside of their vertical stabilizers.

The 318th FIS at McChord AFB, Washington, traded their F-106As for F-15A/Bs in December 1983. The squadron was deactivat-

ed on 7th December 1989 and its aircraft transferred to the 142nd FIG of the Portland ANG. Like the 48th, this squadron received a few F-15As wired for the Vought ASAT missile, although no missiles were forthcoming. Originally the squadron retained their colorful eight-pointed two-tone blue star on the vertical stabilizers. Later in their career they adapted 'TC' (for Tacoma, a nearby city in Washington) tailcodes and a two-tone blue fin stripe with an eight-pointed star in its center.

Air National Guard

The F-15 has become one of the mainstays of the ANG, with eight squadrons operating the F-15A/B.

The 101st Fighter Squadron (previously an FIS) of the 102nd Fighter Wing, Massachusetts ANG, began receiving F-15s in September 1987. Most of the units aircraft originally came from the disbanding 5th FIS at Minot AFB. Massachusetts Guardsmen have on several occasions intercepted and escorted Soviet long-range reconnaissance aircraft off the Atlantic coast of the US. The unit is based at Otis ANGB on Cape Code. An ANG Minuteman is superimposed over a map of the state on the vertical stabilizer of their aircraft, and the centerline tanks carries a 'Cape Cod' inscription superimposed on a harpoon.

The 110th FS is assigned to the 131st FW, Missouri ANG, at the Lambert-St Louis Airport. The 'SL' tailcodes reflects their St Louis home. The squadron is located directly across the runway from the McDonnell Douglas factory that builds F-15s. The unit is assigned battlefield air superiority, and also provides dissimilar air combat training for ANG F-16 units. The 11th began converting from F-4Es in May 1991, and achieved IOC on 15th September 1991.

Below, left: **No.405th TTW logo applied when the aircraft was repainted. Generally the paint logos were on the rear fuselage boom extensions, immediately behind the formation light strips.** Dennis R Jenkins

Below, right: **This was the commander's aircraft (76-0089) from the 405th TTW. Traditionally, the CO's aircraft at Luke AFB carried a stripe for each squadron on its rudder, a tradition carried on by the F-15s.** Dennis R Jenkins

The 122nd FS from Louisiana's 159th FW wear the tailcode 'JZ,' short for 'jazz' in tribute to their New Orleans home. The 122nd was the first ANG squadron to receive F-15s, beginning in June 1985. The first aircraft came mostly from Luke, early FY73 models, with the original speedbrake with external stiffener, and a coat of Air Superiority Blue underneath the Compass Ghost grey. In 1991, the FY73 aircraft were traded for FY77 models, mostly from Holloman. In 1993 the squadron began receiving aircraft that had been processed through the MSIP. The squadron is now known as the 'Bayou Militia'; the term 'Coonass Militia' being deemed politically incorrect (a Coonass being a native of Louisiana). The squadron has deployed to Keflavik, Alborg Denmark, Howard AFB Panama, CFB Cold Lake, Incirlik Turkey, and Bodo Norway. The purple, green and gold stripes on the tails are the colors of Mardi Gras, and each flight of aircraft is designated by one of the colors.

Oregon ANG's 123rd FS is part of the 142nd FW, and is based at the Portland International Airport. The unit received its first F-15 on 1st October 1989, with most of the F-15s coming from the disbanded 318th FIS at McChord AFB. Interestingly, the unit's assigned mission is to provide air defense of the US west coast, the same role previously assigned to the 318th. The squadron is assigned 'OR' tailcodes but does not use them.

The 173rd FW, based at Kingsley Field near Klamath Falls, recently transitioned from the F-16 to become an F-15 training wing. Each ANG unit gave up a 'family model' (F-15B) so that the new training squadron could have a large number of two-seaters. With the arrival of the new F-22 Raptor, the 325th FW at Tyndall will begin transitioning to the Raptor, and Klamath Falls will begin training all F-15 pilots.

This page, top to bottom:

The Fighter Interceptor Squadrons managed to keep their colorful tail markings for a short time. All the squadrons used markings basically similar to those they had used on their General Dynamics F-106 Delta Darts. No.48th FIS example illustrated. US Air Force

The 318th FIS was based at McChord AFB, Washington, until they were disbanded on 7th December 1989. US Air Force

The Minot AFB-based 5th FIS. The lead aircraft was painted for the commander, as evidenced by the '5FIS' serial number. US Air Force

The 128th FS belongs to the 116th FW, Georgia ANG. The squadron is based at Dobbins AFB, just outside Marietta, Georgia, and began receiving F-15s in March 1986. Originally the unit carried a broad dark stripe with 'Georgia' on the vertical stabilizer, but began using 'GA' tailcodes before it lost its F-15s in 1996.

The 159th FS from Florida's 125th FW began receiving their F-15A/Bs in June 1995.

The 188th FS from New Mexico's 150th FW is based at Albuquerque, and began receiving F-15s in 1991.

Based at Hickam AFB, the Hawaii ANG operates the 199th FS from the 154th FW. The unit was one of the last users of the F-4 prior to beginning to receive their F-15A/Bs in the summer 1987. The majority of the aircraft came from the 21st FS at Elmendorf as that unit transitioned from the F-15A/B to the C/D.

Top: **The first eight F-15Es were used in the test program to clear the multitude of air-to-ground weapons envisioned. Here the third 'test' aircraft (86-0188) drops a 2,000 pound iron bomb while still carrying a Sidewinder and LANTIRN pods. Like the air-superiority variants, F-15Es do not have 'turkey feathers' on their F100 engines, although they appear to have been reintroduced on the F-15I variant.** Boeing

Above: **A full load of 12 500 pound bombs and four AIM-9 Sidewinders are carried along with a 600-gallon drop tank by this F-15E(86-0190) undergoing tests at Edwards AFB, California. LANTIRN pods are hung on the intake pylons. This was the last of the 'test' F-15Es, and was fully representative of the production standard except for a mostly non-functional ALQ-135B electronics countermeasures set.** Boeing

US Air Force F-15 Strength as of 1st January 1998

	ACC	AETC	AFMC	PACAF	USAFE	ANG	McAir	NASA	AMARC	Total
F-15A	1	–	3	–	–	101	2	1	102	210
F-15B	–	–	7	–	–	15	2	2	9	35
F-15C	156	63	1	93	39	–	1	–	–	353
F-15D	14	24	3	10	3	–	–	–	–	54
F-15E	125	–	5	21	52	–	1	–	–	204
Total										856

ACC = Air Combat Command
AETC = Air Education and Training Command
AFMC = Air Force Materiel Command
PACAF = Pacific Air Forces
USAFE = US Air Forces, Europe

ANG = Air National Guard
McAir = Bailed to McDonnell Aircraft
NASA = National Aeronautics and Space Administration
AMARC = Stored at the Aircraft Maintenance and Regeneration Center

US Air Force F-15 Unit

Air Force	Wing	Squadron	Primary Markings	Location	Tail Code	F-15 Version	Years From To	Comments
ACC, 9th AF	1st FW	27th TFS	yellow tail stripe	Langley AFB, Virginia	FF	A/B/C/D	76 – Present	
		71st TFS	red tail stripe	Langley AFB, Virginia	FF	A/B/C/D	75 – Present	
		94th TFS	blue tail stripe	Langley AFB, Virginia	FF	A/B/C/D	76 – Present	
ACC, 9th AF	4th Wing	333rd FS	red tail stripe	Seymour Johnson AFB, North Carolina	SJ	E	94 – Present	Formerly 4th TFW/FW
		334th FS	blue tail stripe	Seymour Johnson AFB, North Carolina	SJ	E	91 – Present	
		335th FS	green tail stripe	Seymour Johnson AFB, North Carolina	SJ	E	90 – Present	
		336th FS	yellow tail stripe	Seymour Johnson AFB, North Carolina	SJ	E	89 – Present	
ACC, 9th AF	33rd FW	58th FS	blue tail stripe	Eglin AFB, Florida	EG	A/B/C/D	78 – Present	
		59th FS	yellow tail stripe	Eglin AFB, Florida	EG	A/B/C/D	79 – Present	
		60th FS	red tail stripe	Eglin AFB, Florida	EG	A/B/C/D	81 – Present	
ACC, 12th AF	49th FW	7th FS	blue tail stripe	Holloman AFB, New Mexico	HO	A/B	77 – 91	7th FS originally used a blue & white checker-board tail stripe
		8th FS	yellow tail stripe	Holloman AFB, New Mexico	HO	A/B	78 – 91	
		9th FS	red tail stripe	Holloman AFB, New Mexico	HO	A/B	78 – 91	
ACC, 12th AF	58th TTW	461st TFTS	yellow tail stripe with black stars	Luke AFB, Arizona	LA	A/B/D	77 – 79	
		550th TFTS	black tail stripe with silver wings	Luke AFB, Arizona	LA	A/B/D	77 – 79	
		555th TFTS	green tail stripe w/ five white stars	Luke AFB, Arizona	LA	A/B/D	74 – 79	
ACC, 12th AF	366th Wing	390th FS	blue tail stripe	Mountain Home, Montana	MO	C/D	92 – Present	
		391st FS	orange and black tiger tail stripe	Mountain Home, Montana	MO	E	92 – Present	
ACC, 14th AD(P)	4th TFW(P)	335th FS	green tail stripe	Al Kharj AB, Saudi Arabia	SJ	E	90 – 91	'Desert Shield/Storm'
		336th FS	yellow tail stripe	Al Kharj AB, Saudi Arabia	SJ	E	90 – 91	'Desert Shield/Storm'
		53rd TFS	yellow tail stripe	Dhahran AB, Saudi Arabia	BT	C/D	90 – 91	'Desert Shield/Storm'
ACC TFWC	57th Wing	422nd TES	black & yellow checkerboard	Nellis AFB, Nevada	WA	A/B/C/D/E	77 – Present	Formerly 57th FWW
		433rd WSN	black & yellow checkerboard	Nellis AFB, Nevada	WA	A/B/C/D/E	76 – Present	
ACC, TAWC	79th TEG	85th TES	black & white checkerboard / white tail stripe w/ red diamonds	Eglin AFB, Florida	OT / ET	various / various	75 – Present / 75 – Present	Formerly 'AD' tail code / Formerly 3246th TW
AETC, 19th AF	56th FW	461st TFTS	yellow and black tail stripes	Luke AFB, Arizona	LA	A/B/D/E	91 – 91	Formerly 405th TTW
		550th FTS	black tail stripe w/ silver wings	Luke AFB, Arizona	LA/LF	A/B/E	91 – 95	
		555th TFTS	green tail stripe w/ five white stars	Luke AFB, Arizona	LA/LF	A/B/E	91 – 94	
AETC, 19th AF	325th FW	1st FS	red tail stripe	Tyndall AFB, Florida	TY	A/B/C/D	84 – Present	Formerly ADWC, 1st AF
		2nd FS	yellow tail stripe	Tyndall AFB, Florida	TY	A/B/C/D	84 – Present	Formerly 325th TTW
		95th FS	blue tail stripe	Tyndall AFB, Florida	TY	A/B/C/D	88 – Present	
AETC, 19th AF	405th TTW	426th TFTS	red tail stripe	Luke AFB, Arizona	LA	A/B/D	81 – 90	Originally 58th TTW
		461st TFTS	yellow and black tail stripes	Luke AFB, Arizona	LA	A/B/D/E	79 – 91	Squadrons to 56th FW
		550th TFTS	black tail stripe w/ silver wings	Luke AFB, Arizona	LA/LF	A/B/E	79 – 91	
		555th TFTS	green tail stripe w/ five white stars	Luke AFB, Arizona	LA/LF	A/B/E	79 – 91	
USAFE, 3rd AF	48th FW	492nd FS	blue tail stripe	RAF Lakenheath, England	LN	E	92 – Present	
		493rd FS	yellow tail stripe	RAF Lakenheath, England	LN	C/D	92 – Present	
		494th FS	red tail stripe	RAF Lakenheath, England	LN	E	92 – Present	
USAFE, 17th AF	–	32nd FS	orange outlined in green	Soesterberg AB, Netherlands	CR	A/B/C/D	78 – 94	
USAFE, 17th AF	36th FW	22nd FS	red tail stripe	Bitburg AB, Germany	BT	A/B/C/D	77 – 94	
		53rd FS	yellow or tiger tail stripe	Bitburg AB, Germany	BT	A/B/C/D	77 – 94	53rd FS to 52nd Wing
		525th FS	blue tail stripe	Bitburg AB, Germany	BT	A/B/C/D	76 – 92	
USAFE, 17th AF	52nd Wing	53rd FS	yellow or tiger tail stripe	Spangdahlem AB, Germany	SP	C/D	94 – Present	
PACAF, 5th AF	18th FW	12th FS	yellow tail stripe	Kadena AB, Okinawa	ZZ	C/D	80 – Present	
		44th FS	blue tail stripe	Kadena AB, Okinawa	ZZ	C/D	79 – Present	
		67th FS	red tail stripe	Kadena AB, Okinawa	ZZ	C/D	79 – Present	
PACAF, 11th AF	3rd Wing	17th FS	blue tail stripe	Elmendorf AFB, Alaska	AK	C/D	94 – Present	Formerly the 21st CW
		43rd FS	blue tail stripe	Elmendorf AFB, Alaska	AK	A/B/C/D	82 – 94	
		54th FS	yellow tail stripe	Elmendorf AFB, Alaska	AK	C/D	87 – Present	Alaskan Air Command
		90th FS	red tail stripe	Elmendorf AFB, Alaska	AK	E	90 – Present	
ADTAC, 1st AF	–	5th FIS	yellow lightning w/ five blue stars	Minot AFB, North Dakota	–	A/B	84 – 88	Aircraft to 102nd FS
ADTAC, 1st AF	–	48th FIS	blue tail stripe w/ four white stars	Langley AFB, Virginia	LY	A/B	81 – 91	Aircraft to 110th FS
ADTAC, 1st AF	–	57th FIS	black & white checkerboard	Keflavik NS, Iceland	IS	C/D	85 – 96	CFT equipped
ADTAC, 1st AF	–	318th FIS	eight-point two-tone blue star	McChord AFB, Washington	TC	A/B	83 – 89	Aircraft to 123rd FS
Mass. ANG	102nd FW	101st FS	Minuteman logo on tail	Otis ANGB, Massachusetts	–	A/B/C/D	88 – Present	
Missouri ANG	131st FW	110th FS	red stripe with 'St Louis Arch'	Lambert Field, St Louis, Missouri	SL	A/B	91 – Present	
Louisiana ANG	159th FW	122nd FS	purple/yellow/green tail stripe	New Orleans JRB, Louisiana	JZ	A/B	85 – Present	Used to be NO tail codes
Oregon ANG	142nd FW	123rd FS	'Oregon' with stylized 'Eagle'	Portland IAP, Oregon	OR	A/B	89 – Present	Seldom use Tail Code
ANG Training	173rd FW	–	–	Kingston Field, Oregon	–	A/B	97 – Present	Trains all ANG F-15 pilots
Georgia ANG	116th FW	128th FS	black stripe edged in red	Dobbins AFB, Georgia	GA	A/B	86 – 96	Aircraft to 199th FS
Florida ANG	125th FW	159th FS	–	Jacksonville IAP, Florida	FL	A/B	95 – Present	
Hawaii ANG	154th FW	199th FS	red and yellow checkerboard	Hickam AFB, Hawaii	–	A/B/C/D	87 – Present	
AFMC	46th TW	40th TS	white tail stripe w/ red diamonds	Eglin AFB, Florida	ET	various	73 – Present	
AFMC	78th ABW	339th TS	varied	Robins AFB, Georgia	RG	A	78 – Present	
AFMC	AFFTC	415th TS	blue stripe with white 'X's	Edwards AFB, California	ED	various	72 – Present	Also F-15 JTF/CTF

USAF Serial Numbers

Serial No(s)	Qty	Block Number	Notes
71-0280 - 0281	2	F-15A-1-MC	0281 bailed to DFRC in 1975; Returned in 1983
71-0282 - 0284	3	F-15A-2-MC	
71-0285 - 0286	2	F-15A-3-MC	
71-0287 - 0289	3	F-15A-4-MC	0287 bailed to DFRC in 1976 as NASA 835
71-0290	1	F-15B-3-MC	F-15S/MTD and NF-15B ACTIVE
71-0291	1	F-15B-4-MC	McAir Demonstrator aircraft
72-0113 - 0116	4	F-15A-5-MC	0114 sold to Israel in 1992, 0116 delivered to Israel, 'Peace Fox I'
72-0117 - 0120	4	F-15A-6-MC	0117/0118, 0120 delivered to Israel, 'Peace Fox I'; 0119 modified as Streak Eagle
73-0085 - 0089	5	F-15A-7-MC	0087 sold to Israel in 1992
73-0090 - 0097	8	F-15A-8-MC	0093/0094 sold to Israel in 1992
73-0098 - 0107	10	F-15A-9-MC	0101/0102, 0104/0105, 0107 sold to Israel in 1992
73-0108 - 0110	3	F-15B-7-MC	0110 sold to Israel in 1992
73-0111 - 0112	2	F-15B-8-MC	0111/0112 sold to Israel in 1992
73-0113 - 0114	2	F-15B-9-MC	0113 sold to Israel in 1992
74-0081 - 0093	13	F-15A-10-MC	0085, 0088, and 0093 sold to Israel in 1992
74-0094 - 0111	18	F-15A-11-MC	0097, 0101, 0107, 0109 sold to Israel in 1992
74-0112 - 0136	25	F-15A-12-MC	0122 and 0125 sold to Israel in 1992
74-0137 - 0138	2	F-15B-10-MC	0137 sold to Israel in 1992
74-0139 - 0140	2	F-15B-11-MC	
74-0141 - 0142	2	F-15B-12-MC	0141 bailed to DFRC in 1993 as NASA 836
74-0143 - 0157	0	F-15B-12-MC	Cancelled prior to production
75-0018 - 0048	31	F-15A-13-MC	
75-0049 - 0079	31	F-15A-14-MC	
75-0080 - 0084	5	F-15B-13-MC	
75-0085 - 0089	5	F-15B-14-MC	
75-0090 - 0124	0	F-15A/B	Cancelled prior to production
76-0008 - 0046	39	F-15A-15-MC	
76-0047 - 0083	37	F-15A-16-MC	
76-0084 - 0113	30	F-15A-17-MC	0084, 0086 used for trials with ASM-135A ASAT
76-0114 - 0120	7	F-15A-18-MC	
76-0121 - 0123	0	F-15A-18-MC	Cancelled prior to production
76-0124 - 0129	6	F-15B-15-MC	
76-0130 - 0135	6	F-15B-16-MC	
76-0136 - 0140	5	F-15B-17-MC	
76-0141 - 0142	2	F-15B-18-MC	
76-1505 - 1514	10	F-15A-17-MC	FMS for Israel, 'Peace Fox II'
76-1515 - 1523	9	F-15A-18-MC	FMS for Israel, 'Peace Fox II'
76-1524 - 1525	2	F-15B-16-MC	FMS for Israel, 'Peace Fox II'
77-0061 - 0084	24	F-15A-18-MC	0084 used as test bed for APG-63 radar
77-0085 - 0119	35	F-15A-19-MC	
77-0120 - 0153	34	F-15A-20-MC	
77-0154 - 0156	3	F-15B-18-MC	
77-0157 - 0162	6	F-15B-19-MC	
77-0163 - 0168	6	F-15B-20-MC	0166 used for Integrated Flight-Fire Control
78-0468 - 0495	28	F-15C-21-MC	
78-0496 - 0522	27	F-15C-22-MC	
78-0523 - 0550	28	F-15C-23-MC	
78-0551 - 0560	0	F-15C-23-MC	Cancelled prior to production
78-0561 - 0565	5	F-15D-21-MC	
78-0566 - 0570	5	F-15D-22-MC	
78-0571 - 0574	4	F-15D-23-MC	
78-0575	0	F-15D-23-MC	Cancelled prior to production
79-0004 - 0006	3	F-15D-24-MC	0004/0006 transferred to Saudi Arabia
79-0007 - 0011	5	F-15D-25-MC	0010 transferred to Saudi Arabia
79-0012 - 0014	3	F-15D-26-MC	
79-0015 - 0037	23	F-15C-24-MC	0015, 0017/0019, 0023/0024, 0028, 0031/0033 transferred to Saudi Arabia in August 1990
79-0038 - 0058	21	F-15C-25-MC	0038/0039, 0043, 0045, 0051/0052, 0055 transferred to Saudi Arabia in August 1990
79-0059 - 0081	23	F-15C-26-MC	0060, 0062/0063 transferred to Saudi Arabia in August 1990
79-0280 - 0281	2	F-15J-24-MC	Sold to Japan as 02-8801/8802, 'Peace Eagle'
79-0282 - 0285	4	F-15DJ-26-MC	Sold to Japan as 12-8051/8054, 'Peace Eagle'
79-0286 - 0287	2	F-15DJ-27-MC	Sold to Japan as 22-8055/8056, 'Peace Eagle'
80-0002 - 0023	22	F-15C-27-MC	
80-0024 - 0038	15	F-15C-28-MC	
80-0039 - 0053	15	F-15C-29-MC	
80-0054 - 0055	2	F-15D-27-MC	
80-0056 - 0057	2	F-15D-28-MC	
80-0058 - 0061	4	F-15D-29-MC	
80-0062 - 0067	6	F-15C-28-MC	FMS for Saudi Arabia, 'Peace Sun'
80-0068 - 0074	7	F-15C-29-MC	FMS for Saudi Arabia, 'Peace Sun'
80-0075 - 0085	11	F-15C-30-MC	FMS for Saudi Arabia, 'Peace Sun'
80-0086 - 0099	14	F-15C-31-MC	FMS for Saudi Arabia, 'Peace Sun'
80-0100 - 0106	7	F-15C-32-MC	FMS for Saudi Arabia, 'Peace Sun'
80-0107 - 0110	4	F-15D-27-MC	FMS for Saudi Arabia, 'Peace Sun'
80-0111 - 0112	2	F-15D-28-MC	FMS for Saudi Arabia, 'Peace Sun'
80-0113 - 0114	2	F-15D-29-MC	FMS for Saudi Arabia, 'Peace Sun'
80-0115 - 0117	3	F-15D-30-MC	FMS for Saudi Arabia, 'Peace Sun'
80-0118 - 0119	2	F-15D-31-MC	FMS for Saudi Arabia, 'Peace Sun'
80-0120 - 0121	2	F-15D-32-MC	FMS for Saudi Arabia, 'Peace Sun'
80-0122 - 0124	3	F-15C-27-MC	FMS for Israel, 'Peace Fox III'
80-0125 - 0127	3	F-15C-28-MC	FMS for Israel, 'Peace Fox III'
80-0128 - 0130	3	F-15C-29-MC	FMS for Israel, 'Peace Fox III'
80-0131 - 0132	2	F-15D-27-MC	FMS for Israel, 'Peace Fox III'
80-0133 - 0136	4	F-15D-28-MC	FMS for Israel, 'Peace Fox III'
81-0002	1	F-15C-32-MC	Sold to Saudi Arabia
81-0003	1	F-15D-32-MC	Originally a Saudi F-15C, swapped with 81-0066
81-0020 - 0031	12	F-15C-30-MC	
81-0032 - 0040	9	F-15C-31-MC	
81-0041 - 0055	15	F-15C-32-MC	
81-0056	1	F-15C-32-MC	To USAF - from ex-Saudi F-15C 81-0003
81-0057 - 0060	0	F-15C-32-MC	Cancelled prior to production
81-0061 - 0062	2	F-15D-30-MC	
81-0063 - 0065	3	F-15D-31-MC	
81-0066	0	F-15D-32-MC	Cancelled - delivered as Saudi F-15D 81-0003
81-0067	0	F-15D-31-MC	Cancelled prior to production
81-0068 - 0069	2	F-15DJ-32-MC	Sold to Japan as 32-8057/8058, 'Peace Eagle'
81-0070 - 0071	2	F-15DJ-33-MC	Sold to Japan as 42-8059/8060, 'Peace Eagle'
82-0008 - 0022	15	F-15C-33-MC	
82-0023 - 0038	16	F-15C-34-MC	
82-0039 - 0043	0	F-15C-34-MC	Cancelled prior to production
82-0044 - 0045	2	F-15D-33-MC	
82-0046 - 0048	3	F-15D-34-MC	
83-0010 - 0034	25	F-15C-35-MC	
83-0035 - 0043	9	F-15C-36-MC	
83-0044 - 0045	0	F-15C-36-MC	Cancelled prior to production
83-0046 - 0048	3	F-15D-35-MC	
83-0049 - 0050	2	F-15D-36-MC	
83-0051	0	F-15D-36-MC	Cancelled prior to production
83-0052 - 0053	2	F-15DJ-36-MC	Sold to Japan as 52-8061/8062, 'Peace Eagle'
83-0054 - 0055	2	F-15C-35-MC	FMS for Israel, 'Peace Fox III'
83-0056 - 0062	7	F-15C-36-MC	FMS for Israel, 'Peace Fox III'
83-0063 - 0064	2	F-15D-35-MC	FMS for Israel, 'Peace Fox III'
84-0001 - 0015	15	F-15C-37-MC	
84-0016 - 0031	16	F-15C-38-MC	
84-0032 - 0041	0	F-15C-38-MC	Cancelled prior to production
84-0042 - 0044	3	F-15D-37-MC	
84-0045 - 0046	2	F-15D-38-MC	
84-0047 - 0048	0	F-15D-38-MC	Cancelled prior to production
85-0093 - 0107	15	F-15C-39-MC	
85-0108 - 0128	21	F-15C-40-MC	
85-0129 - 0131	3	F-15D-39-MC	
85-0132 - 0134	3	F-15C-40-MC	
86-0143 - 0162	20	F-15C-41-MC	
86-0163 - 0180	18	F-15C-42-MC	
86-0181 - 0182	2	F-15D-42-MC	
86-0183 - 0184	2	F-15E-41-MC	Lot I
86-0185 - 0190	6	F-15E-42-MC	Lot I
87-0169 - 0189	21	F-15E-43-MC	Lot II
87-0190 - 0210	21	F-15E-44-MC	Lot II
87-0211 - 0216	0	F-15E-44-MC	Cancelled prior to production
88-1667 - 1687	21	F-15E-45-MC	Lot III
88-1688 - 1708	21	F-15E-46-MC	Lot III
89-0046 - 0063	0	F-15E-47-MC	Cancelled prior to production
89-0064 - 0081	0	F-15E-48-MC	Cancelled prior to production
89-0471 - 0488	18	F-15E-47-MC	Lot IV
89-0489 - 0506	18	F-15E-48-MC	Lot IV
90-0227 - 0244	18	F-15E-49-MC	Lot V
90-0245 - 0262	18	F-15E-50-MC	Lot V
90-0263 - 0267	5	F-15C-49-MC	Sold to Saudi Arabia
90-0268 - 0271	4	F-15C-50-MC	Sold to Saudi Arabia
90-0272 - 0274	3	F-15D-50-MC	Sold to Saudi Arabia
90-0275 - 0279	5	F-15D-50-MC	FMS for Israel, 'Peace Fox IV'
91-0300 - 0317	18	F-15E-51-MC	Lot VI
91-0318 - 0335	18	F-15E-52-MC	Lot VI
91-0600 - 0605	6	F-15E-53-MC	Lot VII (paid for by selling ex-USAF F-15Cs to Saudi Arabia)
92-0364 - 0366	3	F-15E-53-MC	Lot VII (attrition aircraft for Gulf war losses)
93-0852 - 0863	12	F-15S-54-MC	FMS for Saudi Arabia, 'Peace Sun IX'
93-0864 - 0875	12	F-15S-55-MC	FMS for Saudi Arabia, 'Peace Sun IX'
93-0876 - 0887	12	F-15S-56-MC	FMS for Saudi Arabia, 'Peace Sun IX'
93-0888 - 0899	12	F-15S-57-MC	FMS for Saudi Arabia, 'Peace Sun IX'
93-0900 - 0911	12	F-15S-58-MC	FMS for Saudi Arabia, 'Peace Sun IX'
93-0912 - 0923	12	F-15S-59-MC	FMS for Saudi Arabia, 'Peace Sun IX'
94-0286 - 0294	9	F-15I-56-MC	FMS for Israel, 'Peace Fox V'
94-0295 - 0306	12	F-15I-57-MC	FMS for Israel, 'Peace Fox V'
94-0500 - 0503	4	F-15I-57-MC	FMS for Israel, 'Peace Fox VI'
96-0200 - 0205	6	F-15E-58-MC	Attrition aircraft
97-xxxx - xxxx	5	F-15E-61-MC	Attrition aircraft
98-xxxx - xxxx	6	F-15E-62-MC	Added by Congress
McAir-built F-15s:	**1,357**		

F-15s on Display and in Museums

Serial No	Location	City	State
71-0280	USAF History and Traditions Museum	Lackland AFB	TX
71-0281	Langley Air Park	Langley AFB	VA
71-0286	Chanute Aerospace Museum	Chanute AFB	IL
72-0119	United States Air Force Museum	Wright-Patterson AFB	OH
73-0085	Museum of Aviation	Warner-Robins AFB	GA
73-0086	Louisiana National Guard Museum	New Orleans	LA
73-0099	W-R ALC Headquarters	Warner-Robins AFB	GA
73-0100	NAS New Orleans Joint Reserve Base	NAS New Orleans	LA
73-0108	Luke Air Park	Luke AFB	AZ
74-0083	Camp Zeist	Netherlands	
74-0090	Tyndall Air Park	Tyndall AFB	FL
74-0109	Sinsheim Museum	Germany	
74-0118	Pima Air and Space Museum	Tucson	AZ
74-0121	Georgia ANG Base	Dobbins AFB	GA
74-0124	USAF Armament Museum	Eglin AFB	FL
74-0131	RAF Lakenheath	United Kingdom	
76-0014	Evergreen Helicopters Headquarters	McMinnville	OR
76-0024	Peterson Space Command Museum	Peterson AFB	CO
76-0037	Holloman AFB	Holloman AFB	NM
76-0040	Otis ANG Base	Boston	MA
76-0042	USAF Academy	USAF Academy	CO
76-0048	McChord Air Museum	McChord AFB	WA
76-0088	Missouri ANG Base	Bridgeton	MO
76-0108	Kelly Field Heritage Museum	Kelly AFB	TX
77-0068	Rickenbacker ANG Base	Dayton	OH
77-0090	Hill AFB Museum	Hill AFB	UT
???	Kadena AB	Okinawa, Japan	

F-15 Models and Designations

Model	Notes
F-15A	Initial Air Superiority Model for USAF and IDF/AF
TF-15A	Two-Seat Variant of F-15A (now F-15B)
F-15B	Two-Seat Variant of F-15A (ex-TF-15A)
F-15C	Improved Air Superiority Model for USAF, IDF/AF, and RSAF
F-15D	Two-Seat Variant of F-15C
F-15E	Strike Interdiction Model for USAF
F-15F	Proposed Strike Interdiction Model for RSAF
F-15G	Proposed Defense Suppression Model for USAF
F-15H	Proposed Strike Interdiction Model for RSAF
F-15I	Strike Interdiction Model for IDF/AF
F-15J	Air Superiority Model for JASDF
F-15DJ	Two-seat Variant of F-15J
F-15K	Proposed Strike Interdiction Model for South Korea
F-15(N)	Proposed Model for US Navy
F-15(N-PHX)	Proposed Model for US Navy with Phoenix Missiles
RF-15	Proposed Reconnaissance Model for USAF
F-15(R)	Proposed Reconnaissance Model for USAF
F-15S	Strike Interdiction Model for RSAF (formerly F-15XP)
F-15U	Proposed Strike Interdiction Model for UAE
F-15U(Plus)	Proposed Strike Interdiction Model for UAE
F-15XP	Proposed Strike Interdiction Model for RSAF (now F-15S)
YF-15A	Unofficial Designation Belatedly Used for Test Aircraft
YTF-15A	Unofficial Designation Belatedly Used for Test Aircraft
YF-15B	Unofficial Designation Belatedly Used for Test Aircraft
GF-15A	Informal Designation for Ground Trainers (ex-Test Aircraft)
NF-15B	Modified F-15B (71-0290) for S/MTD and ACTIVE

'Desert Storm' F-15 Kills

Kill No	Date	Serial No	Pilot(s)	Pilot's Kill	Country	Squadron	Wing	Weapon	Aircraft Destroyed
56	17 Jan 91	85-0125	Capt Jon K Kelk	1	USAF	58th TFS	33rd TFW	AIM-7M	Iraqi MiG-29
57	17 Jan 91	85-0105	Capt Robert E Graeter	1	USAF	58th TFS	33rd TFW	AIM-7M	Iraqi Mirage F.1EQ
58	17 Jan 91	85-0105	Capt Robert E Graeter	2	USAF	58th TFS	33rd TFW	AIM-7M	Iraqi Mirage F.1EQ
59	17 Jan 91	83-0017	Capt Steven W Tate	1	USAF	71st TFS	1st TFW	AIM-7M	Iraqi Mirage F.1EQ
60	17 Jan 91	85-0108	Capt Rhory R Draeger	1	USAF	59th TFS	33rd TFW	AIM-7M	Iraqi MiG-29
61	17 Jan 91	85-0107	Capt Charles J Magill (USMC)	1	USAF	58th TFS	33rd TFW	AIM-7M	Iraqi MiG-29
62	19 Jan 91	85-0122	Capt Craig W Underhill	1	USAF	58th TFS	33rd TFW	AIM-7M	Iraqi MiG-29
63	19 Jan 91	85-0114	Capt Casar A Rodriguez	1	USAF	58th TFS	33rd TFW	ground	Iraqi MiG-29
64	19 Jan 91	85-0099	Capt Lawrence E Pitts	1	USAF	58th TFS	33rd TFW	AIM-7M	Iraqi MiG-25
65	19 Jan 91	85-0101	Capt Richard C Tollini	1	USAF	58th TFS	33rd TFW	AIM-7M	Iraqi MiG-25
66	19 Jan 91	79-0069	Capt David S Prather	1	USAF	525th TFS	36th TFW	AIM-7M	Iraqi Mirage F.1EQ
67	19 Jan 91	79-0021	Lt David G Sveden	1	USAF	525th TFS	36th TFW	AIM-7M	Iraqi Mirage F.1EQ
68	24 Jan 91	80-0068	Capt Ayehd Salah al-Shamrani	1	RSAF	No.13 Sqn	–	AIM-9L	Iraqi Mirage F.1EQ
69	24 Jan 91	80-0068	Capt Ayehd Salah al-Shamrani	2	RSAF	No.13 Sqn	–	AIM-9L	Iraqi Mirage F.1EQ
70	26 Jan 91	85-0119	Capt Rhory R Draeger	2	USAF	59th TFS	33rd TFW	AIM-7M	Iraqi MiG-23
71	26 Jan 91	85-0104	Capt Anthony E Schiavi	1	USAF	58th TFS	33rd TFW	AIM-7M	Iraqi MiG-23
72	26 Jan 91	85-0114	Capt Casar A Rodriguez	2	USAF	58th TFS	33rd TFW	AIM-7M	Iraqi MiG-23
73	27 Jan 91	84-0025	Capt Jay T Denney	1	USAF	53rd TFS	36th TFW	AIM-9L	Iraqi MiG-23
74	27 Jan 91	84-0025	Capt Jay T Denney	2	USAF	53rd TFS	36th TFW	AIM-9L	Iraqi MiG-23
75	27 Jan 91	84-0027	Capt Benjamin D Powell	1	USAF	53rd TFS	36th TFW	AIM-7M	Iraqi MiG-23
76	27 Jan 91	84-0027	Capt Benjamin D Powell	2	USAF	53rd TFS	36th TFW	AIM-7M	Iraqi Mirage F.1EQ
77	29 Jan 91	79-0022	Capt Donald S Watrous	1	USAF	32nd TFS	32nd TFG	AIM-7M	Iraqi MiG-23
78	29 Jan 91	85-0102	Capt David G Rose	1	USAF	60th TFS	33rd TFW	AIM-7M	Iraqi MiG-23
79	02 Feb 91	79-0064	Capt. Masters	1	USAF	525th TFS	36th TFW	AIM-7M	Iraqi Il-76
80	06 Feb 91	84-0019	Lt Robert W Henemann	1	USAF	53rd TFS	36th TFW	AIM-9L	Iraqi Su-25
81	06 Feb 91	84-0019	Lt Robert W Henemann	2	USAF	53rd TFS	36th TFW	AIM-9L	Iraqi Su-25
82	06 Feb 91	79-0078	Capt Thomas N Dietz	1	USAF	53rd TFS	36th TFW	AIM-9L	Iraqi MiG-21
83	06 Feb 91	79-0078	Capt Thomas N Dietz	2	USAF	53rd TFS	36th TFW	AIM-9L	Iraqi MiG-21
84	07 Feb 91	85-0102	Capt Anthony R Murphy	1	USAF	58th TFS	33rd TFW	AIM-7M	Iraqi Su-22
85	07 Feb 91	85-0102	Capt Anthony R Murphy	2	USAF	58th TFS	33rd TFW	AIM-7M	Iraqi Su-22
86	07 Feb 91	85-0124	Col Rick N Parsons	1	USAF	58th TFS	33rd TFW	AIM-7M	Iraqi Su-22
87	07 Feb 91	80-0003	Maj Randy W May	1	USAF	525th TFS	36th TFW	AIM-7M	Iraqi Mi-24
88	14 Feb 91	89-0487	Capt Richard T Bennett	1	USAF	335th TFS	4th TFW	GBU-10	Iraqi Hughes 500
			Capt Daniel B Bakke (WSO)	1					
89	20 Mar 91	84-0014	Capt John T Doneski	1	USAF	53rd TFS	36th TFW	AIM-9L	Iraqi Su-22M
90	22 Mar 91	84-0010	Capt Thomas N Dietz	3	USAF	53rd TFS	36th TFW	AIM-9M	Iraqi Su-222
91	22 Mar 91	84-0015	Lt Robert W Hehemann	1	USAF	53rd TFS	36th TFW	ground	Iraqi PC-9

The F-15's first kill was a Syrian MiG-21 on 27th June 1979 by No. 133 Squadron of the IDF/AF

Kill numbers 1-55 were made by the IDF/AF, mainly against Syrian MiGs, but there is remarkably little independent data available.

Special thanks to Tom Brewer at the United States Air Force Museum for compiling this list.

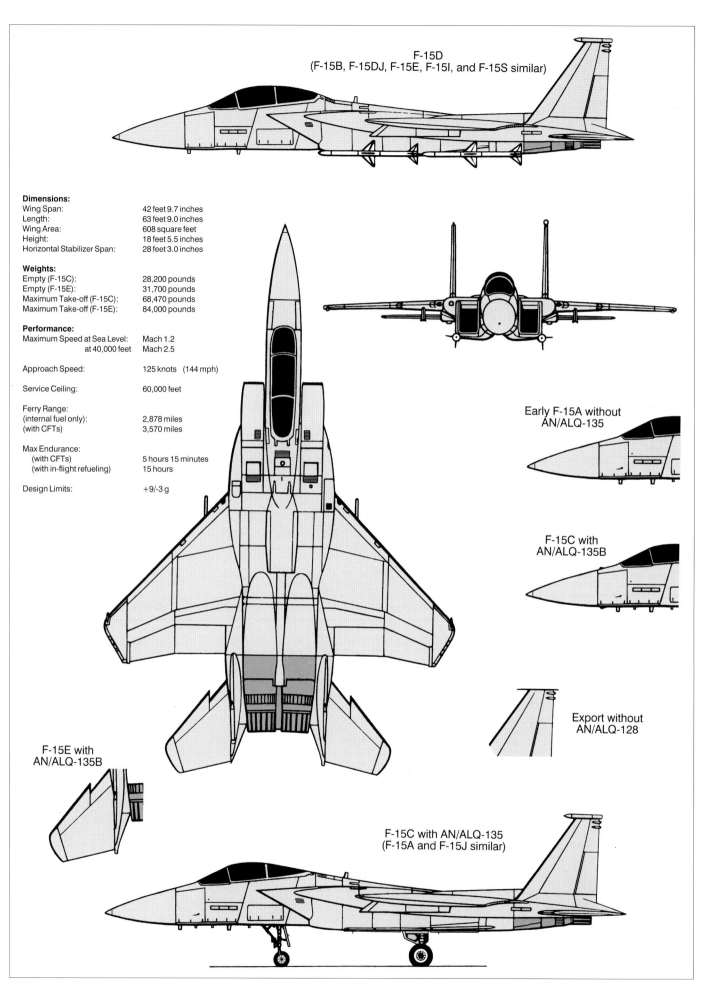

F-15D
(F-15B, F-15DJ, F-15E, F-15I, and F-15S similar)

Dimensions:

Wing Span:	42 feet 9.7 inches
Length:	63 feet 9.0 inches
Wing Area:	608 square feet
Height:	18 feet 5.5 inches
Horizontal Stabilizer Span:	28 feet 3.0 inches

Weights:

Empty (F-15C):	28,200 pounds
Empty (F-15E):	31,700 pounds
Maximum Take-off (F-15C):	68,470 pounds
Maximum Take-off (F-15E):	84,000 pounds

Performance:

Maximum Speed at Sea Level:	Mach 1.2
at 40,000 feet	Mach 2.5
Approach Speed:	125 knots (144 mph)
Service Ceiling:	60,000 feet
Ferry Range:	
(internal fuel only):	2,878 miles
(with CFTs)	3,570 miles
Max Endurance:	
(with CFTs)	5 hours 15 minutes
(with in-flight refueling)	15 hours
Design Limits:	+9/-3 g

Early F-15A without
AN/ALQ-135

F-15C with
AN/ALQ-135B

Export without
AN/ALQ-128

F-15E with
AN/ALQ-135B

F-15C with AN/ALQ-135
(F-15A and F-15J similar)

Chapter Eleven

Construction and Systems

Except when specifically noted, references to the F-15E include the F-15I/S/U/K variants.

Cockpit

A crew of one (A and C) or two in tandem (all other variants), is accommodated on McDonnell Douglas IC-7 (through block-17 and all Israeli) or ACES-II (block-18 and subsequent, except Israeli) ejection seats. The ACES-II ejection seat automatically selects one of three ejection modes: mode 1 is a low speed mode during which the parachute is deployed almost immediately after the seat departs the aircraft; mode 2 is a high speed mode during which a drogue chute is first deployed to slow the seat, followed by the deployment of the main parachute; mode 3 is a high altitude mode in which the sequence of events is the same as mode 2 except that man-seat separation is delayed until a safe altitude is reached. There are two ejection control handles, one mounted on each forward upper side of the seat. The controls are interconnected so that actuation of either control initiates ejection. A 10-minute supply of emergency oxygen is furnished by a storage bottle on the left rear of the ejection seat, and is activated automatically upon ejection. Later aircraft have a system called SEAWARS installed that automatically releases the parachute risers from the pilot upon immersion in sea water. SEAWARS was retrofitted to ACES II seats.

The single piece wrap-around windscreen provides 10% more viewing area and a 32% weight reduction compared to a three-piece design. The windscreen is made of fusion bonded cast acrylic outer layers and a polycarbonate center layer. This windscreen was susceptible to cracking where the acrylic joined with a fiberglass frame, causing frequent leaks and maintenance problems. The F-15E introduced a slightly different windscreen, which was later retrofitted to some earlier aircraft. This windscreen eliminated the fiberglass frame, greatly reducing the probability of cracking. The bubble type canopy is made of 0.29-inch-thick polycarbonate with an abrasion resistant coating. This material is 29% lighter than laminated Plexiglas, and 56% lighter than laminated tempered safety glass. The canopy is made of two pieces, with a small frame separating the two pieces just aft of the pilot's head, since

there is not a production capability to form such a large object from one piece. The two-seater's canopy has different contours to provide additional headroom for the second crew member. Retractable boarding steps are provided on the left side forward fuselage.

McDonnell Douglas Electronics Company builds the HUD, which projects all essential flight information in the form of symbols onto a combining glass positioned above the instrument panel at the pilot's eye level. The HUD's field of vision is approximately 20° by 20°. The display presents the information needed to conduct flight operations and to intercept and engage targets without the need to look inside the cockpit. The HUD continuously displays the following information: magnetic heading, indicated airspeed, barometric altitude, velocity vector, aircraft load factor (g) and indicated Mach number. Additional information is presented depending upon the mode (air-to-air, air-to-ground, landing, etc.) selected. The HUD in the F-15E is of an improved, wide field of vision (25° by 40°) design, though it displays essentially the same information as the earlier units. LANTIRN information is also projected onto the F-15E HUD.

The front cockpit of the two-seat models is identical to the cockpit on the single-seater with the addition of an intercom control panel. The F-15A/B and early F-15C/Ds contain conventional flight and weapons instrumentation. The

MSIP-II program added a Sperry multi-purpose color display (MPCD) screen and programmable armament control set (PACS) to the front cockpit of the F-15C/D to replace the original armament control panel. This screen is also capable of displaying video images from a long-range optics system (yet to be installed in any F-15), or video presentations from some weapons. The rear cockpit of two-seaters contains flight controls and essential flight instrumentation. Both cockpits are illuminated with blue filtered white lighting which is preferred over red because white maintains high legibility to lower light levels and also allows color coding of displays. Light intensity can be adjusted for each display.

The F-15E contains four multi-purpose displays (MPD) and three multi-purpose color displays (MPCD). There are two MPDs in each cockpit, one MPCD in the front cockpit and two MPCDs in the rear cockpit. The MPDs display system data, sensor video, and weapon information in a monochromatic format. The MPDs have 20 peripheral pushbuttons by which the crew can control weapons systems, sensors, and data to be displayed. Legends are positioned adjacent to each pushbutton to advise the crew of the modes and options selectable for operation of the onboard radar, FLIR, navigation, and weapons systems.

The exact content of the data in the display formats is software programmable. The MPCDs

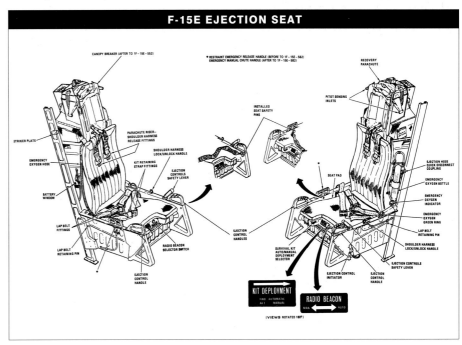

Right: **Illustration from the F-15E flight manual.**
US Air Force

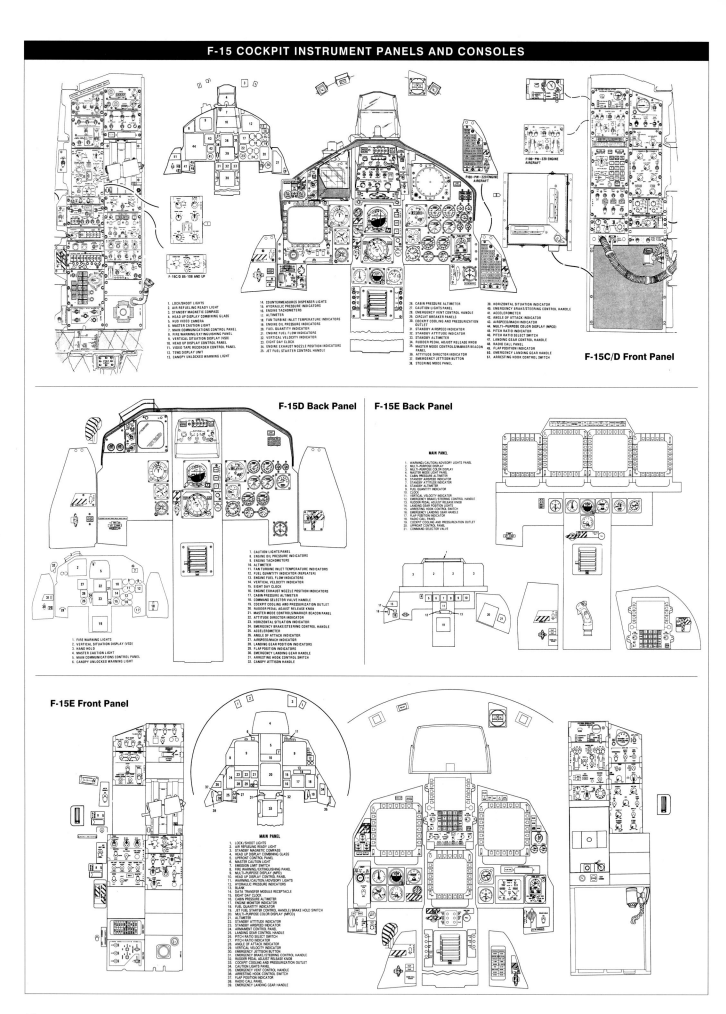

F-15C/D 85-108 AND UP

F-100-PW-220 ENGINE AIRCRAFT

F-100-PW-220 ENGINE AIRCRAFT

1. LOCK/SHOOT LIGHTS
2. AIR REFUELING READY LIGHT
3. STANDBY MAGNETIC COMPASS
4. HEAD UP DISPLAY COMBINING GLASS
5. HUD VIDEO CAMERA
6. MASTER CAUTION LIGHT
7. MAIN COMMUNICATIONS CONTROL PANEL
8. FIRE WARNING/EXTINGUISHING PANEL
9. VERTICAL SITUATION DISPLAY (VSD)
10. HEAD UP DISPLAY CONTROL PANEL
11. VIDEO TAPE RECORDER CONTROL PANEL
12. TEWS DISPLAY UNIT
13. CANOPY UNLOCKED WARNING LIGHT

14. COUNTERMEASURES DISPENSER LIGHTS
15. HYDRAULIC PRESSURE INDICATORS
16. ENGINE TACHOMETERS
17. ALTIMETER
18. FAN TURBINE INLET TEMPERATURE INDICATORS
19. ENGINE OIL PRESSURE INDICATORS
20. FUEL QUANTITY INDICATOR
21. ENGINE FUEL FLOW INDICATORS
22. VERTICAL VELOCITY INDICATOR
23. EIGHT DAY CLOCK
24. ENGINE EXHAUST NOZZLE POSITION INDICATORS
25. JET FUEL STARTER CONTROL HANDLE

26. CABIN PRESSURE ALTIMETER
27. CAUTION LIGHTS PANEL
28. EMERGENCY VENT CONTROL HANDLE
29. CIRCUIT BREAKER PANELS
30. COCKPIT COOLING AND PRESSURIZATION OUTLET
31. STANDBY AIRSPEED INDICATOR
32. STANDBY ATTITUDE INDICATOR
33. STANDBY ALTIMETER
34. RUDDER PEDAL ADJUST RELEASE KNOB
35. MASTER MODE CONTROLS/MARKER BEACON PANEL
36. ATTITUDE DIRECTOR INDICATOR
37. EMERGENCY JETTISON BUTTON
38. STEERING MODE SWITCH

39. HORIZONTAL SITUATION INDICATOR
40. EMERGENCY BRAKE/STEERING CONTROL HANDLE
41. ACCELEROMETER
42. ANGLE OF ATTACK INDICATOR
43. AIRSPEED/MACH INDICATOR
44. MULTI-PURPOSE COLOR DISPLAY (MPCD)
45. PITCH RATIO INDICATOR
46. PITCH RATIO SELECT SWITCH
47. LANDING GEAR CONTROL HANDLE
48. RADIO CALL PANEL
49. FLAP POSITION INDICATOR
50. EMERGENCY LANDING GEAR HANDLE
51. ARRESTING HOOK CONTROL SWITCH

F-15C/D Front Panel

F-15D Back Panel

F-15E Back Panel

7. CAUTION LIGHTS PANEL
8. ENGINE OIL PRESSURE INDICATORS
9. ENGINE TACHOMETERS
10. ALTIMETER
11. FAN TURBINE INLET TEMPERATURE INDICATORS
12. FUEL QUANTITY INDICATOR (REPEATER)
13. ENGINE FUEL FLOW INDICATORS
14. VERTICAL VELOCITY INDICATOR
15. EIGHT DAY CLOCK
16. ENGINE EXHAUST NOZZLE POSITION INDICATORS
17. CABIN PRESSURE ALTIMETER
18. COMMAND SELECTOR VALVE HANDLE
19. COCKPIT COOLING AND PRESSURIZATION OUTLET
20. RUDDER PEDAL ADJUST RELEASE KNOB
21. MASTER MODE CONTROLS/MARKER BEACON PANEL
22. ATTITUDE DIRECTOR INDICATOR
23. HORIZONTAL SITUATION INDICATOR
24. EMERGENCY BRAKE/STEERING CONTROL HANDLE
25. ACCELEROMETER
26. ANGLE OF ATTACK INDICATOR
27. AIRSPEED/MACH INDICATOR
28. LANDING GEAR POSITION INDICATORS
29. FLAP POSITION INDICATORS
30. EMERGENCY LANDING GEAR HANDLE
31. ARRESTING HOOK CONTROL SWITCH
32. CANOPY JETTISON HANDLE

1. FIRE WARNING LIGHTS
2. VERTICAL SITUATION DISPLAY (VSD)
3. HAND HOLD
4. MASTER CAUTION LIGHT
5. MAIN COMMUNICATIONS CONTROL PANEL
6. CANOPY UNLOCKED WARNING LIGHT

MAIN PANEL

1. WARNING/CAUTION/ADVISORY LIGHTS PANEL
2. MULTI-PURPOSE DISPLAY
3. MULTI-PURPOSE COLOR DISPLAY
4. MASTER MODE LIGHT PANEL
5. CABIN PRESSURE ALTIMETER
6. STANDBY AIRSPEED INDICATOR
7. STANDBY ATTITUDE INDICATOR
8. STANDBY ALTIMETER
9. FUEL QUANTITY INDICATOR
10. CLOCK
11. VERTICAL VELOCITY INDICATOR
12. EMERGENCY BRAKE/STEERING CONTROL HANDLE
13. RUDDER PEDAL ADJUST RELEASE KNOB
14. LANDING GEAR POSITION LIGHTS
15. ARRESTING HOOK CONTROL SWITCH
16. EMERGENCY LANDING GEAR HANDLE
17. FLAP POSITION INDICATOR
18. RADIO CALL PANEL
19. COCKPIT COOLING AND PRESSURIZATION OUTLET
20. UPFRONT CONTROL PANEL
21. COMMAND SELECTOR VALVE

F-15E Front Panel

MAIN PANEL

1. LOCK/SHOOT LIGHTS
2. AIR REFUELING READY LIGHT
3. STANDBY MAGNETIC COMPASS
4. HEAD UP DISPLAY COMBINING GLASS
5. UPFRONT CONTROL PANEL
6. MASTER CAUTION LIGHT
7. EMISSION LIMIT SWITCH
8. FIRE WARNING/EXTINGUISHING PANEL
9. MULTI-PURPOSE DISPLAY (MPD)
10. HEAD UP DISPLAY CONTROL PANEL
11. WARNING/CAUTION/ADVISORY LIGHTS
12. HYDRAULIC PRESSURE INDICATORS
13. BLANK
14. DATA TRANSFER MODULE RECEPTACLE
15. EIGHT DAY CLOCK
16. CABIN PRESSURE ALTIMETER
17. ENGINE MONITOR INDICATOR
18. FUEL QUANTITY INDICATOR
19. JET FUEL STARTER CONTROL HANDLE/BRAKE HOLD SWITCH
20. MULTI-PURPOSE COLOR DISPLAY (MPCD)
21. ALTIMETER
22. STANDBY ATTITUDE INDICATOR
23. STANDBY AIRSPEED INDICATOR
24. ARMAMENT CONTROL PANEL
25. LANDING GEAR CONTROL HANDLE
26. PITCH RATIO SELECT SWITCH
27. PITCH RATIO INDICATOR
28. ANGLE OF ATTACK INDICATOR
29. VERTICAL VELOCITY INDICATOR
30. EMERGENCY JETTISON BUTTON
31. EMERGENCY BRAKE/STEERING CONTROL HANDLE
32. RUDDER PEDAL ADJUST RELEASE KNOB
33. COCKPIT COOLING AND PRESSURIZATION OUTLET
34. CAUTION LIGHTS PANEL
35. EMERGENCY VENT CONTROL HANDLE
36. ARRESTING HOOK CONTROL SWITCH
37. FLAP POSITION INDICATOR
38. RADIO CALL PANEL
39. EMERGENCY LANDING GEAR HANDLE

display a monochromatic or multicolor presentation of sensor and weapon video overlaid with symbology, advisory readouts, and navigation data. Color coding of display data aids in quick interpretation of complex formats. Color presentation of navigational maps also contributes to easy and accurate assessment of the tactical situation. The MPCDs also have 20 peripheral pushbuttons which provide control in the same manner as the MPD. Each MPD/MPCD has a power switch, a brightness control, and a built-in test indicator. The contents and organization of the various displays can be controlled by the multi-purpose switch on the forward control stick or the rear right hand controller. Two F-15Bs (71-0290 and 71-0291) have been fitted with F-15E-style instrumentation for their continued roles as test and demonstration aircraft.

The front control stick consists of a stick grip and force transducer, and contains six (seven in the F-15E) controls: an autopilot/nose gear steering disengage switch (paddle switch); nose gear steering/weapons button; a trigger; a weapon release button; a trim switch; an auto acquisition button; and a castle switch to control the FLIR (F-15E only). The rear cockpit stick has only four controls: an autopilot/nose gear steering disengage switch (paddle switch); a weapons release button; a trim switch and a refueling release button. The rear cockpit trigger, although present, is non-functional. The front throttles contain switches for: rudder trim; flap actuation; microphone; speed brake actuation; undesignate/missile rejection; weapon mode; target designation, and antenna elevation. The F-15C and F-15E added a switch to control the chaff/flare dispenser. The F-15E also added switches for laser designator control, and a multi-purpose switch. The rear throttles provide controls for rudder trim, speed brake actuation, and the microphone. The rear cockpit of the F-15E also contains a hand controller on the forward inboard section of each console. These controllers are used to provide sensor/display control. Both controllers contain a trigger switch, a laser designator switch, a target designate switch and a 'coolie' switch. The left controller also contains a castle switch to control the FLIR, a chaff/flare dispenser control switch, and a mode reject switch. The right controller also contains an IFF interrogate switch, a multi-purpose switch, and an auto-acquisition switch.

By 1997, all US Air Force F-15s had been retrofitted by TCTO 1F-15-1262 with the F-15E style stick and throttle controls, although the switch functions differ slightly.

In addition to the normal caution and warning lights contained on the instrument panel and HUD, the F-15 is equipped with a voice warning system that can announce some emergencies (fire, low fuel, etc.) to the pilot over the intercom system. On block-24 (79-0004) and subsequent aircraft, a video tape recording system was installed with the capability of recording the display on either the HUD or the vertical situation display. Maximum recording time was 30 minutes.

This system replaced the 16mm film-based KB-27B HUD camera system installed on aircraft prior to block-24. The KB-27B system was installed forward and to the right of the HUD and recorded the combined HUD symbology and forward field of vision. A 100 foot film capacity magazine was provided. By 1997, most aircraft were equipped with two Sony 8mm video recorders in the rear of the right console to record the HUD and VSD.

The F-15 oxygen system includes a 10 liter liquid oxygen supply with a normal system operating pressure of 70 psi.

Opposite Page top and left center: **The instrument panel illustrations from the F-15C/D flight manual.** US Air Force

Opposite Page bottom and right center: **The instrument panel illustrations from the F-15E flight manual.** US Air Force

Below, left: **The throttle quadrant for the F-15E. The F-15 introduced a concept known as 'hands on throttle and stick' that permitted the pilot to actuate most of the important switches without removing his hands from the throttle and control stick during air combat.** US Air Force

Below, right: **The control stick of the F-15E is nearly as busy as the throttle. Many of the switches have different actions when the aircraft is on the ground and in the air. For example, the paddle switch actuated by the little finger disengages the nose wheel steering when on the ground, but disengages the autopilot when in the air.** US Air Force

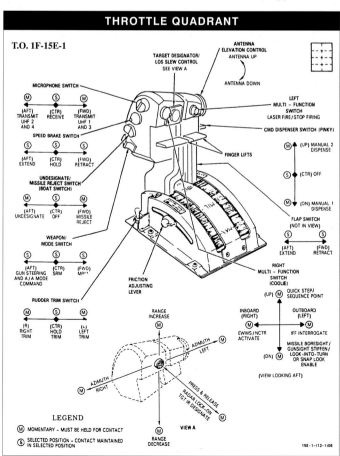

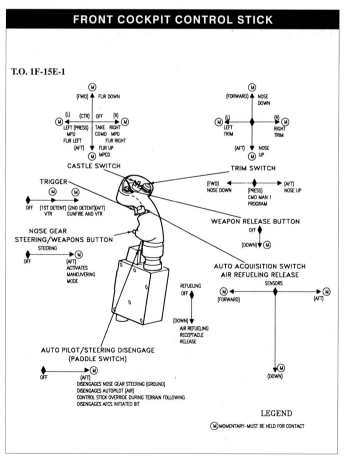

Fuselage

The F-15's fuselage is built in three sections, primarily for ease of manufacturing. All three sections are all-metal, semi-monocoque structures, constructed primarily of aluminum with some titanium in high-stress areas. The forward fuselage is built to enhance accessibility to the avionics, and contains 90% of the black boxes and 85% of the wiring. Six non-structural doors are provided to access the avionics. The forward fuselage of the F-15E was redesigned to allow fitting of the ALQ-135B system, although the external appearance is the same. The center fuselage contains the mechanical parts of the M61 cannon, the 20mm ammunition drum, and fuel cells. A truss structure allows the wing loads to be carried around the engine air ducts, permitting a lower weight, smaller cross-section configuration. To preclude possible engine damage, no removable fasteners are used forward of the air intakes.

The wing torque box is a multi-cell, three-spar, structure utilizing multi-stiffened skins to carry the bending loads into the fuselage through three pairs of pinned lugs. To increase aft fuselage structural efficiency, engine removal and installation is made from the rear of the aircraft, with the engines sliding on rails installed on each side of each engine bay. The engines are separated by a keeled titanium web which supports the arresting hook. The keel also protects the second engine from damage caused by a catastrophic failure of the first, enhancing survivability. A fire extinguishing system is fitted in both engine bays, a first for an American fighter. The aft fuselage of the F-15E was completely redesigned to allow it to accommodate either the P&W F100 or the GE F110 engine.

The special nose radome is constructed from a synthetic foam material sandwiched between outer skins and features a weight savings of 35% in comparison with earlier radome structures. It also provides heat resistance up to 500°F, and an undistorted passage for radar signals. A small ALQ-135B antenna radome is mounted on the right fuselage extension just aft of the base of the rudder on F-15C/D aircraft and F-15Es carry a similar radome on both sides. The shape of this radome changed on some F-15C/Ds that were also fitted with upper and lower ALQ-135B antennas on the forward fuselage. Six small antennas are carried on the underside of the nose of F-15As and early F-15Cs, from front to rear: TACAN/UHF blade antenna; ALQ-135 band-2 antenna; ALQ-135 band-1 antenna; UHF blade antenna; ALR-56 low-band antenna on the front nose gear door; and an ALQ-135 band-3 antenna just aft of the nose landing gear. The location of these antennas was changed slightly on single-seat aircraft fitted with ALQ-135B system, with one of the ALQ-135 antennas being deleted and the forward UHF blade antenna being moved approximately 18-inches aft. Two seat aircraft (including the F-15E) do not have the ALQ-135 antennas on the lower fuselage. A UHF/VHF communications antenna is also located on the upper fuselage, just behind the cockpit. To simplify maintenance access, the F-15 has 185 access doors and panels covering a total of 570 square feet on its wings and fuselage, 85% of which can be reached without work stands. Interestingly, no removable fasteners are used on the aircraft forward of the air intakes.

A speed brake on the upper center-fuselage is constructed of graphite-epoxy, aluminum honeycomb, and titanium. It is electrically controlled, hydraulically operated, and can be positioned to any intermediate position between fully retracted and fully extended if the angle of attack (AOA) is below 25 units. If the AOA is above 25 units, the speed brake will not extend if selected. Three different styles of speed brakes have been used: the first 20 test aircraft (71-0280/0291, 72-0113/0120) used a 20-square-foot rectangular speed brake that was found to cause a mild buffeting at some airspeeds; the first 30 operational aircraft (73-0085/0114) used a 31.5-square-foot speed brake with an external stiffener; while aircraft beginning with block-10 (74-0081) use an identical speed brake without the external stiffener. The newer speed brake extension angle was limited to 25° on aircraft prior to block-13, but was increased to 45° by TCTO 1F-15A-734 and on block-13 (75-0018) and later aircraft. All block-7 through block-9 aircraft were retrofitted with the later speed brake without the external stiffener during depot level maintenance. The speed brake has suffered from delamination of the composite material, and is considered a

---

F-15 EAGLE MANUFACTURING BREAKDOWN

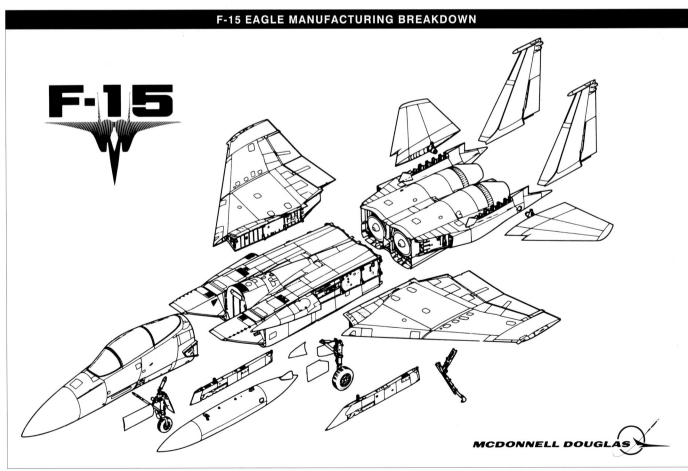

MCDONNELL DOUGLAS

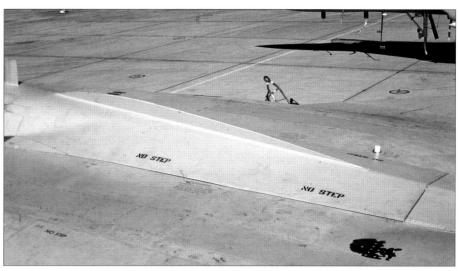

heavy maintenance item. The last block of F-15As and all subsequent aircraft have a slight change in contours to the area immediately behind the speed brake to simplify production. No F-15Bs were built to the newer design.

Integrally machined aluminum and titanium are used throughout the F-15 to reduce weight and cost. This construction technique eliminates many of the joints common to the build-up construction of earlier types. The F-15E's upper rear fuselage, rear fuselage keel, main landing gear doors, and some rear fuselage fairings incorporate superplastic formed/diffusion bonded (SPF/DB) titanium structure. The fairing extending rearward between the engine nozzles was deleted from the F-15E during the redesign of the aft fuselage. This fairing has been removed from most earlier aircraft as they have progressed through MSIP or depot-level maintenance. Surprisingly, the removal of the fairing has slightly decreased the overall drag coefficient of the aircraft.

Wings

The wings are shoulder mounted with a NACA-64A airfoil section of varying thickness-to-

chord ratios, ranging from 6.6% at the root, to 3.0% at the tip. A total of 608 square feet of wing area is provided (six less than the original wingtip design). The leading edges have a conical camber, and there are no leading edge lift devices. The wing has 1° of anhedral, and 0° of incidence. Sweepback is 45° at the leading edge, and 38° 42' at quarter-chord. The wing is a fail-safe structure comprised of a torque-box with integrally stiffened machined skins and conventionally machined ribs, both of light alloy and titanium. Three titanium main spars are provided, and the aircraft can continue flying (but not maneuvering) with any one of these severed. Leading and trailing edges are of conventional light alloy rib and skin construction. The wingtips are of aluminum honeycomb construction. No spoilers, trim tabs, or anti-ice system are fitted.

A single aileron outboard and flap section inboard are hydraulically operated by National Water Lift actuators. Each wing has a two-position flap with 35.84 square feet of area and a straight trailing edge. The flaps are electrically controlled and hydraulically operated. When the flaps are down, they are protected from structural damage by a blow-up airspeed switch which is set to automatically retract the

flaps at approximately 250 KIAS. The ailerons each have an area of 26.48 square feet, and have a swept back trailing edge. When the aircraft is at rest, the ailerons bleed down, while the flaps remain locked in position.

Wing loading at combat weight is extremely low for a modern fighter, at approximately 56 pounds per square foot of effective lifting surface (not necessarily just the wing). Antennas for the AN/ALR-56 radar warning receiver are located on the leading edge of each wingtip, just inboard of the position lights. Low voltage electroluminescent formation lights are located on the tapered portion of the wingtip. Many aircraft have suffered some minor fatigue cracking around the wing tip and have received metal doublers/patches in this area.

Tail Surfaces

Twin vertical stabilizers are of cantilever construction, making extensive use of boron-epoxy and honeycomb composite materials. The fins have 36° 34' of sweep on the leading edge, and provide 125.22 square feet of area, including rudders. The two vertical tails are identical and are interchangeable, as are the horizontal stabilizers. The mechanical aileron-rudder interconnect (ARI) adjusts the control

Above left: **The inside of the late model speed brake well.** Todd Enlund

Above right: **The first 30 production aircraft used an external stiffener on the speed brake. Changes in the manufacturing processed allowed the stiffener to be deleted on later units.** Don Logan

Right: **The left vertical stabilizer has a pod that contains the rear-looking antenna for the Magnavox ALQ-128 electronic warfare warning system (EWWS). Additional antennas are located behind panels on each side of the forward fuselage. This pod is absent from all foreign F-15s except for the 24 ex-USAF F-15C/Ds sent to Saudi Arabia during the Gulf War and some F-15S aircraft.** US Air Force

ALQ-128 ELECTRONIC WARFARE WARNING SYSTEM POD

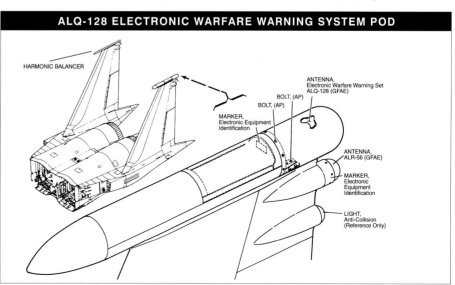

HARMONIC BALANCER

ANTENNA, Electronic Warfare Warning Set ALQ-128 (GFAE)

BOLT, (AP)

BOLT, (AP)

MARKER, Electronic Equipment Identification

ANTENNA, ALR-56 (GFAE)

MARKER, Electronic Equipment Identification

LIGHT, Anti-Collision (Reference Only)

system such that lateral stick motion results in varying rudder deflection dependent on longitudinal stick position. With the stick aft of neutral, lateral motion causes rudder deflection in the same direction as stick motion. With the stick forward of neutral, lateral stick motion causes rudder deflection in the opposite direction. In addition, if the flaps are down, the amount of rudder deflection for a given lateral input is increased. Rudder servo actuators are manufactured by Ronson Hydraulic Units.

The vertical stabilizers have been capped with pods of differing configurations. The 20 test, and some early production, aircraft had dummy pods on both tails, with the left pod having an angled aft section, and the right's terminating abruptly, although these got mixed and matched periodically. Later production aircraft have a larger pod on the left that contains antennas for the ALQ-128 warning system, and the right fin is capped with a harmonic mass balancer only. Some early aircraft have been retrofitted with an ECM-style pod on the left fin, but still retain the dummy pod on the right. A few aircraft have been seen with later style ECM-style pods on both fins. The production F-15s acquired by Israel and Japan have mass balancers on top of both fins, although some Japanese aircraft have been seen with a

modified ECM-style pod on top of the left fin, presumably containing components of the J/ALQ-8 ECM system.

There are two small fairings on the trailing edge near the top of each vertical tail. The upper fairing contains a receiving antenna for the ALR-56 radar warning system, while the lower fairing houses position lights. In late 1987, a corrosion problem around the attach point for the vertical stabilizer was discovered on some older F-15s, and these aircraft required substantial rework to cure the problem. Later, fatigue cracking along the top of both vertical stabilizers resulted in metal doublers being applied to most aircraft. Some aircraft also have been observed with doublers near the base of the vertical stabilizer.

The all-flying horizontal stabilizers (stabilators) have a dog-tooth leading edge, with extended chord outboard. The leading edge sweepback is 50° and a total of 111.36 square feet of area is provided. The stabilators are capable of symmetrical or differential movement, with the leading edge capable of ±20° of deflection. Longitudinal control stick motion positions the stabilators symmetrically to provide pitch control. The pitch ratio is automatically adjusted for altitude and speed. The ratio is high at low speeds, and low at high speeds or low altitude. If hydraulic pressure is lost, the pitch ratio will drive to an intermediate position and lock. If the mechanical linkage becomes jammed, mechanical longitudinal control is lost; however, the control augmentation system can provide enough stabilator control for moderate flight maneuvers and landing.

Landing Gear

All F-15s use an electrically controlled, hydraulically operated, tricycle-type landing gear with a single wheel on each unit. All units retract forward, and incorporate oleo-pneumatic shock absorbers made by Cleveland Pneumatic Tool Company. The F-15C introduced a slightly heavier-duty main landing gear strut, which was also retrofitted to most F-15As. The nosewheel and 22 x 6.6-10 tire are made by Goodyear and inflated to 260 psi. The main wheels are by Bendix, with 34.5 x 9.75-18 tires supplied by Goodyear and inflated to 340 psi. Several different styles of wheels have been used during the F-15's service life, although by 1996 only one type remained in service on the F-15A/B/C/D.

Bendix carbon heat-sink brakes with a Hydro-Aire anti-skid system are fitted to the main gear. The anti-skid system is not considered effective below 30 knots, and heavy braking is not recommended below that speed. After the main and nose gear are extended, the forward doors are closed, although it was common to see the main gear doors open on the initial development aircraft. A nosewheel steering system is provided, and is automatically engaged when weight is on the nosewheel. Normal steering authority is ±15°, with a maneuvering mode allowing ±45 degrees. An emergency system provides hydraulic accumulator pressure to power the brakes in the event the normal hydraulic system is lost. Anti-skid is not available when using the emergency hydraulic system.

Due to its significantly higher gross weight, the F-15E uses Bendix wheels and Michelin AIR-X radial tires on all three units. Nosewheel tire size is 22 x 7.75-9 and the main units use a 36 x 11-18 tire. All are inflated to 305 psi. The main landing gear doors of the F-15E have a noticeable bulge in order to accommodate the larger wheel/tire assemblies.

A retractable arresting hook is enclosed in the underside of the aft fuselage. It is electrically controlled, extended by gravity and a hydraulic dashpot, and retracted by utility

Left: **The nose gear has remained relatively unchanged throughout the F-15s career.** Dennis R Jenkins

Sequence below: **The F-15 main wheels have been changed several times. The one in the center photograph is the current operational wheel. Noteworthy is the McAir insignia in the early production wheel at right.** Dennis R Jenkins

hydraulic pressure. F-15A/B aircraft prior to block-15 had doors to cover the arresting hook in its retracted position, but these were removed, along with their associated mechanisms, by TCTO 1F-15A-764 dated 13th May 1977. Block-15 and later aircraft never had the doors installed. This was accomplished primarily because it was deemed that the small increase in drag was more than offset by simplified maintenance. The tail hook on the F-15E is of a new design to handle the significant increase in gross weight of that variant, and also deleted the fairing that extended between the engine nozzles above the tail hook. The fairing has also been removed from most earlier F-15s.

AMAD/JFS

The F-15's generators and hydraulic pumps are attached to an airframe-mounted accessory drive (AMAD) unit. This unit receives power from the engines via two drive shafts, and contains four hydraulic pumps and two integrated drive generators (IDG). The IDGs provide ac power and are rated at 40/50 kva each. The jet fuel starter (JFS), a self-contained auxiliary power unit, is mounted between the engines and is connected to the AMAD for ground power. The JFS gives the F-15 a self-starting capability, and can start either engine, but not both simultaneously. Starting power for the JFS is provided by a hydraulic motor driven by either of two hydraulic accumulators. The JFS shuts down automatically when the second engine reaches 50% rpm. The JFS may be used in-flight to perform a JFS assisted airstart. A set of louvers that originally covered the JFS exhaust port has been removed from most aircraft during the mid-1990s.

The electrical power system consists of the two ac generators, two (three in the F-15E) transformer-rectifiers, an emergency ac/dc generator and a power distribution system. The JFS can provide sufficient RPM to the IDGs to power the electrical system. External electrical power may be connected to the aircraft through a receptacle near the nose gear well.

The two ac generators that are the primary source of electrical power are connected for split bus, non-synchronized, operation that enables them to supply different buses during normal operations, or for a single generator to supply both buses if one generator should fail.

Current limiters are provided to prevent a fault in one generator system from shutting down both generators. Either generator is capable of supplying power to the entire system except for external ECM pods, which will be switched off-line. A utility hydraulic motor-driven emergency ac/dc generator provides power to a separate emergency power bus. If both main generators are inoperative, or both transformer-rectifiers fail, or some other combination of faults render the primary system inoperative, the emergency generator automatically comes on-line. No battery or ram-air turbine (RAT) is fitted, and the flight manual calls for an angle-of-attack that ensures the engines windmill at 12% to provide electrical power.

Three independent hydraulic systems are provided, each pressurized to 3,000 psi by four Abex AMAD driven pumps. Reservoir level sensing is employed in all three systems for the purpose of isolating a leak. When a leak develops in a circuit, a valve senses the reservoir level and shuts off the affected circuit.

Miscellaneous Systems

The F-15 uses two totally independent flight control systems. One is a traditional mechanical linkage to the hydraulic actuators at each control surface and serves as a backup system. The primary system is a triple redundant fly-by-wire (FBW) electronic system, the first incorporated on an American fighter. The mechanical and FBW systems normally work together, but either system alone is capable of providing sufficient aircraft control for flight. Spring cartridges provide simulated aerodynamic forces to the control stick and rudder pedals. The spring cartridges have trim actuators which actually move the neutral positions and thus the control surfaces. Lateral stick motion positions the ailerons, rudders and stabilators to provide roll control. The ratio of aileron/differential stabilator deflection is adjusted automatically for different airspeeds. At subsonic speeds the roll ratio is high, and at supersonic speeds the ratio is reduced. The FBW control

system is somewhat adaptive, and is able to provide limited compensation for damaged or missing control surfaces.

A Garrett environmental control system (ECS) provides conditioned air and pressurization for the cockpit and avionics, windshield anti-fog and anti-ice, the pilot's anti-g suit, and the canopy seal. Inlet air temperatures to avionics equipment are controlled to 82.5 ±2.5°F at altitudes below 35,000 feet (to minimize condensation when operating in high ambient humidities), and to 53 ±3 °F above 35,000 feet. The cooling capacity of the system is approximately 150,000 BTUs per hour.

The wiring system used on the F-15 was a major advance in miniaturization. As an example, a 22-pound 0.772-square-inch bundle used on the F-4 was miniaturized to a 9.6-pound bundle with a cross section of 0.224 square inches. There are approximately 19 miles of wiring on board the aircraft.

External lighting includes six green electroluminescent formation lights. One is on each wingtip behind the position light, one on each side of the fuselage just forward of the cockpit, and one on each side of the fuselage just aft of the wing trailing edge. MSIP resulted in a different formation light being installed on the left side to accommodate a new removable access panel. Position lights include a green light on the forward edge of the right wingtip, a red light on the forward edge of the left wingtip, and a white light just below the tip of the left vertical tail. There are three red anti-collision lights, one on the leading edge of each wing just outboard of the air intake, and another just below the tip of the right vertical tail fin. Taxi and landing lights are located on the nose gear strut.

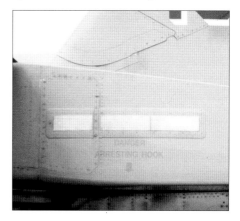

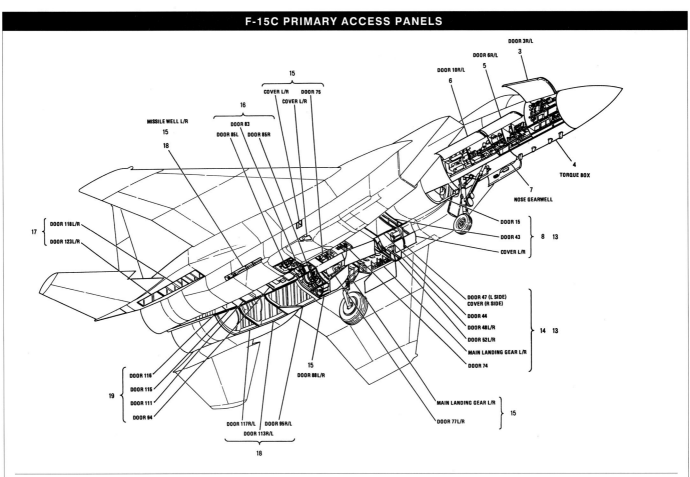

INDEX NUMBER	NOMENCLATURE	VOLUME–FIGURE NUMBER
1	Wing Wiring Installation	4-17
2	F.S. 209.900 and Nose Barrel Deck Wiring Installation	4-32
3	Nose Barrel Left Side and Right Side Wiring Installation	4-33, 4-34
4	Nose Barrel Forward Lower Panel Wiring Installation	4-35
5	Avionics Access Door 6L and 6R Wiring Installation	4-36, 4-37
6	Avionics Access Door 10L and 10R Wiring Installation	4-38, 4-39
7	Nose Landing Gear Well Wiring Installation	4-40
8	Environmental Control System Bay Wiring Installation	4-41, 4-42
9	F.S. 254.500 Bulkhead and Main Instrument Panel Wiring Installation	4-43
10	Canopy Wiring Installation	4-44
11	Cockpit Left Side and Right Side Wiring Installation	4-45, 4-46
12	Aft of Cockpit Left Side and Right Side Wiring Installation	4-47, 4-48 & 4-49
13	F.S. 415.000 to F.S. 481.500 Center Fuselage Wiring Installation	4-51, 4-52
14	F.S. 481.500 to F.S. 558.500 Center Fuselage Wiring Installation	4-53, 4-54
15	F.S. 558.500 to F.S. 626.900 Center Fuselage Wiring Installation	4-55, 4-56
16	Airframe Mounted Accessory Drive System Bay Wiring Installation	4-57, 4-58
17	Aft Fuselage Left Hand and Right Hand Boom Wiring Installation	4-62, 4-63
18	Aft Fuselage Left Engine and Right Engine Bays Wiring Installation	4-64, 4-65
19	Aft Fuselage Keel Web Wiring Installation	4-66
20	Vertical Fin Wiring Installation	4-67

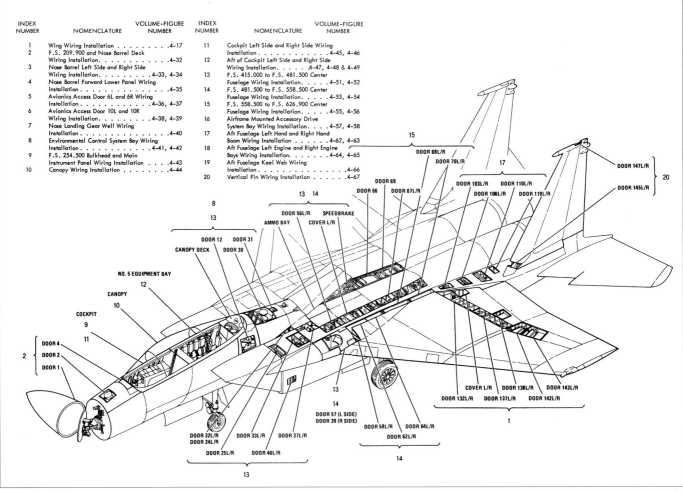

Avionics

The Hughes Aircraft AN/APG-63 (all F-15A/Bs, F-15J/DJs, and early F-15C/Ds) radar set is a high frequency, pulse-Doppler attack radar designed primarily for air-to-air combat. The radar provides target range, range rate, antenna angles and angular rates to the central computer for the computation of weapon attack mode parameters. Radar video is synthetically produced on the VSD (vertical situation display) located in the upper left of the pilot's instrument panel. The display is presented in symbol format, meaning it does not display actual targets but rather a computer-derived 'scene'. The radar set consists of several line replaceable units and connecting waveguide assemblies, mostly mounted inside the radome or in the forward left equipment bay.

The unit provides long-range detection and tracking of small, high-speed, targets operating at all altitudes down to tree-top level. Since late-1979, aircraft have been fitted with a programmable signal processor (PSP), which provides the system with the ability to respond quickly to new tactics or to accommodate improved modes and weapons through software reprogramming rather than by extensive hardware retrofit. The APG-63 was the first US airborne radar to incorporate a PSP. A radar ECCM (electronic counter-countermeasure) feature provides the capability of detecting the presence and location of ECM devices. Special ECCM circuits automatically configure the radar for optimum search, acquisition, and track performance against repeater and noise jamming devices.

The APG-63 has a nominal 100 mile range, but is optimized for short and medium range combat. It employs a gridded traveling wave tube transmitter, digital Doppler signal processing, and digital mode/data management. These features enable the radar to operate over a wide range of pulse repetition frequencies (PRF), pulse widths, and processing modes. The antenna is a planar array type, gimbaled in all three axes to maintain lock during air combat maneuvering. The ability of Hughes to provide a wide variety of PRFs in one unit was the primary consideration in winning the F-15 radar contract. The radar can operate in:

- The long range search (LRS) pulse-Doppler mode is the primary air-to-air surveillance mode. In this mode the radar operates in both high and medium PRF. The pilot can

select search ranges from 10nm to 160nm. The detection range is highly sensitive to the target cross-sectional area, Doppler conditions, ground clutter signal strength, and tactical conditions (look-up versus look-down). The mixing of PRFs maximizes the potential for target detection for both tail aspect and nose aspect targets.

- The velocity search (VS) mode is a pulse-Doppler, long-range surveillance mode in which the search display is presented in terms of target relative ground speed versus azimuth. This mode uses high PRF exclusively. It is used to provide early detection of targets in the long range, high closure rate, head-on aspect environment.

- The short range search (SRS) pulse-Doppler mode is optimized for a short range, high maneuvering attack using AIM-9 missiles or the internal cannon. This mode uses medium PRF and features displays selectable for 10, 20, and 40nm scales. Medium PRF provides a better capability to break out targets in a multi-target environment, and

also provides improved range resolution.

- The pulse mode is a low PRF, non-Doppler, mode provided as a back-up search and track capability in non-cluttered (look-up) conditions with no capability in look-down situations since no clutter rejection features are provided.

- The manual track mode is utilized when target tracking is inhibited due to problems in the radar tracking system.

- The sniff mode is a passive/active mode used to detect jamming of the radar channels or to provide a minimum of radar radiation time to prevent detection. This mode is gaining acceptance as an effective method of searching without giving away the current position of the F-15 by continuously broadcasting radar energy.

Technology continues to improve, and by 1983 a new radar was available for the Eagle. The AN/APG-70 (late F-15C/Ds and all subsequent aircraft) is an extensively modified APG-63, but utilizes the same antenna assembly and

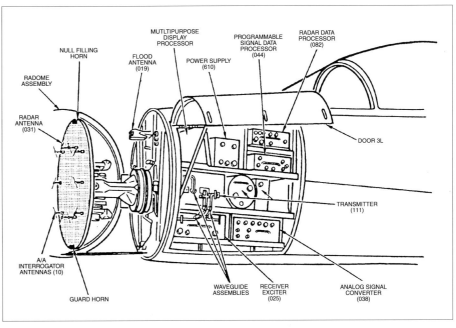

Opposite page: **The F-15 has many access panels to ease maintenance.** US Air Force

Right: **Almost all of the F-15's radar electronics can be reached through a large door on each side of the forward fuselage without the need for access stands. The door itself contains the forward AN/ALQ-128 antennas and the pitot tubes.** US Air Force and Dennis R Jenkins

power supplies. Features of the modified transmitter include higher average power and increased stability with better dynamic range. The redesigned receiver/exciter has increased bandwidth, improved tracking in ECCM mode, greater sensitivity, and generally longer detection ranges.

A synthetic aperture radar (SAR) mode is incorporated into the version installed in the dual-role F-15E, but not in the MSIP-II F-15C/D. SAR allows the detection of tank-sized targets at ranges in excess of 30 miles and targets separated by 10 feet can be distinguished individually. The radar also incorporates a 'ground moving target detection' mode to assist the crew in finding ground-based vehicles. The SAR imagery is unaffected by adverse weather, smoke, haze, or fog.

The F-15I and F-15S program developed variants of the APG-70 radar to meet the specific needs of the Israeli and Saudi air forces. Con-

trary to many reports, these versions are generally more capable than the USAF version, not less. Both of the new systems (APG-70I and APG-70S) were flight tested on a USAF F-15E prior to being delivered to the final customer.

Interestingly, by the time that the 210th F-15E was ordered, many of the individual sub-assemblies in the APG-70 were obsolete and not supportable. The solution came from adopting six electronic modules developed for the Saudi APG-70S unit. This new hybrid radar did not receive a new designation, but is informally known as the APG-70(E210).

Parts obsolesence was also affecting earlier

Right and below: **Most of the major components of the F-15 radar (the APG-70 in an F-15C is shown) can be reached by maintenance personnel without the use of work stands. The F-15 was one of the first jet fighters designed with maintenance in mind.** Hughes Aircraft Company via the Terry Panopalis Collection (right); Hughes Aircraft Company (below)

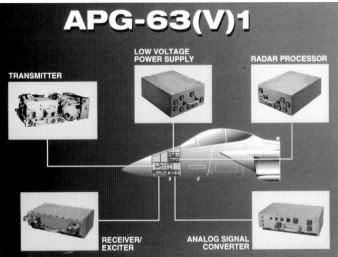

Top left: **The AN/APG-63 was tested aboard a modified C-141A equipped with an F-15 nose radome. The aircraft is now in the AFFTC Museum collection at Edwards AFB.**
Dennis R Jenkins

Below: **Early F-15As are beginning to show up in aviation museums and as gate guards at military bases. This F-15A (74-0124) is displayed at the USAF Armament Museum.** Dennis R Jenkins

Above: **The revised Hughes AN/APG-63(V) radar is being installed in all US Air Force F-15As and F-15Cs that are not equipped with the AN/APG-70 set. The Air Force is evaluating installing the radar in all remaining air-superiority F-15s, as are the Israeli and Saudi Air Forces. It is unlikely Japan will fund such a major upgrade for their F-15Js, preferring to wait for the introduction of the new Mitsubishi F-2 (FS-X) fighter.**
Hughes Aircraft Company

Above: **One of the early test F-15As was used for continued testing of the ACES II ejection seat after the aircraft was retired. Noteworthy is the amount of debris created by the force of the ejection. This can be identified as a 'real' aircraft by the cover over the pitot tube and the early national insignia and maintenance markings on the fuselage section. The serial number of the aircraft could not be ascertained from available records.** US Air Force

F-15 radars. In an attempt to fix this, on 18th July 1997 the first F-15C equipped with an improved Hughes AN/APG-63(V)1 radar successfully completed its first flight test, four days ahead of schedule. The radar provides improved supportability and operational capabilities that surpass early APG-70 units. The radar was developed under a $200 million contract awarded in 1994. Special attention was placed on a design to balance the need of system performance, cost and reliability, and on a rigorous parts management program to maximize the availability of parts for the radar for years to come. In addition to greater reliability and maintainability, the APG-63(V)1 also offers substantial increases in processing capacity and electronic counter-countermeasures. An improved air-to-ground mode was also provided. The APG-63(V)1 interfaces with the existing F-15C/D radar antenna and displays with only minor modifications. The upgrade kit uses the APG-70 tactical software with limited changes.

There is a potential that the APG-63(V)1 will eventually replace all versions on the APG-63 and APG-70 in USAF, Israeli, and Saudi service by the end of 2003. There is, however, a move underway to adopt the Israeli radar originally developed by Elta for the Lavi fighter program. This radar has better SAR resolution than the APG-70 in the air-to-ground mode, and air-to-air capabilities roughly equivalent to the APG-68 used in late model F-16s. The radar has been selected for the Turkish F-4 upgrade, and will be flight tested by the USAF in an F-16 in late 1998. It would, however, require significant development for use in the F-15.

As of the end of 1996, 497 USAF F-15s were equipped with APG-63 radar sets, and 245 (FY86 and higher) used APG-70 sets. As far as is known, all foreign F-15s, except the F-15I and F-15S, use versions of the APG-63.

The Lockheed Martin LANTIRN system is carried by the F-15E. LANTIRN consists of an AN/AAQ-13 navigation pod carried on a stub pylon under the starboard air intake, and an AN/AAQ-14 targeting pod carried under the port air intake.

The LANTIRN navigation pod provides high-speed penetration and precision attack on tactical targets at night and in adverse weather. The navigation pod also contains a terrain-following Ku-band radar and a fixed wide-field-of-view (WFOV) infrared sensor, which provides a visual cue and input to the aircraft's flight control system, enabling it to maintain a preselected altitude above the terrain and avoid obstacles. This sensor displays an infrared image of the terrain in front of the aircraft to the pilot on the HUD. The navigation pod enables the pilot to fly along the general contour of the terrain at high speed, using mountains, valleys and the cover of darkness to avoid detection. Martin Marietta (now Lockheed Martin) initiated the LANTIRN research and development program in September 1980. Initial operational test and evaluation of the LANTIRN navigation pod was successfully completed in December 1984, and the Air Force approved low-rate initial production in March 1985 with full-rate production following in November 1986.

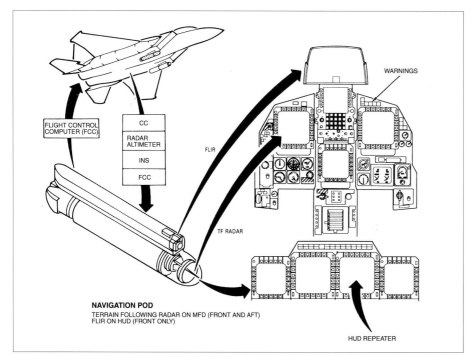

NAVIGATION POD
TERRAIN FOLLOWING RADAR ON MFD (FRONT AND AFT)
FLIR ON HUD (FRONT ONLY)

Left above: **The F-15E introduced a new cockpit based on multi-function CRTs instead of conventional flight instruments. This permits the display of terrain-following radar images from the LANTIRN navigation pod. The F-15E front cockpit also introduced a new wide-angle field-of-view heads up display (HUD) that can also display infrared images from the LANTIRN pod. The 'guy in back' can display the HUD image on one of his multi-function displays.** US Air Force

Left middle: **The LANTIRN AAQ-13 navigation pod is carried on the starboard stub pylon on the F-15E.** Dennis R Jenkins

Left: **The LANTIRN AAQ-14 targeting pod is carried on the port stub pylon on the F-15E. A travel pod is on the CFT.** Dennis R Jenkins

The first production pod was delivered to the Air Force on 31st March 1987. The navigation pod is 78.2 inches long, 21.5 inches high, 14.0 inches wide, and weighs 470 pounds. The pod cost $1,380,000 each in 1996.

The LANTIRN targeting pod contains a high-resolution, 8.1-inch-aperture forward-looking infrared sensor (FLIR) for long-range target acquisition, WFOV FLIR (6° x 6°) for target detection and tracking, and a narrow-field-of-view FLIR (1.7° x 1.7°) for target selection. The pod also contains a laser designator-rangefinder for precise delivery of laser-guided munitions, a missile boresight correlator for automatic lock-on of AGM-65D imaging infrared Maverick missiles, and software for automatic target tracking. These features simplify the functions of target detection, recognition and attack and permit pilots of single-seat fighters to attack targets with precision-guided weapons on a single pass. In April 1986, initial operational test and evaluation of the LANTIRN targeting pod proved that a low-altitude, night, under-the-weather, precision attack mission was feasible. The Air Force approved low-rate initial production in June 1986, and full-scale production was approved in early 1990. The targeting pod is 98.5 inches long, 15.0 inches in diameter, and weighs 524 pounds. The targeting pod cost $3,200,000 in 1996.

The LANTIRN targeting pod is subject to electrical arcing above 25,000 feet, and automatically shuts down. In late 1996, some F-15E units began receiving updated pods that are designed to operate up to 40,000 feet. High on the 'wish list' of Strike Eagle pilots is an upgraded FLIR unit that would allow targets to be spotted at longer ranges, even in degraded thermal conditions. The new LANTIRN system being fielded on US Navy F-14s during 1996 is equipped with such a sensor, so it would be a relatively easy task to fit it to the F-15E. In early 1997, Lockheed unveiled an improved LANTIRN 2000 pod set with substantially improved capabilities. Unfortunately, the USAF has not committed to purchasing the improved pod.

By the end of 1995, Lockheed Martin had built or had orders from the US and eight allies for 578 LANTIRN targeting pods, 742 navigation pods, 111 Sharpshooter pods (a modified targeting pod), and 12 Pathfinder pods (modified navigation pods).

A General Electric automatic flight control system (AFCS) provides for control augmentation, pitch/roll attitude hold and altitude hold. Two separate AN/ARC-164 UHF radios are provided, both equipped with KY-58 (KY-28 in F-15A/B and non-MSIP F-15C/D) speech security units (scramblers). Both of the transmitter-receivers operate on manually selected frequencies, or on 20 preset frequency channels within the 225.000 to 399.975MHz range. All F-15Es, late F-15C/Ds, and most aircraft processed under the MSIP-II program incorporate a Have Quick jam-resistant frequency-hopping radio. Have Quick radios and speech security units were not exported.

IBM manufactures the high-speed, stored program, general purpose central computer. F-15A/Bs and F-15C/Ds before the MSIP-II program, and all F-15D/DJs, had central computers fitted with 32k of memory. MSIP-II increased this to 128k and tripled the speed of the processor. The computer provides air-to-air and air-to-ground steering and weapons delivery, navigation, flight director, and control and display management functions. It also provides the pilot with steering and weapon delivery cues, target data, avionics system status, and weapons configuration. A separate air data computer receives inputs from the pitot-static system, the angle of attack probes, the left total temperature probe, the altimeter setting knob, the nose landing gear door switch, and the flap switch. The computer then corrects these inputs for sensor error as required, computes various derived parameters from this data, and furnishes required parameters to the aircraft central computer. A Hazeltine AN/APX-76 IFF/SIF system is provided. This interrogator supports mode 1, mode 2, mode 3/A, mode 4, and mode C. Modes 1, 2, and 3/A are selective identification feature (SIF) modes, mode 4 is used for high confidence identification (crypto), and mode C is used for civilian ATC reporting.

The instrument landing system provides the capability for the aircraft to make a precision landing approach and descent. The radios and IFF controls are mounted in a stack directly in front of the pilot, just below the top of the instrument panel glare shield, as opposed to the more traditional location in one of the consoles. A self-contained Litton AN/ASN-109 inertial navigation system (INS) provides continuous present position monitoring and the capability for visual, TACAN, or radar updating in all aircraft except the F-15E.

The F-15E contains a self-contained, fully automatic, ring laser gyro (RLG) INS which supplies the primary attitude reference for the aircraft and provides continuous present position monitoring. In addition, the INS provides aircraft attitude, heading, velocity, and acceleration information to the LANTIRN, radar, and AFCS. The RLG is a rate-integrating gyro which does not use a spinning mass like a conventional gyroscope. The RLG detects and measures angular rotation by measuring the effective frequency difference between two contrarotating (one clockwise, one counter-clockwise) laser beams in a ceramic block. As the two laser beams travel simultaneously around the cavity, mirrors reflect each beam around the enclosed path. When the gyro is at rest, the two beams have the same frequency because the optical path is the same in both directions. However, when the gyro is subjected to an angular turning rate about an axis perpendicular to the plane of the two beams, one beam sees a greater path length and the other sees a shorter path length. The two resonant frequencies change to adjust to the longer or shorter optical path, with the frequency differential being directly proportional to the angular turning rate.

TCTO 1F-15E-737 (ECP-2593) adds Global Positioning System (GPS) capabilities to F-15E aircraft beginning in late 1998.

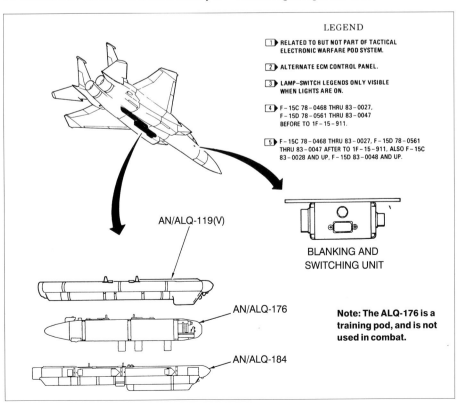

LEGEND

1 ▶ RELATED TO BUT NOT PART OF TACTICAL ELECTRONIC WARFARE POD SYSTEM.

2 ▶ ALTERNATE ECM CONTROL PANEL.

3 ▶ LAMP–SWITCH LEGENDS ONLY VISIBLE WHEN LIGHTS ARE ON.

4 ▶ F-15C 78-0468 THRU 83-0027, F-15D 78-0561 THRU 83-0047 BEFORE TO 1F-15-911.

5 ▶ F-15C 78-0468 THRU 83-0027, F-15D 78-0561 THRU 83-0047 AFTER TO 1F-15-911, ALSO F-15C 83-0028 AND UP, F-15D 83-0048 AND UP.

AN/ALQ-119(V)

BLANKING AND SWITCHING UNIT

AN/ALQ-176

AN/ALQ-184

Note: The ALQ-176 is a training pod, and is not used in combat.

EW Systems

The F-15's electronic warfare equipment is collectively known as TEWS (Tactical Electronic Warfare System). This system consists of the AN/ALR-56 radar warning receiver (RWR), the AN/ALQ-128 electronic warfare warning system (EWWS), AN/ALQ-135 internal countermeasures set (ICS or ICMS), AN/ALE-45 expendable countermeasures set (ECS or CMD), and the AN/ALQ-119 (or equivalent) ECM pod. Apparent problems with systems development and integration caused F-15A/Bs to be deployed without the majority of the system installed, although all aircraft were later retrofitted. The AN/ALR-56 and AN/ALQ-128 were installed by TCTO 1F-15A-700 dated 10th December 1976, and the AN/ALQ-135(V) ICS was installed by TCTO 1F-15A-807 dated 5th September 1977, although it took more than a decade to actually incorporate the systems in all operational aircraft. TCTO 1F-15C-923 installed the AN/ALE-45 set into all aircraft. The two-seat F-15B/D aircraft are not fitted with the AN/ALQ-135 since the second seat occupies the area normally used by the system electronics. The two-seat F-15E has a redesigned forward fuselage that allows all components of TEWS to be carried in USAF aircraft, and indigenous systems in the F-15I.

AN/ALQ-119(V). Westinghouse ECM pod family developed under QRC-335/522 beginning in 1970. These are dual-mode (deception-noise) jamming pods that operate in the E-band through J-band frequency range. Three ALQ-119 configurations are available. The objective is to confuse or deceive threats by disrupting the acquisition-tracking-guidance functions of the enemy radar. The pod is also used by Israel and Japan on their F-15s. The ALQ-119(V) pod is also known as the 'TEWS pod' when used on the F-15, and is carried on the centerline stores station (#5) after inclusion of TCTO 1F-15A-652 dated 16th February 1977. The pod may also be carried on either inboard wing stations (#2 or #8), but can not be operated since no wiring provisions were incorporated in the aircraft, although some controls and indicators exist in the cockpit of C/D aircraft. The F-15E does not appear capable of carrying external ECM pods, relying instead on expanded ALQ-135B coverage. The basic long pod ALQ-119(V)-15 covers the entire threat spectrum, and is normally carried by two-seat aircraft. Two short pods, -16 and -17, cover the low band and mid/high bands respectively.

AN/ALQ-128. Magnavox electronic warfare warning system (EWWS). Antennas for the system are located flush to the side of the forward fuselage just above and forward of the pitot tubes, as well as the pod on top of the left vertical stabilizer. Warning coverage is different from the ALR-56, but actual functions and capabilities are classified. This system was not exported on any F-15C/Ds, resulting in all foreign aircraft having a mass-balance on the left vertical stabilizer instead of the normal USAF ECM pod. The exception to this is the ex-USAF C/Ds provided to Saudi Arabia during the Gulf war, where the ALQ-128 was removed but the pod remained. Photographs of late F-15S models show both the forward fuselage and vertical stabilizer antennas normally associated with this system, leading to speculation that the F-15I and F-15S are being equipped with some version of the EWWS.

AN/ALQ-131(V). Microprocessor controlled dual-mode (deception-noise) pod manufactured by Westinghouse. The ALQ-131 pod employs variations of noise, transponder and repeater techniques to counter SAM radars, AAA and AI fire control system radars, and velocity gate tracking radars. Developed as QRC-559 beginning in 1971, this system received a significant update under a $15.5 million 'Have Exit' contract in August 1980. The block-II pods, which began qualification testing in November 1985, incorporate new hardware as well as new deception techniques. Block-I pods are also used by Israel and Japan on their F-15s. The pod is of modular construction and, depending on the exact mission, can vary from 85 to 154 inches long. Other dimensions are 12 inches wide, 25 inches high while weight is between 100 and 150 pounds, depending on exact configuration.

AN/ALQ-135. Northrop manufactured internal countermeasures set (ICMS). The function of the ICMS is to counter surface-to-air missile, airborne interceptor, and anti-aircraft artillery attacks using active jamming with a minimum of pilot activity. The ALR-56 RWR detects and analyzes the threat environment and determines the most effective ECM that the ALQ-135

Left above: **An AN/ALQ-119(V) pod under an early test F-15A (71-0285) at Edwards AFB during 1976. Originally, the outer wing stations were going to carry a newly developed TEWS pod, but this never materialized. Only the centerline station is currently certified to carry ECM pods.** Dennis R Jenkins

Left: **This F-15E (88-1690) from the 4th TFW shows the two different ALQ-135 antennas that have begun appearing on the Eagle. The left (near) boom uses the normal round antenna that has been seen for years on F-15Cs and F-15Es, while the right (far) boom shows the new 'square' antenna. All F-15Es are equipped with one of each antenna in the configuration shown here. F-15Cs only have an antenna on the right boom, and both styles have been observed. The square antenna is normally seen on aircraft equipped with the band-3 antennas on the nose, so it is assumed to be related to that recent modification.** Dennis R Jenkins

can provide to oppose the threat environment as it exists at that instant. The RWR then controls the ICMS to provide the most effective jamming modulations and frequency assignments. If the RWR is not functioning, the ICMS can operate autonomously or under pilot control. Since the majority of the electronics is carried in the area occupied by the second seat in the F-15B/D, the ALQ-135 was not installed in two-seat aircraft.

The F-15E has a redesigned forward fuselage and ammunition feed system that enabled it to become the first two-seater to carry the AN/ALQ-135B. Initial development commenced in August 1974, with production beginning in September 1975. More than 1,000 sets, worth more than $2 billion, had been produced. Some Israeli and Saudi aircraft have been observed with the band-1 and band-2 antennas under the nose, and Japanese aircraft carry a similar J/ALQ-8 system.

ALQ-135 sets used on F-15As and early F-15Cs operate in two bands, with band-1 covering E- through G-Band, and band-2 operating in G- through I-band, with a frequency overlap in G-band. The system is composed of six line replaceable units (LRU) plus waveguides and antennas. Three of the LRUs are control oscillators, and three are amplifiers. These aircraft have a separate small antenna for each band on the bottom of the forward fuselage, two between the UHF blade antennas (band-1 and band-2), and a third (band-3) aft of the nose wheel well.

An improved ALQ-135B is used by late F-15Cs and the F-15E. This set operates in three bands, with band-1 operating in E- through G-band, band-2 covering G- through I-band, and band-3 operating in H- through J-band. The system uses a combined band-1 and band-2 (also known as band-1.5) antenna on the bottom of the forward fuselage between the UHF blade antennas, and a band-3 antenna behind the nose wheel well. Additional band-3 antennas are carried on the rear of the fuselage boom-extensions, one on the right of the F-15C and one on each side of the F-15E. The shape of this rear boom antenna changed on some aircraft during 1995, although the reason for the change is unknown. On some aircraft, two small forward-facing triangular band-3 transmitter antennas are mounted on the top and bottom of the fuselage immediately aft of the radome. Although the antennas show up in documentation as early as 1986, no aircraft were observed with them until 1992.

AN/ALQ-176. ECM training pod sometimes carried by the F-15 during Red Flag exercises.

AN/ALQ-184. Manufactured by Raytheon, this is a major update to the ALQ-119 pod. Improvements include higher radiated power, enhanced ECM techniques, improved reliability, and easier maintenance. The antennas are of a new multi-beam design. Two different ALQ-184 pod configurations are available: the ALQ-184(V)-1 long pod covers the complete threat spectrum; and the -2 short pod which covers the mid/high bands only. Two-seat aircraft generally carry the long pod to ensure greater threat coverage since they are not equipped with the ALQ-135 set.

AN/ALR-56. Radar warning receiver manufactured by Loral. Upgrade to ALQ-56A in 1981 by TCTO 1F-15-779. Receives, analyzes and stores threat data transmitted by surface-to-air missile radars, air intercept radars, and anti-aircraft artillery control radars. The data is provided to the pilot as warning lights, CRT displays, and audible warnings. The RWR also provides automated control and tuning data for the AN/ALQ-135 system and ALE-45 dispenser set. Determination of jamming requirements is made by comparison of received signals with a stored program threat table. The set is composed of a processor, low-band receiver, high-band receiver, countermeasures display, receiver controller, power supply, and antenna system. The solid-state, digitally controlled, dual-channel receivers cover roughly C- through J-band. The antenna system consists of four circularly polarized spiral high-band antenna assemblies, each within its own radome (one on the trailing edge of each tail, and one on the leading edge of each wingtip), and a small low-band blade antenna on the nose gear door.

A major update is the ALR-56C with a significantly faster processor capable of handling more threats and greater signal densities. Principle functions are: programmed signal search; signal acquisition and analysis; establishing threat priorities; jammer management; passive

---

NOTE:

The F-15C/D internal fuel tanks are shown. The F-15A/B internal tanks are about the same except they do not have the leading edge internal wing tanks or the number 1 auxiliary tank.

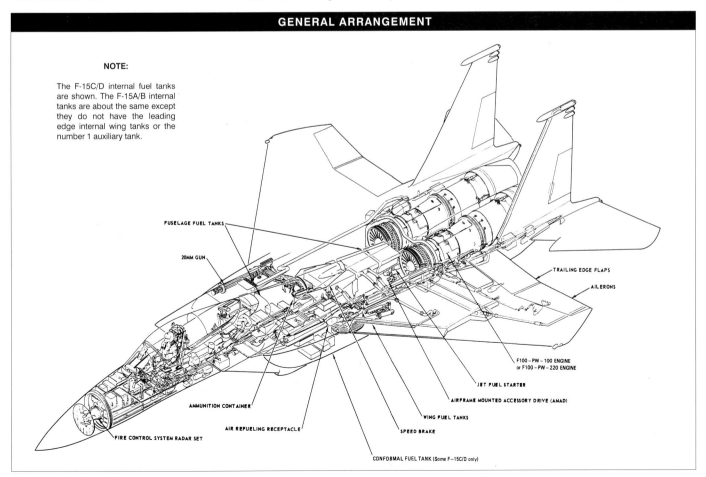

FUSELAGE FUEL TANKS

20MM GUN

TRAILING EDGE FLAPS

AILERONS

F100 – PW – 100 ENGINE or F100 – PW – 220 ENGINE

JET FUEL STARTER

AMMUNITION CONTAINER

AIRFRAME MOUNTED ACCESSORY DRIVE (AMAD)

AIR REFUELING RECEPTACLE

WING FUEL TANKS

SPEED BRAKE

FIRE CONTROL SYSTEM RADAR SET

CONFORMAL FUEL TANK (Some F–15C/D only)

103

countermeasure management; and providing visual and audible alerts. The ALR-56C has been fitted to all F-15C/D aircraft, and was a production feature on all of the F-15Es. Some F-15A/B aircraft have also been fitted with the improved system.

AN/ALE-45. Tracor manufactured expendable countermeasure dispenser set. The ALE-45 is a solid-state microprocessor controlled dispenser which interfaces to the ALR-56 for automatic operation. The set determines the best dispensing program based on operating mode, payload management inputs, available expendables, threat type, altitude, velocity, and aspect angle to the threat. The set can also be controlled manually by the pilot. The dispensing program is incorporated into

replaceable modules that can be changed on the flightline. The set has four dispensers, each with two magazines, and is capable of dispensing RR-170, RR-180 or RR-188 chaff (240 cartridges, maximum), MJU-7 flares (120 cartridges), and MJU-10 flares (48 cartridges). One-quarter of the flare load can not be carried on F-15Es when the LANTIRN targeting pod is installed. Two dispensers are located in the bottom of the fuselage immediately forward of each main landing gear wheel well, although the system is seldom seen fitted while the aircraft are in the United States. Installation provisions exist in all F-15C/Ds and the F-15E, but apparently initially not in USAF F-15A/Bs. At least some part of the wiring was incorporated into USAF F-15As, and the system control

switch exists on the throttle quadrant of all F-15s. The MSIP program installed provisions for the ALE-45 into all the remaining USAF F-15A/Bs. At least some Israeli F-15As are equipped with the ALE-45 dispensers or equivalent indigenous systems.

Foreign EW Systems

AL/L-8202 (Israel). ECM pod manufactured by the Elta Electronics Industries, Ltd. subsidiary of Israeli Aircraft Industries (IAI), Ltd. The pod is designed to provide self-protection against both surface and airborne threats. It has wide frequency coverage (F- through J-band), and a high broadband output with selectable ECM techniques. Antennas are located at both ends of the pod, which is 114 inches long, 10 inches wide, 15 inches high, and weighs 90 pounds. The pod is used by all Israeli variants of the F-15 and other *Heyl Ha' Avir* aircraft.

J/ALQ-8 (Japan). Indigenously designed and produced self-defense system similar in capabilities to the USAF ALQ-135. During the mid-1990s, two small antennas very similar to ALQ-135 antennas began to appear under the forward fuselage in the same general location as their USAF counterpart. Aircraft with these antennas also have two small cooling scoops located on the fuselage bottom next to the bottom of the air intakes.

J/APR-4 (Japan). Radar warning receiver set designed and manufactured by Tokyo Keiki. The system was heavily based on the experience gained during the development of the J/APR-2 for the McDonnell/Mitsubishi F-4EJ

Left, top to bottom: **Three of the four Ferris paint test F-15s (the fourth, 74-0089, is on page 53).**

73-0111, as the 555th TFTS commander's aircraft at Luke AFB. Jack D Morris

74-0139 at Luke AFB. Jim Rotramel

74-0110 at Luke AFB. Mick Roth

Below: **The tip of the F-15 radome is molded separately from the rest of the radome. Due to the lead times involved in ordering the tips, they do not always match the current paint scheme of the aircraft. Here an air superiority blue aircraft has a black tip.** Dennis R Jenkins

and the J/APR-3 for the Mitsubishi F-1. The system is functionally similar to, but less sophisticated than, the USAF ALR-56, and is capable of processing multiple inputs simultaneously in a dense electromagnetic environment. Utilizes a digital computer with a re-programmable software package to permit rapid reconfiguration. The cockpit display is similar in size, shape and location to the TEWS display in USAF F-15s. The display provides for multiple threat data presentations in alphanumeric and graphic formats. The system interfaces with the J/ALQ-8 for coordination of defensive countermeasures.

Paint and Markings

The first 42 Eagles (71-0280/0291, 72-0113/0120, 73-0085/0099, and 73-0108/0114) were painted air-superiority blue, with the exception of 71-0287 which was finished in gloss white for its role as the spin-test aircraft, and 72-0119 ('Streak Eagle') which was not painted. Air superiority blue (officially, simply 'Superiority Blue') consisted of flat AS Blue (FS35450) on the upper surfaces and gloss AS Blue (FS15450) on the lower surfaces. This paint scheme was considered effective in the blue skies over Edwards and Luke, but it was not so effective in cloudy skies, such as those expected to be encountered over Europe most of the year.

Below: **The AIM-120 AMRAAM missile had some vibration problems on the aft fuselage stations of the F-15, but some minor design changes cleared the missile to be carried on all either F-15 missile stations. Here an F-15C (84-0018) fires an AIM-120A during development testing. Noteworthy are the cameras installed on the fuselage missile stations to record the launch.**
US Air Force

The majority of the test aircraft received day-glo orange markings on their wingtips, vertical and horizontal stabilizers, and engine inlets to make them more visible during test flights. After the test program was completed, several of the early test aircraft received new gloss white paint jobs with a contrasting trim color. The fourth F-15A (71-0283) received bright orange (but not day-glo) trim, while 71-0285, 71-0289, and 71-0290 used royal blue trim in the same general scheme. The aircraft were used for training maintenance and ground crews, and many publications show they were redesignated GF-15A,s although official records do not support this, referring to them simply as F-15A.

The first F-15B (71-0290) later received a colorful red, white, and blue paint scheme for its role as the F-15S/MTD. The second F-15B (71-0291) also received a red, white, and blue scheme, this one a duplicate of one developed for (but never used by) the Thunderbirds air demonstration squadron. The aircraft was painted in late 1975 to celebrate the US Bicentennial, and later went on a world-tour in a slightly modified version of the scheme.

Aircraft up to and including 72-0113 had a black tip on the radome. Aircraft beginning with 72-0114 used blue tips that more closely resembled the rest of the paint scheme. Early 'Compass Ghost' aircraft still had light blue tips before grey tips reached the production line. Some of test aircraft sported long test instrumentation booms from the front of all-metal noses at various times in their careers.

All the Air Superiority Blue operational aircraft were repainted into 'Compass Ghost' during their first depot-level maintenance period. It should also be noted that the tail codes initially used at Luke were painted in white, instead of the more normal black. The exception to this was 73-0109, the second to arrive, which had

black tail codes for several months before they were repainted white. Operational squadrons used black tail codes, a practice later adopted by Luke, although some Nellis aircraft were periodically seen with white tail codes.

Early production aircraft after 73-0100 (or 74-0137 for two-seaters), including foreign deliveries, were painted in 'Compass Ghost'. Project 'Compass Ghost' has been a continuing effort by the military to find the most effective camouflage scheme possible.

The standard F-15 scheme prior to 1990 consisted of two shades of grey, called Light Ghost Grey (FS36320) and Dark Ghost Grey (FS36375), applied in a pattern designed to minimize the reflectance of various contours of the aircraft.

Four aircraft were painted in the 'Ferris Attitude Deceptive' scheme dreamed up by aviation artist Keith Ferris. This reintroduced the concept of painting an aircraft to make it difficult to determine its direction of movement during close-in aerial combat. The scheme was also applied to several F-14s, as well as both Air Force and Navy F-4s and aggressor aircraft. An additional feature of the concept was a 'false-canopy' painted on the bottom of the aircraft. There were several legal concerns over the continued use of the paint scheme by the military, and the aircraft were repainted into 'Compass Ghost' in late-1976.

The following Federal Standard (FS) colors were used for the Ferris schemes:

Serial	Light	Medium	Dark	Canopy
73-0111	36440	36231	36118	36118
74-0089	36440	36231	36320	36118
74-0110	36622	36440	36231	36231
74-0139	36440	36231	36118	36118

Three operational aircraft at Luke received high-visibility markings for a short time during 1976: 73-0100 sporting wide yellow bands around the wings and tails; 73-0103 got alternating white and red 'invasion stripes' around the forward fuselage and wings; while 73-0112 received similar (but not identical) stripes in black. Additionally, 74-0113 was painted in standard 'Compass Ghost' with a FS36118 false-canopy on the bottom of the fuselage.

The 'Strike Eagle' demonstrator (71-0291) was originally painted in Compass Ghost, then was repainted in the standard 'European One' scheme of dark grey (FS36081) and two dark greens (FS34092 and FS34102). Three F-15Cs assigned to the 57th FWW at Nellis were painted in different schemes to find the final F-15E camouflage: 82-0029 was essentially Compass Ghost utilizing a lighter and darker shade of grey than usual (FS36251 and FS36176); 82-0028 used three tones of grey (FS numbers unknown) in a pattern very reminiscent of the one used on one of the F-16XL SCAMP prototypes; and the last one (82-0022) was painted in the very dark gunship grey (FS36114) used by production F-15Es.

Beginning in 1990, 'Compass Ghost' was replaced by the 'High and Low Reflectance Gray' scheme that uses two new shades of grey (FS36251 and FS 36176). This so-called 'Mod Eagle' scheme has been applied to almost all F-15s as they progress through depot-level maintenance or the MSIP program. The F-15S aircraft destined for Saudi Arabia use a modified version of the 'Mod Eagle' scheme instead of the F-15E's gunship grey. The F-15Is for Israel use a version of the IDF/AF's standard desert camouflage.

All aircraft have the interior of their air intakes painted in gloss white. This helps to resolve the 'black hole' effect often presented by a fighter approaching head-on, and also aids in detecting the presence of foreign objects, such as blood or feathers. Wheel wells, landing gear struts, and the interior of the speed brake area are also generally painted gloss white. Most interior surfaces are finished with a metallic green coating for corrosion resistance.

Armament

Fixed armament consists of one General Electric M61A1 Vulcan 20mm rotary cannon in the shoulder area of the right wing root. The muzzle is positioned well aft of the main engine air intake to prevent ingestion of exhaust gases. The cannon has six barrels, weighs 275 pounds, is electrically controlled, hydraulically driven, and has a muzzle velocity of 3,380 feet per second. The gun has a selectable firing rates of 4,000 or 6,000 rounds per minute, and a total of 940 rounds of ammunition are carried by all variants except the F-15E. A drum assembly provides storage for the 20mm ammunition, and is directly linked to the ammunition conveyer system and the return conveyer system. An exit unit removes ammunition from the drum and an entrance unit returns spent cases, misfired rounds and cleared rounds to the drum. The complete ammunition cycle forms a closed loop from the drum to the gun and return.

The components that make up a complete round or cartridge used in the M61A1 gun are: a brass or steel cartridge case, an electric primer, propellant powder, and the projectile. The complete cartridge is approximately 6.625 inches long and weighs roughly 1/2 pound.

Five types of M-51 ammunition are currently available. The 20mm target practice cartridge (TP) is ball ammunition with a hollow projectile that does not contain filler. The 20mm armor piercing incendiary (API) projectile is charged with an incendiary composition that ignites on impact. And the 20mm high explosive incendiary (HEI) cartridge explodes with an incendiary effect after it has penetrated the target. The HEI cartridge is normally used against aircraft and light ground targets. HEIT rounds are practice versions of the normal HEI round, and a TPT tracer is also available and is normally carried as every seventh round.

In addition to the M-51 series of 20mm ammunition, the F-15 can also use PGU-28 and PGU-27 rounds. This projectile is much more streamlined, and has a boattail for reduced drag and a significantly higher muzzle velocity. The HUD gunsight compensates for the PGU round's different ballistics. PGU-28 is an HEI round, while PGU-27 is TP.

In order to gain additional space for electronic equipment (primarily the AN/ALQ-135 set), the F-15E has a redesigned ammunition handling system that uses a linkless feed system. The ammunition capacity was initially stated as 512 rounds, but ever increasing need for volume for the electronics has reduced this to the vicinity of 450 rounds in current production aircraft. The new system required the use of a small fairing on the underside of the fuselage directly beneath the ammunition drum, and this is one of the identifying features of the F-15E and its variants.

The basic F-15 is equipped with nine numbered external stores stations: The left outboard wing station is #1; the left inboard wing station is #2, the left forward fuselage missile station is #3 while the left aft fuselage missile station is #4; the centerline is #5; the right fuselage missile stations are #6 (aft) and #7 (forward); the right inboard wing station is #8; and the right outboard wing station is #9.

The inboard wing station pylons are both equipped with two rail launchers for either AIM-9 or AIM-120 missiles, effectively giving four additional stations. Stations #1 and #9

Below **The M61 illustrations for the F-15C and the F-15E.** US Air Force

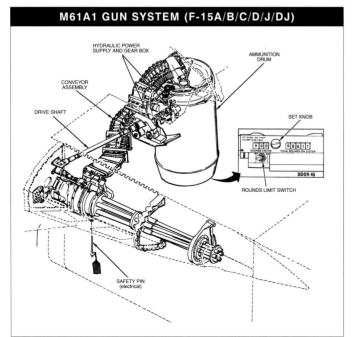

M61A1 GUN SYSTEM (F-15A/B/C/D/J/DJ)

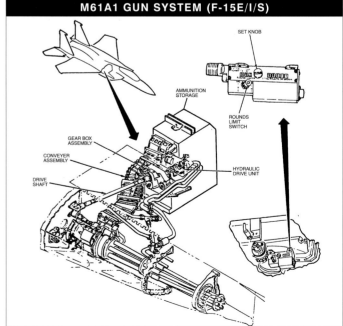

M61A1 GUN SYSTEM (F-15E/I/S)

were intended for a still-born ECM pod, and are not currently cleared to carry any stores. The outboard wing stations (#1 and #9) were finally deleted from the F-15E.

All variants of the F-15 are capable of carrying a variety of air-to-air missiles including the AIM-7F/M Sparrow III, AIM-9L/P/M Sidewinder, and the AIM-120A AMRAAM. The AIM-7s are carried on the four fuselage missile stations. The AIM-9s are rail launched, and are carried mounted on rail on either side of each inboard wing station weapons pylon. AIM-120A/Cs may replace any of the AIM-7s and/or AIM-9s, although there were initially some vibration/flutter problems when they were carried on the two aft fuselage stations. The AIM-120B is basically an AIM-120A that has modified electronics capable of being reprogrammed in the field. The AIM-120C introduced new, smaller, aerodynamic control surfaces in order to fit into the F-22's weapons bay, and is significantly more agile than earlier missiles, while also having a slightly longer range.

Ground crews do not like to mount the AIM-120 on the inboard wing rail because of handling problems, although flight crews do not like AIM-9s mounted on the inboard rails since it restricts the seeker's field of view. The normal combat load in 1996 has developed to be two AIM-7M on stations 3/7 (forward), two AIM-9s on stations 2B/8A (inboard), and four AIM-120s on stations 4/8 and 2A/8B.

Drop tanks containing 610 gallons may be carried on the three inboard stations of all F-15s. The outboard wing stations, rated at 1,300 pounds each, are not currently cleared to carry any stores (according to the flight manual), although both ECM pods and HARM have been observed there on occasion. Each of the inboard wing stations and the centerline accommodate a variety of conventional and special stores carried singularly or on multiple ejector racks (MER). The MER-200 racks used on the F-15 are of a different design than earlier MERs, and are rated to 7.33g as opposed to the 5g of Vietnam-era MERs..

All F-15s except for USAF A/Bs are capable of carrying conformal fuel tanks (CFT), and these provide additional weapons stations. Originally called FAST-packs (Fuel and Sensor Tactical), the low-drag CFTs contain approximately 114 cubic feet of usable volume. They attach to outer side of each engine intake, under the wing root, and are designed to the same load factors as the basic F-15 (i.e.; 9g). The CFTs can be installed or removed in 15 minutes. At subsonic and transonic speeds the CFTs actually improve the aircraft's drag coefficient (being slightly area-ruled), and impose a minimal penalty at supersonic speeds. In theory the CFTs can be configured to include a variety of systems, such as reconnaissance sensors, laser designators, radar detection and

Right: **The stores and pylon illustrations from the F-15E weapons manual.** US Air Force

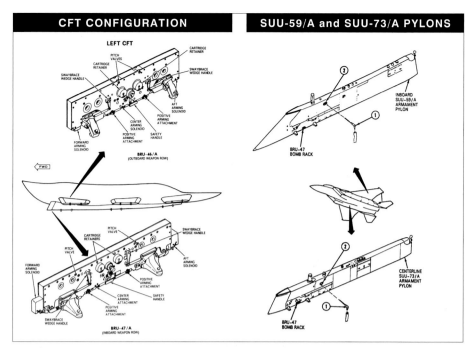

CFT CONFIGURATION

SUU-59/A and SUU-73/A PYLONS

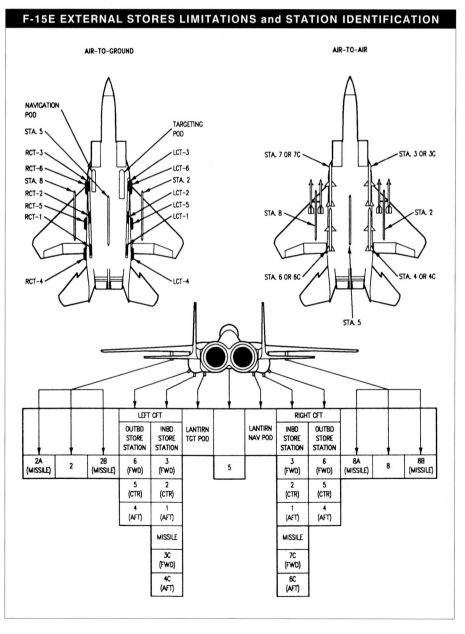

F-15E EXTERNAL STORES LIMITATIONS and STATION IDENTIFICATION

jamming equipment, in addition to 750 gallons of fuel. All external stores stations remain available with the CFTs in place, and McDonnell Douglas has developed a new weapons attachment system which can extend the operating radius with large external loads by up to 40%. Known as tangential carriage, it involves the installation of six stations in two rows of stub pylons on the lower corner and bottom of each type-4 CFT. Each of these stations is capable of carrying 2,000 pounds, and four of them are wired to support AIM-7 or AIM-120A missiles. The use of tangential carriage greatly reduces the drag associated with carrying external stores when compared to the normal MERs. Early type-1 CFTs have attach points for four Sparrows, and are used primarily on F-15C/Ds instead of the F-15E. A type-3 CFT was also developed that had attach points for four Sparrows or a single MER, and were intended for use on the F-15C/D. It does not appear that any great number of type-3 CFTs were ever procured by the USAF.

The AN/ASQ-T11 and the AN/ASQ-T13 air combat maneuvering instrumentation system (ACMI) pods may also be carried. The pod is the same general size and shape as an AIM-9 Sidewinder, and is suspended in the same manner as the AIM-9.

MXU-648/A cargo (personnel) pods may be carried on the inboard wing pylons and/or the centerline station. The pod is a converted BLU-27 fire bomb shell. The empty weight of the pod is 125 pounds, and a maximum of 300 pounds may be loaded into the pod.

This page, top to bottom:

One of the few photographs showing the F-15 (71-0291) carrying weapons (an AGM-88 HARM) on the outboard wing station. Noteworthy are the unusual type-3 CFTs. McDonnell Douglas

Until the introduction of the AIM-120 AMRAAM, the F-15's primary medium-range missile was the AIM-7 Sparrow III. In the mid-1990s it finally began to be replaced by the AIM-120. Dennis R Jenkins

A fairly typical war-load of missiles – AIM-120s on the fuselage stations and inboard pylon, with an AIM-9 on the outboard pylon. Unlike the 1970s, when missiles were generally painted gloss white, modern missiles are a dull light gray to help them blend into the aircraft's camouflage. Dennis R Jenkins

The M61 Vulcan with most of the surrounding sheet metal removed. This well-proved 20mm cannon is being outclassed by newer Russian and European 25mm and 30mm designs. Mick Roth

Opposite page, top: **The Rafael Python 4 short range air-to-air missile can replace the normal USAF AIM-9 Sidewinders on IDF/AF F-15s. These missiles reportedly have better seekers and are more maneuverable than the AIM-9, further increasing the Eagle's kill probability.** Rafael Weapon Development via Tsahi Ben-Ami

Powerplants

Early F-15A/Bs used two Pratt & Whitney (a division of United Technologies) F100-PW-100 turbofans, each rated at 23,830 pounds thrust with afterburner. Since all accessories (generators, etc.) are mounted in the AMAD, the left and right engines of the F-15 are interchangeable, simplifying maintenance considerably.

The F100 is a two-shaft turbofan with a high-augmentation afterburner. The engine is equipped with a direct pitot-type titanium intake

Below: **Most of the improvements to the F100 were a result of the DEEC test program carried out between NASA and P&W with 71-0287 (in the background). These improvements have finally resulted in a powerful and reliable engine.**
NASA / DFRC via Tony landis

with a fixed nose bullet. There are 21 inlet guide vanes in a single row equipped with variable-camber trailing edges. The fan has three stages and the fan blades and discs are of titanium construction. The compressor is a 10-stage axial design constructed primarily of titanium, Inconel and other high-temperature alloys. The first three stages of the compressor are equipped with variable stator blades to allow optimum airflow scheduling.

The annular combustion chamber is fabricated of Haynes-188 cobalt-based alloy with film cooling. It is equipped with dual fuel injectors and a capacitor-discharge ignition system, each containing an independent engine-mounted generator and three igniter plugs, two for the engine and one for the afterburner. The F100 is designed to be smokeless, and this is

achieved by concentrating combustion on the front of the burner, and using extremely high operating temperatures. The high pressure turbine has two stages with directionally solidified alloy blades. The low-pressure turbine has two stages with PWA-73 coated alloy blades and a maximum allowable speed of 10,400 rpm.

The afterburner has five concentric spray rings in flow from the core engine, and two slightly further downstream in the fan bypass airflow. The flameholder assembly is downstream of the spray rings, and is connected with a high-energy ignition system that permits a modulated light-up. The outer bypass duct and other major afterburner assemblies are fabricated in sheet and stringer titanium, while the interior liner is of coated Haynes-188. A small augmentor fuel drain is located on the bottom of the fuselage beneath each engine to ensure that fuel to does not accumulate in the afterburner. Originally this drain protruded downward a couple of inches beneath the fuselage, but its location continued to injure ground crews, so by the mid-1990s most aircraft had the protrusion removed and the drain is now flush with the surrounding fuselage

The convergent-divergent axi-symmetric exhaust nozzle is a multi-flap, balanced beam, arrangement giving a wide range in area and profile. The nozzles are positioned pneumatically by engine bleed air. With the landing gear down and the engine in IDLE, the nozzles will be approximately 80% open. With the landing gear up, the nozzle is at minimum area at all times except at MIL power or above. The nozzles are full open only when in full afterburner. Originally, 17 small titanium covers protect the actuators for the nozzles, but these 'turkey feathers' were removed from the engines by a TCTO since they were a maintenance burden (and cost $1,200 each). All early F100 variants

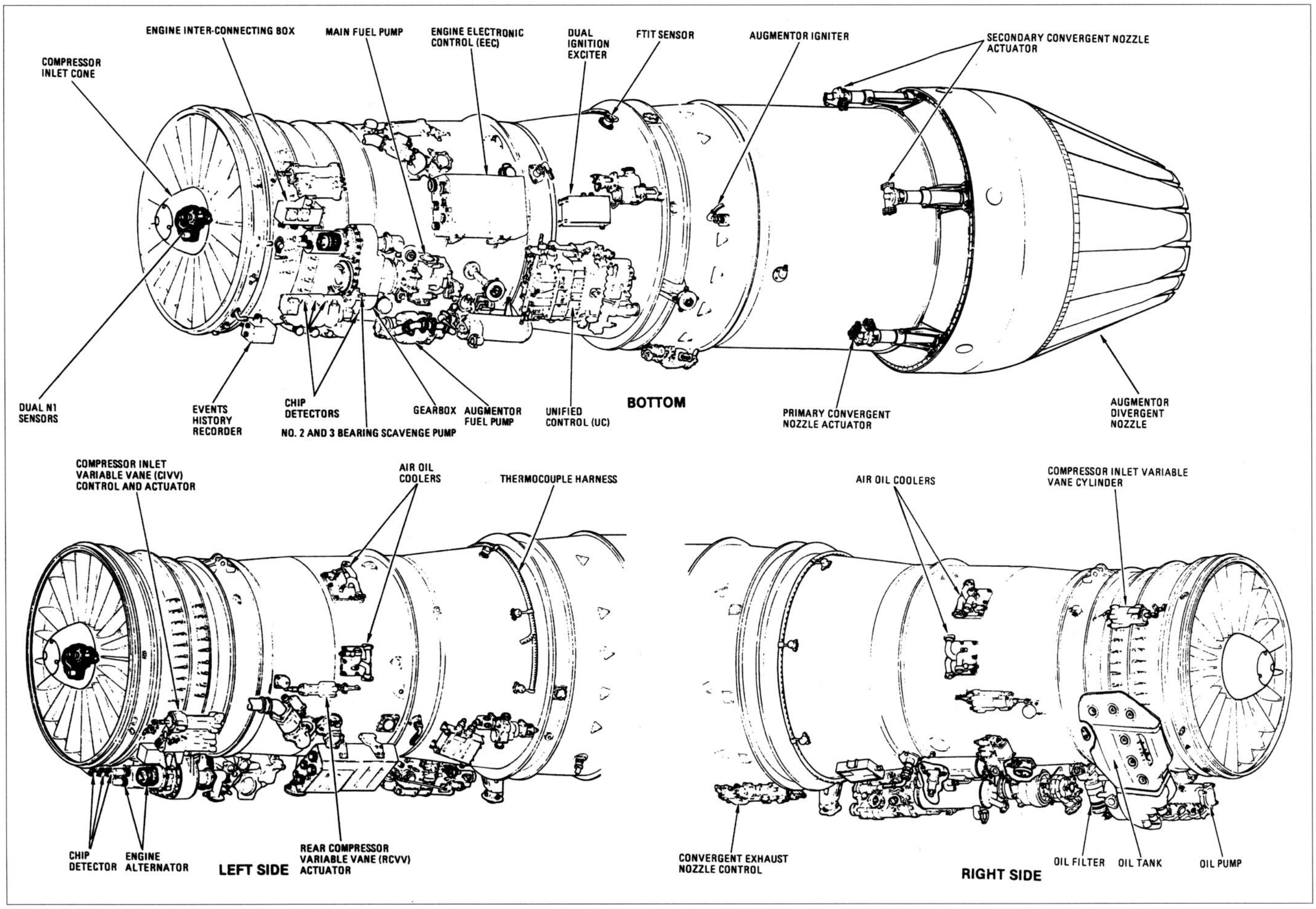
ENGINE INTER-CONNECTING BOX
MAIN FUEL PUMP
ENGINE ELECTRONIC CONTROL (EEC)
DUAL IGNITION EXCITER
FTIT SENSOR
AUGMENTOR IGNITER
SECONDARY CONVERGENT NOZZLE ACTUATOR
COMPRESSOR INLET CONE
DUAL N1 SENSORS
EVENTS HISTORY RECORDER
CHIP DETECTORS
NO. 2 AND 3 BEARING SCAVENGE PUMP
GEARBOX
AUGMENTOR FUEL PUMP
UNIFIED CONTROL (UC)
BOTTOM
PRIMARY CONVERGENT NOZZLE ACTUATOR
AUGMENTOR DIVERGENT NOZZLE
COMPRESSOR INLET VARIABLE VANE (CIVV) CONTROL AND ACTUATOR
AIR OIL COOLERS
THERMOCOUPLE HARNESS
AIR OIL COOLERS
COMPRESSOR INLET VARIABLE VANE CYLINDER
CHIP DETECTOR
ENGINE ALTERNATOR
LEFT SIDE
REAR COMPRESSOR VARIABLE VANE (RCVV) ACTUATOR
CONVERGENT EXHAUST NOZZLE CONTROL
RIGHT SIDE
OIL FILTER
OIL TANK
OIL PUMP

are 191.2 inches long, 46.5 inches in diameter, and weigh 3,033 pounds.

Beginning in October 1986, F-15s were delivered with the improved F100-PW-220 version, which delivers 23,450 pounds thrust with afterburner. Although it generates slightly less thrust, the new engine provides a small improvement in specific fuel economy, and generally increased reliability. Most earlier -100 engines have been modified to the newer -220 configuration in US and foreign service. The F100-PW-220 and -229 are 208 inches long, 46.5 inches in diameter, weighs 3,184 pounds, and shares 81% of its parts and 90% of its GSE with the earlier engine. The engine's ignition system consists of four igniters, two for the engine and two for the afterburner, as opposed to the three igniters of the F100-PW-100. The exhaust nozzles are not designed to be equipped with turkey feathers. Major improvements incorporated into the production F100-PW-220 include:

- Increased core life – 4,000 cycles (9 years) for the first inspection and an 8,000 cycle engine life expectancy. The use of single crystal 1st and 2nd stage turbine blades is a major contributor.
- Digital electronic engine control reduces control system complexity by replacing both the engine electronic control (EEC) and the hydro-mechanical unified fuel control (UFC) units employed on the F100-PW-100.
- Gear-type main fuel pump – 400 fewer parts than the high-speed variable-vane pump. This pump doubles the life expectancy to 2,000 hours.
- Improved augmentor (afterburner) with better cooling and stronger materials.
- A light-off detector (LOD) that senses augmentor ignition and, with the DEEC, permits faster throttle transients. If the LOD does not sense a 'light-off', it automatically retards the throttles to MIL, terminates fuel flow to the afterburner, and checks all systems. If everything checks good, the LOD will automatically attempt two additional relights. If these attempts are unsuccessful, the LOD is disabled by the DEEC, and one additional relight is attempted, using tailpipe pressure to verify an afterburner light-off.

The F100-PW-220 incorporates an engine monitoring system which consists of the DEEC and an engine diagnostic unit (EDU). The DEEC and EDU continuously monitor electrical control components and engine operation to detect engine failures. Abnormal engine operation and either intermittent or hard failures of components are detected and flagged for maintenance personnel. During abnormal engine operation or component failure, the EDU will record engine and aircraft data as an aid to maintenance troubleshooting. The EDU also maintains engine life-cycle information.

In early-1984, the Air Force announced that a second engine was being procured for all future F-15 and F-16 aircraft, and the Navy also selected the engine to power the F-14B (formerly the F-14A(Plus)) and F-14D. This engine was the General Electric F110-GE-100, which generates 23,100 pounds of thrust with afterburner. The F110 is designed for modular assembly to facilitate maintenance and repair, and numerous borescope ports are positioned along the engine for inspecting critical areas, such as the compressor, combustor and turbine assemblies. The core is basically a scaled-down version of the F101 that powers the B-1B coupled with a scaled-up version of the F404 (F/A-18A) fan assembly. The engine is 181.9 inches long, 46.5 inches in diameter and weighs 3,300 pounds. It has identical attachment points and fittings to the F100-PW-220,

Above: **All F-15s have, so far, used the Pratt & Whitney F100 turbofan engine. Although initially a fairly troublesome engine, the introduction of digital electronic engine controls has allowed it to perform well in the twin-engine F-15. However, it was felt that the GE F110 engine was more reliable, and this engine has been used in most later single-engine F-16s.** US Air Force

Opposite page: **The F-15's engines slide out of the engine bays directly onto their ground servicing carts on rails. Most major accessories are mounted to the airframe instead of the engine, simplifying removal and installation.** McDonnell Douglas

and can be interchanged. An annual competition has been staged to determine the number of powerplants produced by each contractor, with General Electric winning a 50.4% share to date. Although there is no reason why they could not be, no GE engines have been used in operational F-15s as of April 1998.

The F100-PW-220E began to be introduced to squadron service during 1995. These engines offer the same thrust as the standard -220 engine, but incorporate several of the improvements developed for the -229 engine for better throttle response and improved reliability. Another benefit is another slight improvement in fuel economy.

The Improved Performance Engine (IPE) program produced engines from each manufacturer that have an increase to approximately 29,000 pounds sea-level static thrust. These engines, the F100-PW-229 and F110-GE-129, have been successfully demonstrated in an F-16C and a modified F-15A. Both engines are available to power the F-16C/D and F-15E.

As of the end of 1996, a total of 449 operational USAF F-15s were powered by -100 engines, 201 by -220s, 17 by -220Es, and 75 late-model F-15Es by -229s. All F-15I and F-15S aircraft delivered as of early 1998 use -229s.

Air is fed to the engines by two straight two-dimensional external compression inlets, one on each side of the fuselage. Air inlet controllers are provided by Hamilton Standard, with actuators by National Water Lift. The inlets are identical, but completely separate, and are capable of operating asymmetrically. Each system consists of three variable ramps, a variable diffuser ramp and a variable bypass door. The entire intake rotates about a pivot on the lower cowl lip to provide optimum airflow at all angles of attack. The upper leading edge can rotate up to 11° below and 4° above the horizontal. The variable ramps provide air at optimum subsonic flow to the face of the engine throughout the aircraft speed range.

Ramp position is controlled by the air inlet controller, as is the bypass door. The bypass door controls the inlet duct Mach number by opening to automatically bypass excess air. The air inlet controller, one for each inlet, utilizes angle of attack, temperature, ramp actuator position, aircraft Mach number and inlet Mach number to schedule the ramps and bypass door operation. The first ramp is locked in the up position until the engine is started, and the diffuser ramp remains locked in the up position unless the aircraft is above 0.5 Mach.

A series of tests in the Air Force Arnold Engineering Development Center wind tunnel has established that the inlet is essentially stall-free at any flight attitude and all altitudes. The inlets

also provide a small measure of lift, and serve to unload the horizontal stabilizer, much the same as a canard, allowing a smaller stabilator. Most F-15s have received various doubler panels (some of them very large) on the side of their intakes to correct various stress cracks.

Internal fuel in the F-15A/B is carried in four Goodyear fuselage tanks and two wet-wing tanks with a total capacity of 1,759 gallons. Block-10 and later aircraft incorporated ECP-253M4 and carry approximately 30 gallons (200 pounds) more fuel in tank #1 for a total of 1,789 gallons. Aircraft prior to block-10 were not retrofitted with the modification. The F-15C/D (and J/DJ) has six fuselage tanks, two wet-wing tanks, and small leading and trailing edge wing tanks for a total of 2,070 gallons. The F-15E (and I/S/U) has a slightly redesigned #1 fuselage tank, and carries 51 gallons less than the F-15C. Recommended fuel is JP-8, although the aircraft is capable of limited operations on commercial Jet-A. The internal wing tanks and fuselage tank #1 are transfer tanks. The tanks are arranged so that fuel from all internal tanks will gravity transfer even if the transfer pumps fail. Regulated engine bleed air transfers fuel from the external tanks to any internal tank that will accept it, and also provides a positive pressure on all internal tanks. The fuel transfer system is completely automated. Engine feed tanks are self-sealing for protection from up to 0.50 caliber projectiles, and all internal tanks have reticulated foam for fire/explosion suppression. Wherever possible, fuel lines have been routed inside the fuel tanks, and wherever that was not possible, the lines are covered with a self sealing material. Single point refueling is provided, and an in-flight refueling receptacle is mounted in the left wing root. The in-flight refueling receptacle incorporates pyrotechnic devices which can open a stuck slipway door to permit emergency refueling. The refueling door can not then be closed in flight.

Optional conformal fuel tanks (CFT) may be attached to the sides of the air intakes of all variants except the A/B, and contain 750 gallons each. Some F-15A/Bs in US and Israeli service have been modified to carry the CFTs. Each CFT is pressurized be a self-contained ram air pressurization and vent system. The CFT fuel compartments incorporate explosion suppression foam slabs for enhanced survivability. A total of 592 sets of CFTs were procured for USAF service.

All internal, CFT and external fuel (except from the engine feed tanks) may be dumped overboard from an outlet at the trailing edge of the right wing tip. Provisions are provided for up to three 610 gallon drop tanks, one on the centerline, and one on each inboard wing station. The drop tanks are rated to the maneuvering capabilities (+9/-3g) of the aircraft. External tanks built after January 1977 have improved lightning strike protection, and earlier tanks were modified by TCTO 1F-15A-659 dated 16th February 1977.